"The war over Syria has been, in truth, a fight for control over the global economic and political order—a last, failing stand for a declining American empire to forestall the current shift toward a new global balance of power. Unlike so many hastily-written books on Syria that miss this point, Stephan Gowans' work will prove to be an essential primer on the Syrian conflict for years to come. A must read."

—**Sharmine Narwani**, Journalist and Analyst of Mideast Geopolitics

"Washington's Long War on Syria is a well-researched and deeply considered analysis of the tragedy that has befallen Syria. Stephen Gowans reveals the political and economic interests that are motivating Washington's intervention in Syria. No praise is too high for this much-needed corrective to Western propaganda. This fascinating book is a must-read for anyone seeking a deeper understanding of the war in Syria."

—**Gregory Elich** is on the Board of Directors
of the Jasenovac Research Institute
and the Advisory Board of the **Korea Policy** Institute

"Stephen Gowans paints a very clear portrait of the Syrian Arab Republic, and documents the extensive efforts from the Pentagon to bring it down. With the mainstream media spewing regime change propaganda 24-hours a day, Gowan's book is a must-read. It tells the true story of the Syrian people and their struggles for independence and development, a story that desperately needs to be heard. This book would make even the most ardent interventionist question Washington's policies. Gowan's tells truths that are so deeply hidden in western countries, but yet are so vital in understanding world events."

—**Caleb Maupin**, Journalist & Political Analyst

"Washington's Long War on Syria" is a well-researched and highly readable account of why the United States has launched a major crusade to overthrow the Baathist government in Damascus. Needless to say, the story it tells is completely at odds with the US-sponsored fairy tale about a brutal dictator crushing a democratic protesters, leaving noble Americans no choice but to ride to the rescue."

—**Dan Lazare**, Journalist and Author

Stephen Gowans

WASHINGTON'S LONG WAR ON SYRIA

Baraka
Books

Montréal

ISBN 978-1-77186-108-3 pbk; 978-1-77186-113-7 epub; 978-1-77186-114-4 pdf; 978-1-77186-115-1 mobi/pocket

Book Design and Cover by Folio infographie
Editing and proofreading: Renée Picard, Robin Philpot
Cover photos : iStock

Legal Deposit, 2nd quarter 2017

Bibliothèque et Archives nationales du Québec
Library and Archives Canada

Published by Baraka Books of Montreal
6977, rue Lacroix
Montréal, Québec H4E 2V4
Telephone: 514 808-8504
info@barakabooks.com
www.barakabooks.com

Printed and bound in Quebec

Société
de développement
des entreprises
culturelles
Québec

We acknowledge the support from the Société de développement des entreprises culturelles (SODEC) and the Government of Quebec tax credit for book publishing administered by SODEC.

Financé par le gouvernement du Canada
Funded by the Government of Canada | Canada

Trade Distribution & Returns
Canada and the United States
Independent Publishers Group
1-800-888-4741 (IPG1);
orders@ipgbook.com

CONTENTS

Are wars of aggression, wars for the conquest of colonies, then, just big business? Yes, it would seem so,
however much the perpetrators of such national
crimes seek to hide their true purpose under banners of high-sounding abstractions and ideals.

Norman Bethune, 1939

FOREWORD

This book was completed late in 2016, at a point the Islamist insurgency in Syria, backed by the United States and its Arab monarch allies, was in its fifth year. It is less an account of the events that marked the conflict from 2011 through late 2016, and more an examination of the processes that shaped it. It is also an inquiry into three political forces which have vied for control of the Syrian state, not only from 2011, but from the end of World War II; these forces are secular Arab nationalism, Sunni political Islam, and U.S. imperialism.

A lapse of a period of four to five months between completion of the book and its publication presented a risk that what was current at the time of its writing might no longer be current at the point the book was released. This posed no trouble from the point of view of the analysis. The focus of the book was on the sweep of events over many decades, and the passage of a few months would hardly alter the account. But a problem arose in relation to the verb tense in which events would be described. Writing in the present tense, as if events of the ground and the balance of forces in the war that prevailed late in 2016 would continue to prevail indefinitely, carried with it the risk that the book would appear dated from the very first moments of its release, depending on what happened in the interim period between completion of the book and its publication. This, of course, was the challenge of how to write about an event of contemporary significance that was still in progress. To deal with the challenge, I chose to write the book retrospectively, with events and processes that were current as late as the final months of 2016 treated as history, as indeed they would be, technically, by the time the book appeared in print.

INTRODUCTION

On behalf of Wall Street, the United States' most politically influential sector, successive U.S. governments waged a war on Arab nationalist Syria, not to support the spread of democracy, which Syria's Arab nationalists had developed to a far higher degree than had Washington's prized Arab allies, but to eliminate opposition to a Washington-led global economic order which prioritized the pursuit of profit above all other considerations. From 1963, Syrian governments in which Ba'ath Arab Socialist Party members Hafez al-Assad and his son Bashar played principal roles, were committed to the Arab nationalist values of freedom from foreign domination and Arab socialism. Syria's secular Arab nationalist governments forged alliances with the Islamic Republic of Iran, which, likewise, rejected integration into the U.S.-superintended global economic order, and valued economic and political independence. They also established alliances with the Soviet Union (leading hardliners in Washington to label Hafez al-Assad an Arab communist) and, after the USSR's dissolution, with Russia. Both countries were considered by U.S. strategists to be "peer competitors" of the United States, and the Assads' alliance with them only added to the enmity Washington felt for the Arab nationalist leaders. The values which the Assad-led Syrian governments embraced were inimical to the U.S. foreign policy goal of creating highly favorable business climates for U.S. corporations, bankers and investors around the world. In place of pandering

to Wall Street, Syria's Arab nationalists sought to free Syria—
and as an ultimate goal, the entire Arab world—from the political and economic agendas of foreign powers.

In the spring of 2011, upheavals shook the Arab world. The
distemper became known as the Arab Spring. Riots broke out
in Syria in March 2011, and quickly turned into an insurgency.
Washington almost immediately called for its old Arab nemesis, Bashar al-Assad, to step down. U.S. president Barack
Obama declared that Assad had lost legitimacy, citing the
armed rebellion as proof.

Throughout the Western world, Washington's opposition to
Assad—who U.S. state officials portrayed as a brutal dictator—
and its support for the armed opposition, were seen to be motivated by distaste for tyranny and love of democracy. But
considerations of promoting democracy played no role in
Washington's decision to back the opposition to the Assad government. This was evident in multiple ways.

Washington's allies on the ground in the fight against the
Syrian government were Islamists, not democrats. The
Islamists' goal was to create a Sunni Islamic state, similar to
Saudi Arabia, in which the Quran, not democratic decision-
making, would be the basis of law. Even the Free Syrian Army,
touted in the early days of the rebellion as a sort of liberal democratic movement, not only included Islamists, but was Islamist-
dominated.[1] The Associated Press reported that "Many of the
[Free Syria Army's] participating groups" had "strong Islamist
agendas." Most of the Free Syrian Army groups were ideological
cognates of the Muslim Brotherhood, the progenitor of al-
Qaeda and Islamic State.[2] *The Wall Street Journal* pointed out
that not only was the Free Syrian Army "dominated by Islamist
groups" it was also "in close coordination with al-Nusra,"[3] the
al-Qaeda affiliate in Syria. Moreover, the group had no program
for the establishment of a multi-party democracy, or of any sort
of democracy, for that matter. Its aims were purely negative,
defined by a single goal—toppling the secular Syrian government. The idea, then, that even the so-called "moderate" and

"relatively secular" Free Syrian Army was not Islamist was mistaken. As the veteran Middle East correspondent Patrick Cockburn remarked, there was no "dividing wall between" Islamic State and al-Nusra "and America's supposedly moderate opposition allies."[4]

Washington's principal Arab ally in the region and in the war against Syria, Saudi Arabia, was an anti-democratic tyranny which crushed its own Arab Spring demonstrations, and sent tanks to neighboring Bahrain to quell demonstrations there which called for an end to monarchy and a transition to democracy. Saudi authorities beheaded Nimr al-Nimr, a Saudi cleric who played a lead role in calling for democracy, and sentenced his nephew to death by crucifixion for taking part in demonstrations against the monarchy as a seventeen-year-old. The United States turned its head, as it had for decades, to the Saudi royal family's disdain for democracy and oppression of its subjects.

Washington positively doted on the immensely wealthy Saudi royal family, whose extensive investments in the United States had led to its integration into the U.S. economic elite. Washington indulged the Saudi dynasty, because it cooperated with U.S. policy goals related to advancing U.S. corporate profit-seeking objectives. As one U.S. official explained, "Countries that cooperate with us get a free pass."[5] And when it came to relations with Washington, the Saudis were cooperators *par excellence*.

Sitting atop the world's largest reserves of oil, the Saudi royals provided U.S. oil firms access to a cornucopia of profits. In addition, by boosting or throttling back production, they managed the world's oil supply—and hence the price of oil, on the world market, in ways that were favorable to the U.S. corporate community. What's more, the Saudi royal family was the U.S. arms industry's top customer. They kept Lockheed Martin, Boeing, Raytheon, General Dynamics, and other weapons manufacturers afloat on a sea of petrodollars, and ensured that the industry's shareholders remained awash in dividends and capital gains.

The Saudis also picked up the tab for various covert operations that facilitated the attainment of U.S. foreign policy
objectives, and acted as a surrogate for U.S. intelligence agencies in running covert operations, when U.S. law tied the CIA's
hands. In return, Washington provided the Saudi royal family
with the protection it needed to safeguard its privileged position atop Saudi society against the resentment and opposition
of its subjects. Washington also protected the Saudi tyranny
against the designs of Arab nationalists who might seek to
wrest the kingdom's oil wells from the House of Saud in order
to mobilize the proceeds of Arabia's petroleum resources to
uplift the Arab nation as a whole, rather than to add to the
riches of the Saudi royal family and their Western oil company
partners.

The other countries Washington had opposed in the region—
Iran, Gaddafi's Libya and Saddam's Iraq—were, like Syria, committed to economic and political independence and state-
directed development at odds with the paradigm favored by the
U.S. State Department on behalf of U.S. banks, corporations,
and investors. That paradigm stressed the necessity of open
markets, free enterprise and a welcoming business climate for
U.S. investment, as well as military cooperation with the
United States. None of these countries allowed the Pentagon
to establish military bases on their soil. States in the Arab and
Muslim worlds which Washington counted as allies—the
cooperators—accepted U.S. hegemony, welcomed virtually
untrammeled foreign investment, and most hosted the U.S.
military within their borders. They were almost invariably
anti-democratic—led by kings, emirs, sultans and military
dictators.

In an effort to arrive at a political solution to the Syrian
uprising, the government in Damascus proposed amendments
to its constitution to create a system of representative democracy that moved Syria closer to the multi-party model favored
in the West. The Ba'ath Arab Socialist Party, Syria's ruling
party under the Assads, would no longer have a constitution-

ally prescribed status as *primus inter pares*, that is, as a lead party to which others were subordinate. Presidential elections—previously referenda to approve or reject a single candidate put forward by the party—would be open to multiple candidates, and not limited to Ba'ath Party members.

Despite the concession, the rebellion continued. This, in conjunction with the reality that the insurrection was led by sectarian Sunni Islamists whose goal was the creation of a Sunni Islamic—and not a multiparty democratic—state, refuted the idea that the desired destination of the rebellion was a democratic one. That the United States and its Arab allies—the monarchs, emirs, and sultans of the Arab world—were funneling weapons to Sunni Islamist militants, refuted the claim that Washington's support for the uprising in Syria was related to solidarity with democrats in a fight against dictatorship.

The United States' efforts to oust the government of Bashar al-Assad antedated the Arab Spring by many years, and Washington had had a hand in inciting the Muslim Brotherhood, which had a long history of violent antagonism toward the Syrian government dating to 1963. Washington's motivations to topple Bashar al-Assad's government prior to 2011 were related to Damascus's embrace of anti-imperialist and anti-Zionist positions and its program of state-directed economic development. Opposition to these elements of Syria's political program continued to undergird the authentic motivation for Washington's support for the armed rebellion that broke out in 2011. Washington had likewise schemed to depose Hafez al-Assad because he implemented socialist policies and aligned his government with the Soviet Union. The senior Assad had inaugurated Syria's alliance with the Islamic Republic of Iran, a country which Washington opposed. Bashar followed many of his father's policies, and Washington complained that he had failed to break with the Ba'ath Party's ideology of opposing Israel, seeking Arab independence from Western influence, and promoting economic development through public-ownership and state planning of the economy (what the U.S. Congressional Research Service would call the adoption of "Soviet models").[6]

In the spring of 2011, Syria had a shorter distance to travel toward the Western model of multi-party representative democracy than did almost any other Arab state. It had an elected legislature with multiparty representation, and a president whose legitimacy was based on a popular mandate obtained in a referendum. Many observers acknowledged that Assad enjoyed widespread support. By contrast, Saudi Arabia, Washington's principal ally in the Arab world, was an absolute monarchy that tolerated only impotent democratic forms that existed on the margins of the Saudi state. There were no political parties in the kingdom, and no meaningful legislature or popular input into who would lead the country. What's more, the king didn't have the support of his subjects, especially those of the Shi'a Muslim sect, who predominated in the oil-rich Eastern Province, and were treated by the Saudi clerical establishment as heretics, if not worse. According to the United States' own intelligence community, Arabs saw Saudi Arabia as a tyranny (and they saw Egypt, Jordan, the Gulf Arab states and Pakistan—all U.S. allies—in the same way).[7] U.S. President Barack Obama claimed, against the evidence, that the Syrian president had lost legitimacy, and therefore had to step down. Yet, according to U.S. intelligence, it was the Saudi leadership, and that of Washington's other Arab allies, which lacked legitimacy. Obama never once said, let alone intimated, that any of Washington's prized royal potentates should step aside.

The profit-seeking imperative of capitalism was the basis for U.S. foreign policy's emphasis on sweeping away nationalist impediments to a global economic order of favorable climates for U.S. trade and investment. Capitalism concentrates wealth in the hands of a tiny minority of bankers, investors and high-level corporate executives, which uses its wealth and control of important economic assets to obtrude its policy preferences on the state. This is not to suggest that a cabal of rich capitalists secretly meets to dictate policy prescriptions to the U.S. government. Instead, the business community takes advantage of a multitude of mechanisms to ensure its policy preferences prevail in competition with other groups. These mechanisms include lobbying and buying influence with politicians by funding their election campaigns and establishing a *quid pro quo* whereby politicians are tacitly promised lucrative positions in the corporate world in post-political life in exchange for support for pro-business positions while in office.

Another mechanism is the revolving door between high-level positions in the corporate world and high-level positions in the state. CEOs, corporate lawyers, and top business people are vastly over-represented relative to their numbers in U.S. cabinets and in the upper echelons of the U.S. bureaucracy. They serve time in government, return to the Olympian heights of the corporate world, return again to government, and circulate back into top-level corporate jobs a few years later. As a consequence, corporate values, concerns and goals remain at the top of government agendas.

Additionally, corporate America is able to set the ideological agenda by establishing and supporting think tanks to prepare policy recommendations, as well as through the use of endowments to universities to steer scholarship in directions that support corporate interests. Corporate America can also shape the ideological environment through its ownership and control of the mass media. The ability to control the ideological agenda means that people who run for elected office or work in consequential positions in the state are usually already committed to pro-business positions.

Finally, the capitalist class is able to use its control of vast economic resources as a club to threaten governments—if they aren't already inclined—to toe the capitalist line. Major corporations, banks and investors, can bring to bear crippling economic pressure as a form of terrorism to induce voters to pressure governments to abandon policies that undermine business interests.

Through all of these mechanisms, the capitalist elite dominates public policy formation. As political scientists Martin Gilens and Benjamin I. Page put it in their 2014 study of over 1,700 policy issues, "economic elites and organized groups representing business interests have substantial impacts on government policy, while average citizens and mass-based interest groups have little or no independent influence."[8]

The substantial impacts of the capitalist class on government policy extend to foreign policy, and is evidenced in U.S. support for countries that build business climates that are favorable to the U.S. economic elite and evinced in U.S. hostility to governments that elevate the interests of local populations above those of U.S. corporations, banks and investors. A hero of African national liberation, Robert Mugabe, a longtime president of Zimbabwe, argued that his country was subjected to crippling economic sanctions by the West "for doing what all other nations [are supposed to] do, that is responding to and looking after the basic interests of [their] people." Mugabe pointed out that the United States and its allies, which had "imposed these sanctions, would rather have us pander to their interests at the expense of the basic needs of the majority of our people."[9] On the other hand, such countries as Saudi Arabia and Bahrain, which make a point of accommodating U.S. business interests, are spared sanctions, threats of war, subversion, destabilization, and invasion, even though they fall well short of liberal democratic virtues; indeed, even though their leaders can be dispassionately described as brutal autocrats.

The influence of business agendas may be even more strongly felt in foreign than domestic policy because ordinary citizens are less likely to be interested in foreign policy issues, or to perceive foreign policy linkages to their everyday lives. As a consequence, they're less likely to mount opposition to foreign policy agendas which serve corporate interests at their expense than they are to oppose domestic policies which encroach upon their immediate economic interests. Another reason foreign policy guided by the sectional interests of corporate America is less likely to be publicly opposed is because, in order to mobilize popular support for their foreign policies, U.S. leaders have veiled the aggressive pursuit of private economic interests abroad behind the myth that the United States is inherently virtuous and is a force for good around the world and therefore is pursuing disinterested goals.[10] Accordingly, the exploitative nature of U.S. foreign policy, and its connection to the sectional interests of wealthy investors and top-level corporate executives, is largely hidden from the U.S. public.

Ideology and the Syria Conflict

Apart from U.S. imperialism, four ideologies played major roles in Wall Street's war on the Syrian governments of both Bashar al-Assad, and his father, Hafez. Two of these, secular Arab nationalism and the Sunni political Islam of the Muslim Brotherhood, arose from the Arab world's encounter with European colonialism.

Secular Arab nationalism sought to unify an Arab nation which had been carved up into individual countries separated by borders drawn in imperial map rooms, and whose Asian and African halves were bisected by a European colonial settler state, Israel. Syria was ruled by Arab nationalists after military officers belonging to the Ba'ath Arab Socialist Party staged a coup d'état in 1963. Committed to unity of the Arab nation, freedom from outside domination, and Arab socialism, Ba'athists posed an ideological challenge within the Arab world to the United States and its Western allies, as well as to Israel, and to the Arab monarchies which were integrated into the United States' informal empire.

Ba'athists, such as Bashar al-Assad, threatened the United States and its Western allies in distal and proximal ways. The distal threat presented by Assad and other Arab nationalists related to their aspiration to unify the world's approximately 400 million Arab-speakers into one single large state with control over the Arab world's vast petroleum resources. This state, which would combine the sophistication of Cairo, Damascus and Baghdad, with the oil wealth of the Arab Gulf states, would be large enough and rich enough to challenge U.S. hegemony in West Asia and North Africa. Moreover, an Arab super state of 400 million people, stretching from the Atlantic Ocean to the Persian Gulf, and containing a vast trove of oil and natural gas, would play a significant role on the world stage. It would be a peer competitor of the United States.

Arguably, the aggressive foreign policy the United States adopted in connection with Iraq, beginning with the first Gulf War, was aimed at eclipsing the threat to U.S. domination of the Middle East that arose when the Iraqi government, led by secular Arab nationalists ideologically committed to the Ba'athist program of unity, freedom, and socialism, invaded Kuwait. Washington feared Iraq's invasion of the Gulf state placed Iraqi forces in a position to continue their march into Saudi Arabia, an eventuality which would place the oil-rich Arabian Peninsula under Baghdad's—and Arab nationalist—control. The annexation of the Arabian Peninsula by Iraq—or recovery of Arab territory on behalf of the Arab nation, in Arab nationalist terms—would create the nucleus of a pan-Arab state. Already, Iraq had exited the Western orbit, insisting on its sovereignty, in concert with its Ba'athist principles. This effectively removed Iraq's petroleum resources from the grasp of Western oil firms, who were no longer free to exploit Iraqi oil on their own terms. The exit of the Arabian Peninsula from Washington's informal empire would compound the problem, removing from the U.S. orbit a source of immense oil profits.

There was an additional danger, as well. The inchoate pan-Arabic state would likely prove to be immensely attractive throughout the Arab world, and this might infuse the Arab nationalist movement with momentum. A domino effect might be set in motion, in which Arabs revolted against the kings, emirs, and sultans who ruled over them and who the United States kept in power as their marionettes. That there was a good chance that a Baghdad-led nascent pan-Arabic state would become an inspiration to Arabs rested on the fact that Iraq's Arab nationalists, pursuing a program of Arab socialism, had already used their country's oil wealth to significantly improve the standard of living of ordinary Iraqis beyond their forebears wildest imaginings. Unlike Marxist socialism, which is class-based, Arab socialism amounted to public-ownership and planning of post-colonial economies with the aim of overcoming the Arab world's colonial legacy of underdevelopment. If Marxist socialism was aimed at liberating the working class from its exploitation by capitalists, Arab socialism was aimed at liberating Arabs from their exploitation by imperialists. By extending the reach of the Arab socialist program to the Arabian Peninsula—and using the peninsula's undoubted oil riches to finance munificent infrastructure development and social welfare programs—the Arab nationalists could infuse their program with unquestioned credibility. Hence, Baghdad could hold out the promise of the peninsula's riches being used as a motor to develop programs of uplift in all parts of the Arab world, including those parts, such as Egypt, where oil was scarce. In other words, the oil wealth monopolized by the House of Saud, the anti-democratic dynasty which ruled Saudi Arabia with U.S.-backing, would become the property of the Arab nation as a whole. This was an inspiring vision Washington could not allow to grip the imaginations of the world's 400 million Arabs. The United States, accordingly, embarked on a decades-long campaign of invasions and economic warfare to drive Iraq's experiment in Arab nationalism into ruin, and eventually to purge the state of its secular Arab nationalist influence. The process was given a formal name: de-Ba'athification. The thesis of this book is that Wall Street's war on Syria was motivated by the same aim: the de-Ba'athification of Syria and the elimination of secular Arab nationalist influence from the Syrian state, as a means of expunging the Arab nationalist threat to U.S. hegemony, not only within the Arab world, but on the world stage.

The more immediate way Arab nationalists threatened the United States was in their insistence on freedom from outside domination, hardly an acceptable ideology in Washington, where imperial thought prevailed, barely concealed behind rhetoric of U.S. leadership, primacy and indispensability. A country which insisted, as the United States had in its various official documents, that "American leadership" is "indispensable,"[11] "U.S. leadership is essential,"[12] and that the United States "will lead the world,"[13] could hardly tolerate the Ba'ath Party's call, from its founding document, for Arabs to "struggle with all their power to raze...every foreign political and economic influence in their countries."

In keeping with its self-appointed status as world leader, the United States also, in officially promulgating its global economic order, demanded universal acceptance of open markets and free enterprise. Washington made no secret that it viewed these institutions as comporting with corporate America's interests, and that it intended to promote U.S. corporate interests around the world—indeed, to make them the basis of its global economic order. The State Department proclaimed, in its Fiscal Year 2004-2009 Mission Statement, that the United States would "act boldly to foster a...world integrated into the global economy;" and that it would "promote economic freedom" and "support programs that encourage...free enterprise." Even more boldly, the 2015 National Security Strategy announced that the United States "can and will lead the global economy" and that it would do so by "opening markets and leveling the playing field for American...businesses abroad." Washington would also "[lower] tariffs on American products, [and break] down barriers to [U.S.] goods and services." U.S. leadership would additionally entail action to discourage "state capitalism," a reference to the state-owned enterprises which dominated China's economy and played a large role in Syria's.

Juxtapose U.S. prescriptions for how the Washington-led global economy would be structured against the economic program espoused in the founding document of the Ba'ath Party: Industry "will be protected together with the national production from the competition of foreign production." Natural "resources, and means of transportation shall be directly administered by the State," in the public interest. Workers "shall take part in managing the factories and they will be given, [on top of] their wages, a share of profits to be determined by the State." The Interim 1990 constitution of secular Arab nationalist Iraq declared that the "State assumes the responsibility for planning, directing, and steering the national economy." These views were inimical to the economic policies Washington promoted as the world's self-appointed leader. They did not fit with the global economic order Washington insisted on creating.

Cynics may insist that the Arab nationalists' commitment to socialism was more rhetorical than authentic, but that would ignore the fact that Arab socialism—that is, the planning, directing and steering of Arab economies—was unquestionably carried out by Arab nationalists in power. One can debate whether to label the ideology that structured the Arab nationalists' economic policies as socialism, but U.S. officials unquestionably regarded the economic demarche of the Arab nationalist countries, including Syria, as socialist. As mentioned, some even went so far as to brand Assad's father, Hafez, an Arab communist. Others described Syria's economic policies under Bashar as inspired by Soviet models.

A second key ideological force in the war on Syria was the political Islam of the Muslim Brothers. It arose as a reaction to Britain's domination of the Arab world's largest country, Egypt. Like the Arab nationalists, the Muslim Brothers reacted to the intrusion into the Arab world of European colonialism. But unlike the Arab nationalists, whose program was based on mobilizing the Arab world on the basis of a common language, the Muslim Brothers sought to unify a larger world, that of Islam, on the basis of Islamic, and not Arab, identity. The Brothers' solution to reversing the decline of Islam relative to the West was to return to the pure Islam, defined as that practiced by the first few generations of Muslims, the so-called Salaf, from which the word Salafism, meaning Islamic fundamentalism, is derived. The Muslim Brotherhood rejected communism, socialism and

Arab nationalism as alien importations from the West, and as false ideologies, springing from the imperfect minds of humans, rather than from the Quran, the revealed word of a perfect God. Muslim Brotherhood-influenced Islamists argued that the solution to the indignities which the West had inflicted upon the inhabitants of the Muslim world was Islam—not nationalism, not socialism, and not communism. Abhorrence of left-wing ideologies made Islamists valuable allies of convenience for Western governments seeking to lance the boil of leftist projects of emancipation from Western domination, though, at the same time, these very same Western governments would have to contend with political Islam as an alternative project of anti-imperialist liberation. The dual role played by political Islam, as ally and adversary of the West, was clearly demonstrated in Osama bin Laden's alliance with the United States against the Soviet Union and Moscow's leftist Afghan government ally in the 1980s, and bin Laden's subsequent militant opposition to the U.S. military presence in the Muslim world.

The Muslim Brotherhood preached a harsh, puritanical code, and promoted the idea that the Quran, and the record of the Prophet Muhammad's thought and practices, the Sunna, were sufficient to govern the moral, political and economic life of a contemporary society. The organization's founder, Hasan al-Banna, promulgated the following motto for his movement: "God is our purpose, the Prophet our leader, the Quran our constitution, jihad our way and dying for God's cause our supreme objective."[14] Westerners might understand the Muslim Brothers by imagining a Christian movement with a parallel motto: God is our purpose, Jesus our leader, the Bible our constitution, religious struggle our way and dying for Jesus our supreme objective. Robert Baer, who worked as a CIA officer in the Middle East, has argued that the Muslim Brotherhood's motto is, in effect, the motto by which the 9/11 hijackers lived and died.[15] Indeed, the thinking of the Muslim Brotherhood, particularly that of the movement's chief ideologue in the 1960s and 1970s, Sayyid Qutb, heavily influenced al-Qaeda's world view. Osama bin Laden's lieutenant, Ayman al-Zawahiri, who succeeded bin Laden as leader of the organization, joined the Muslim Brotherhood at the age of fourteen. Other top al-Qaeda leaders also belonged to the Muslim Brotherhood. As *The Wall Street Journal's* Jay Solomon reported, "Osama bin Laden and other al-Qaeda leaders cite the works of the Brotherhood's late intellectual, Sayyid Qutb, as an inspiration for their crusade against the West and Arab dictators. Members of Egyptian and Syrian Brotherhood arms have also gone on to take senior roles in Mr. bin Laden's movement."[16]

The Brotherhood had long been active in Syria. Its militants engaged in street battles with the partisans of the Ba'ath Arab Socialist Party in the years prior to Ba'athist members of the military seizing power in 1963. After 1963, the Syrian Brotherhood waged an unrelenting life and death struggle against the Ba'ath Party. The Ba'athists remained the dominant power in the Syrian state, and the Muslim Brothers their chief challenger within Syria. The battle waxed and waned, erupting in an armed uprising in Hama in 1982 and again, throughout Syria, in 2011.

Two other movements of political Islam, centered in two regional powers, played important roles in the struggle for Syria.

The first was the political Islam of revolutionary Iran, to which the Arab nationalists of the Syrian state were allied as a consequence of sharing with Iran's Islamic Revolution three core values: a commitment to freeing the Middle East from Western domination; an implacable opposition to the colonial settlement of Palestine (a country, which, from the perspective of Syria's ruling Arab nationalists, was Arab, and from the vantage point of Iran's Islamists, was Muslim); and a state-directed model of economic development. Syria and Iran, along with Hezbollah, the Lebanese Islamist national resistance movement inspired by Iran's Islamic Revolution, made up the so-called "Axis of Resistance" against Western domination of the Middle East. Hezbollah was formed in 1982 to repel the Israeli occupation of southern Lebanon. Opposition to the Zionist settler state in Palestine—a state which played a significant role in enforcing the hegemony of its patron, the United States, over West Asia and North Africa—was an important aspect of the Resistance Axis.

One of the dangers Washington perceived in Iran's 1979 Islamic Revolution was that the Revolution's anti-imperialist and anti-Zionist content might inspire the Arab world. Arab nationalists had failed to eject Israel, a European settler implantation in the Arab world, and had failed to wholly break the chains forged by European colonialism and maintained by Washington. Perhaps Iran's revolution, which succeeded in toppling a U.S.-puppet dictator, the Shah, and which set the country on a path of self-directed economic development and political independence, would inspire the Arab world to throw off the oppressive weight of parasitic kings, emirs, sultans, and dictators, who presided over the divided Arab nation on behalf of imperial masters in Washington. Hezbollah (along with Islamic Jihad, a Palestinian national liberation organization inspired by Iran's Islamic Revolution) demonstrated that the revolution in Iran could galvanize Arabs to political action against outside interference in their lives. And the Syrian government of Hafez al-Assad demonstrated that there were secular Arabs who were willing to form an alliance with Iran's movement of political Islam in pursuit of a shared goal of emancipation from Western domination.

An additional—if not the main—target of the U.S. war on Syria was Iran. Iran was by far a more formidable threat than Syria was to U.S. ascendancy over the petroleum-rich region of West Asia. It was larger and stronger than Syria and its appeal to Islam resonated with many in the Arab world. The U.S. war on Syria had the potential to weaken Iran by exhausting, if not altogether eliminating, one of Tehran's closest allies. Moreover, since Iran's ability to transfer weapons to Hezbollah was facilitated by access to the intervening space of Syria, removing the Arab nationalist republic from the Axis of Resistance would weaken Iran by isolating it from the Lebanese national resistance.

From Washington's point of view, Wahhabism, the puritan-ical, truculently anti-Shi'a state religion of Saudi Arabia appeared as the perfect counter-weight to Iran's brand of pol-itical Islam. For one thing, Wahhabism, unlike the Muslim Brotherhood movement and Iranian Islamic Revolution, was not a reaction to Western domination. Wahhabism arose in the eighteenth century as a viciously sectarian, fundamentalist interpretation of Islam, unrelated to the Arab and Muslim world's encounter with European colonialism. It was a desert ideology, adapted to legitimizing the rule of the House of Saud by emphasizing obedience to authority. Wahhabism had coexisted comfortably with imperialism, providing religious legitimacy to the Kingdom of Saudi Arabia. There was no dan-ger that by itself, Wahhabism would inspire an Arab insurrec-tion or Muslim revolt against Western interference in the Middle East. Wahhabism, however, shared with the Muslim Brotherhood the aim of returning to the early days of Islam, but the Wahhabis' rationale for this demarche was different from that of the Muslim Brothers. The latter wanted to embrace the pristine Islam of the Prophet Muhammad and his companions because the Brothers believed that it was by this route that Islam's decline relative to the West could be reversed. Like Adam and Eve who were expelled from Paradise because they failed to heed God's word, the Muslim Brothers believed that Islam sank into decline and lost its former glory because Muslims were insufficiently pious. (Likewise, some Marxists believe that the decline of communism is due to Marxists devi-ating from the original writings of Marx, and have advocated a return to the "pure" Marx, along with the rejection of the "encrustations" of Leninism, Stalinism, Trotskyism, and so on, as the path to communist revival. Marxism, too, has its own "Salafists.") If the etiology of the disease was divagation from the one true, pure, and original path, then the cure was to return to the path from which the faithful had strayed. Hence, for the Muslim Brothers, Salafism was a means to an anti-imperialist end, and not an end in itself. By contrast, the Salafism of

Wahhabism was a means to realize nothing more than what Abd-al-Wahhab, the itinerant preacher who founded the doctrine, believed was the only correct version of Islam.

Wahhab not only believed that he knew Islam in its pure form, but that those who didn't see Islam as he did were either infidels or apostates, who ought to be treated harshly for failing to heed God's word. He formed an alliance with the Saud family, which in turn formed an Islamic militia, the Ikhwan (Brethren) which launched a reign of terror on the Arabian Peninsula, slaughtering unbelievers, decapitating "apostates," and committing all manner of atrocities, adumbrating the Islamic State terror campaigns of the twenty-first century. In 1802, the Brethren raided "the Shi'ite holy city of Karbala in what is now Iraq, killing most of the city's population, destroying the dome over the grave of the founder of Shiism."[17]

The Saudi kingdom used its vast oil wealth to spread Wahhabism far and wide, and the viciously sectarian ideology partly informed the actions of Islamic State. This is not to say, however, that Islamic State's ideology was pure Wahhabism. It was not. The Islamist organization embraced Wahhab's anti-Shi'a sectarianism, but also incorporated into its thought elements of the Muslim Brotherhood's rejection of political regimes that act on behalf of non-Muslim powers, as Washington's satellite, Saudi Arabia did. Islamic State ideologues reviled the Saudi monarchy as a collaborator with the West and Israel and regarded the country's form of government, a kingdom, as un-Islamic.

What made Wahhabism particularly attractive to U.S. strategists was its anti-Shi'ism. The leaders of Iran's Islamic Revolution were Shi'a Muslims. One way to blunt the appeal of Iran's Islamic Revolution to Arabs and Muslims, most of whom were Sunni, was to foster anti-Shi'a animosity. Galvanized by animus of Shi'a "apostates," Islamic State spent a good deal of its energies attacking Shi'a targets. This, in turn, engendered mistrust and animosity on the part of Shi'ites against Sunnis. The outcome was an escalating sectarian conflict, which acted to keep the Arab and Muslim worlds divided, their members fighting amongst themselves, rather than uniting to shake off their common oppressors.

Divide et Impera

Creating new divisions among subjugated populations, and deepening old ones, are hoary imperialist practices. The Romans called these deliberately centrifugal practices *divide et impera*—divide and rule. The clarion call, "Arabs of the world unite, you have nothing to lose but your chains!" (to modify a famous line from the *Communist Manifesto*) had little chance of being heeded if Arabs were consumed by sectarian warfare, a truth of which imperial powers were only too aware. The same applied to the parallel call for Muslims of the world to unite. We can assume that no one was happier that Wahhabi anti-Shi'ism was propagated globally than the Saudi dynasty's patrons in Washington who had an interest in the continued division of the Arab and Muslim worlds, and of Sunni rejection of the anti-imperialist Shi'a-led Islamic Revolution.

The Alawites, who followed a heterodox branch of Shi'a Islam, belonged to an accidentally significant minority in Syria. Alawites were over-represented relative to their numbers in the dominant Ba'ath Party. Alawites had historically faced discrimination from Syria's Sunni majority. As a consequence, they were attracted to political parties which were explicitly secular and anti-sectarian and which sought to overcome the Arab world's religious divisions. The founders of the Ba'ath party stressed Arab ethnic identity over sectarian identity as a path to Arab unity. Accordingly, the party appealed to members of religious minority sects, which had often suffered discrimination at the hands of the Arab world's Sunni majority. Alawites, like Hafez al-Assad, were inspired by the party's goals and the vision of an Arab world free from sectarian discrimination.

As is true of people from poor communities in many Third World countries, talented Alawites found that a career in the military at an officer's rank offered an escape from poverty. By contrast, the richer Sunnis, who dominated the merchant and landowner classes, were less likely to pursue a military career. As a consequence, both the Syrian officer corps and Ba'ath party came to have a disproportionally strong representation of Alawites (along with members of other religious minorities) and a disproportionally weak representation of Sunnis. It was highly probable, then, that if a military coup d'état were to occur, that the coup leaders would represent minority communities and would carry with them the pro-minority, anti-sectarian ideology of the Ba'ath Party.

In 1963, a cabal of secular Arab nationalist officers from Syria's minority communities, members of the Ba'ath Arab Socialist Party, seized power in a coup d'état. Among the coup leaders was Hafez al-Assad. Seven years later, Assad led a second coup, this time against his former comrades, which he styled a "correction." Assad resolved to take the country in a less hardline leftist direction than his now erstwhile comrades had taken it, largely because he believed the government's policies had alienated a large part of the population. Conservative Muslims needed to be won over by persuasion, not force, and a go-slow approach was, in his view, called for.

Having engaged in court intrigues, Assad knew that it was imperative to surround himself with men of unquestioned loyalty, otherwise, his tenure in government would be brief. Quite naturally, the people Assad could trust the most were his friends and relatives. And Assad's friends and relatives quite naturally came from his own Alawite community. As a consequence, appointees to top security positions were Alawites. They weren't Alawite because Assad chose them on the basis of their religious identity, but because he chose them on the basis of their kinship and amity ties. The over-representation of Alawites in key state security positions, then, was a concomitant, or epiphenomenon, of Assad's decision to surround himself with trusted intimates, which, in turn, was an imperative of political survival, in what, hitherto, had been a highly unstable Syrian state.

Nevertheless, the fact that many top-level positions in the state's security apparatus were taken over by Assad's closest friends and relatives proved to be a boon to the Muslim Brothers, and a great weakness for Assad's government, for it allowed the Brothers to appeal to the Sunni majority by propagating the myth that the new government was an instrument of Alawite rule, guided by a sectarian agenda. Accusing the Ba'ath Party of being an instrument of the Alawite community was tantamount to accusing the mid-twentieth century U.S. Communist Party of pursuing a Jewish agenda because Jews were over-represented in the party relative to their numbers in the U.S. population.

The myth that the Assad governments, both those of Hafez and Bashar, were sectarian, persisted for decades, and the myth's longevity was due in no small part to its political utility to Washington and its Sunni Islamist allies. The myth was insinuated into the journalism of North America and Western Europe where it was often used to frame the U.S. war on Bashar al-Assad's Syria as a sectarian civil conflict pursued by a state captured by an Alawite minority to advance its sectarian interests at the expense of the Sunni majority. Accordingly, the Syrian government was often described in the Western press as "Alawite-led" while the armed opposition was just as often referred to as "largely Sunni." This ignored the reality that both the Syrian Arab Army, and Assad's cabinet, were also largely Sunni, and that this was a political (rather than sectarian) conflict between secular Arab nationalists on the one hand, and jihadists (backed by the U.S. and its allies) on the other. But propagation of the myth of sectarian warfare comported with the predilection of Western discourse for Orientalist depictions of the Global South as a territory riven by ancient inter-communal animosities, which necessitated the intervention of the United States—the self-proclaimed force for good in the world—to establish order. It was useful for U.S. strategists to propagate this understanding for a few reasons.

First, it undergirded the imperialist strategy of divide and rule. Ideological agendas conveyed in Western media reached not only Western audiences, but audiences beyond the West, including in Syria. If the Syrian Sunni majority could be led to understand the Assad government as an instrument of the Alawite community, all the better for the U.S. foreign policy goal of extirpating Arab nationalism from the Syrian state.

Second, the myth of the Assad government as an Alawite instrument of oppression concealed the central role that secular Arab nationalism played in the Middle East and in the politics of the Assad government. This obfuscated the true dimensions of the conflict. If there were any references in Western media to the Assad government's commitment to the Ba'ath Arab Socialist Party's values of freedom from foreign domination, state direction, planning and control of the economy, and working toward the unity of the Arab nation, I'm not aware of them. Acknowledging the ideological framework within which the Syrian government operated, rather than presenting Syrian leaders as motivated by a lust for power to advance a sectarian agenda on behalf of the Alawite minority, would have presented Syria's Arab nationalists as rational actors pursuing what many may have considered defensible, if not praiseworthy, goals. However, to serve U.S. foreign policy objectives, U.S. strategists favored the portrayal of Assad as a power hungry Alawite despot, covering up the Arab nationalist themes that genuinely pervaded his politics.

Third, the false depiction of the Assad government as animated by a sectarian rather than a secular Arab nationalist agenda encouraged an understanding that U.S. leadership, which is to say, Western interference in Syrian politics, was necessary and desirable for the supposed lofty humanitarian reason of bringing about peace in a country troubled by the oppression of a religious majority by a religious minority.

In short, the myth of Alawite oppression of the Sunni majority both encouraged the phenomenon of inter-communal strife, and then used it to justify a U.S.-led program of regime change to overcome it.

Ultimately, the aim of Washington was to assert its leadership over a Syria where Arab nationalists pursued an agenda which was antithetical to U.S. imperialist goals. Syria's Arab nationalists completely rejected U.S. primacy, and, moreover, favored *dirigiste* economic policies wholly at odds with Washington's declared intention of acting "boldly to foster a... world integrated into the global economy," structured to promote U.S. business interests. The de-Ba'athification of Syria would not only remove an obstacle to U.S. leadership in the Levant, it would also weaken Syria's Persian ally, Iran, and fatally weaken the Arab nationalist dream of building a pan-Arabic super state that, apart from emancipating the Arab world from hundreds of years of foreign domination, would challenge U.S. global hegemony.

The Islamic revolutionaries in Tehran, like their Arab nationalist allies in Damascus, also vehemently rejected Washington's self-declared global leadership role, and similarly favored robust state intervention in the economy. Indeed, Iran's revolutionaries defined Iran's private sector as subordinate and subservient to the state sector—an anathema from the perspective of Washington's Wall Street-defined economic orthodoxy. Where Washington declared that "America can and will lead the global economy,"[18] both Damascus and Tehran retorted in no uncertain terms that it would not. Decisions about the Syrian and Iranian economies would fall respectively within the domains of Syrian and Iranian decision-making, and would not be ceded to Washington and its Wall Street patrons. To underscore the point, Assad asserted his Arab nationalist commitment to Syria's independence, telling an Argentine journalist that "Syria is an independent state working for the interests of its people, rather than making the Syrian people work for the interests of the West."[19] Assad's defiance hardly meshed with Washington's demand that all governments fall into line behind U.S. leadership.

Defining War

War is often equated to what J.B.S. Haldane, the British scientist and socialist, called the soldier's business—killing, by pushing or throwing pieces of metal, at an enemy.[20] But Clausewitz, the great Prussian theoretician of war, had another view. He defined war more broadly as an effort to impose one's will on an enemy.[21] By this definition, the soldier's business is only one possible method of warfare among many. Blockade, or siege—an attempt to starve an enemy into submission—is an important form of warfare with historical resonance. Britain imposed a naval blockade on Germany in the First World War which was estimated to have cost the lives of 750,000 German civilians,[22] a form of warfare the British persisted in waging even after an armistice was signed.

In the modern era, economic warfare has often taken the form of what political scientists John and Karl Mueller called "sanctions of mass destruction."[23] In the 1990s, Iraq, then under Arab nationalist rule, was subjected to a vicious U.S.-led sanctions regime, whose ostensible purpose was to coerce Baghdad into destroying its arsenals of chemical and biological weapons, misnamed, for political reasons, as weapons of mass destruction. Chemical and biological weapons have nowhere near the destructive capabilities of nuclear weapons, and only nuclear weapons can be meaningfully labeled WMD. To illustrate the point, in WWI, it took 70,000 tons of gas to produce as many fatalities as were produced in Hiroshima by a single atom bomb.[24] To put it another way, a single atom bomb dropped on Hiroshima killed 70,000 people.[25] By contrast, a rocket with a typical payload of nerve gas will kill between 108 and 290 people if delivered under ideal weather conditions (overcast skies with no wind) over a heavily populated area against unprotected people. If there is a moderate wind or the sun is out, the death rate will be 11 to 29 people.[26] Weapons of mass destruction kill tens of thousands or hundreds of thousands of people, not tens or hundreds.

The reality that Baghdad had no legitimate weapons of mass destruction, however, was of little moment to propagandists in Washington. The point was to make it look like the Iraqi military was a signal menace, and this was accomplished by a simple expedient: slapping the label WMD on Iraq's chemical and biological weapons, an exercise equivalent to calling a pea-shooter a form of artillery. But it worked. Overnight Arab nationalist Iraq was transformed into a looming threat to world peace.

The sanctions led to the deaths of more Iraqis, observed the Muellers, than all the deaths attributable to the use of weapons of mass destruction throughout history.[27] The deaths were labeled by a U.S. Secretary of State as "worth it"—in other words, a small price to pay to maintain U.S. hegemony in the oil-rich Arab world. It was, indeed, a small price to pay...for the United States. Not a single banker on Wall Street, not a single state official in Washington, indeed, not a single U.S. citizen, died as a result of Washington's program of siege warfare on Iraq. Of course it was worth it...if you were planning U.S. foreign policy.

Many peace activists embraced sanctions as an alternative to the soldier's business, viewing them erroneously, not as a form of warfare, with destructive consequences as great if not greater than pushing or throwing pieces of metal at the enemy, but as peaceful coercion. The siege was carried out to impose the will of the United States on Iraq. It created significant harm. By Clausewitz's definition, the sanctions were unambiguously a form of warfare.

If we define warfare as an effort to impose one's will on an enemy by creating or threatening harm, then warfare encompasses a broad range of activities, including:

- Threatening nuclear annihilation
- Training and arming guerillas to project metal at the enemy
- Economic sanctions
- Threatening invasion

- Supporting internal opposition groups to carry out campaigns of internal destabilization
- Sabotage

By this definition, the U.S. war on Syria began long ago, before 2011. It began the moment Arab nationalists came to power in Damascus, proclaiming a motto they were determined would guide their efforts to liberate the Arab world from its centuries of domination by outside powers. The motto was unity, freedom and socialism.

CHAPTER ONE

THE DEN OF ARABISM

The constitution of the Ba'ath Party made a proclamation in its very first line which Washington could have only regarded with deep hostility: "The Arabs are one nation which has its natural right to live under one state." This was a vision for a very different world from the one which existed in the Middle East and North Africa in 2011, and was different from the Arab world which Britain and France created out of the collapse of the Ottoman Empire at the end of World War I. Rather than being divided into twenty-two small, weak, and oft-times squabbling states, the Ba'athists envisaged the roughly 400 million Arabic-speakers who occupied a territory stretching from the Atlantic Ocean to the Persian Gulf—the world's second largest pan-ethnicity after the Han Chinese—uniting as a single bloc into one unified state. And what's more, the Ba'athists believed that an Arab super-state should be truly independent, free from foreign political and economic interference. That meant an end to the string of U.S. (and other foreign) military bases that dotted the Persian Gulf and North Africa. And significantly, it meant that Arabs as a whole would take control of the region's vast petroleum reserves, rather than the resources being monopolized by kings, emirs and sultans installed in petro-kingdoms by the British and kept in power by the United States. Equally alarming to Washington, the Ba'athists proposed to build their independent, united Arab state through public ownership and planning—that is, via socialism, a concept which stirred deep antipathy on Wall Street and therefore at the U.S. State Department, where Wall Street's influence was strong.

One of the first theoreticians of Arab nationalism was a Syrian, Sati al-Husri. For 400 years, Arabs were ruled by the Ottoman Turks, until the Turks' empire collapsed at the end of WWI. In the final years of the Great War, the Arab leader Sherif Hussein led a revolt against Turkish rule, seeking to establish Arab political independence within a single Arab state, spanning the Levant and Arabia. The leaders of the revolt established a kingdom at Damascus.[1] The Allied powers, however, had other plans for the Arab world—plans which included implanting a Jewish homeland in the middle of it. The British and French carved up what al-Husri saw as "a natural cultural entity with an inalienable right to political sovereignty"[2] into a series of separate states, with borders delineated in imperial map rooms in London and Paris, without the slightest regard for the wishes of the Arab inhabitants. Some of the states became *de facto* colonies of the Great Powers. Others were little more than territory surrounding oil wells presided over by monarchs who ruled at the pleasure of London.

Within the Ottoman Empire, Syria was a large territory, which the British and French, to suit their own purposes, split up into what are now modern Syria, Lebanon, Palestine and Jordan. Syria and Lebanon became states under French rule. France invaded the Arab kingdom at Damascus in 1920, making Syria its *de facto* colony—the first of many campaigns of regime change the West would pursue in the country.[3] Palestine and Jordan fell under British governance, with London committing Palestine to a Jewish homeland to be peopled by mainly European immigrants who would displace the indigenous Arabs.

Al-Husri argued that the colonial powers deliberately divided the Arab homeland in order to render the Arab nation politically and militarily impotent. As a collection of individual states, each with its own local concerns and each seeking to safeguard its own autonomy, the countries of the Arab nation would forever work at cross-purposes and would never be able to achieve the coordination and unity necessary to muster a serious challenge to their domination by Europe. Nor would the Arab world be able to repel foreign intruders—among them, European Jews engaged in the colonial project of building a settler state at the very heart of the Arab homeland. As proof of his argument that unless they coalesced into a single state, Arabs would be forever at the mercy of their enemies, al-Husri posed the following question: Why had seven Arab states been unable to defeat Zionist forces in the 1947-1948 war? Answer: Because there were seven Arab states.[4] In al-Husri's view, in order to overcome their divisions, to win manumission from colonial domination, and to gain political independence, Arabs needed to unite into a single state in order to achieve the coordination, focus, military might and economic heft necessary to attain—and then guarantee—their self-determination. Only with unity, coordination, leadership, and scale, could the Arab world achieve independence.

Al-Husri's analysis was not without merit. The failure of Arabs to achieve self-determination in one small but important part of their homeland, Palestine, owes much to the divisions among and within Palestinian communities. Historian Rashid Khalidi argued that a large part of the reason Zionist forces prevailed against the Arabs in the 1947-1948 war was because Zionists possessed the leadership, coordination and unity of purpose the Palestinians lacked.

> "The great majority of the Jewish population was ideologically homogeneous, united around Zionism, while the Palestinian population was ideologically heterogeneous, combining elements of Ottoman Arab, Islamic, Christian, local Palestinian and European thought. The Zionist community in Palestine was drawn mainly from the secular element of the Jewish communities of Europe, while the Palestinians were divided on religious grounds between Islam and Christianity. The Zionists brought

with them a tradition of organization, expressed in strong unions, cooperative movements and socialist-oriented agricultural settlements. By contrast, Palestinian society was largely made up of peasants, lacking any tradition of formal organization. The Zionists had developed a government bureaucracy, representative institutions and the core of a regular army. Palestinian society had neither of these things. The Zionists had a single identity and goal: Jews seeking a homeland in Palestine. By contrast, while the Palestinians had begun to think of themselves in national terms, this was only one of several overlapping identities, which included identities related to being members of Greater Syria and beyond that, a greater Arab nation, as well as religious, local and familial identities."[5]

Leila Khaled, a Palestinian who played an important role in bringing the plight of her people to world attention, pointed out how the absence of leadership, authority, coordination and unity impeded the achievement of Palestinian political goals. In her autobiography, *My People Shall Live,* she cited the failure of Palestinian Arabs to keep and recover their homeland as a signal lesson in the perils of lack of organization. The "Palestinian people," she argued, "were an example of a society in chaos without authority and leadership, which, as a result, was left at the mercy of the Zionist oppressor."[6]

The Ba'ath Party was founded in the 1940s by two Sorbonne-educated school teachers from Damascus, Michel Aflaq and Salah al-Din al-Bitar. Contrary to the myth that the party was established to advance the interests of Alawites, Aflaq was a Christian and al-Bitar a Sunni Muslim, both of whom viewed sectarianism as the very antithesis of the party's *raison d'être;* one of the principal goals of the party would be to unite Arabs across sectarian and other lines on the basis of their common Arab identity.

The Ba'ath Party's origins were very much like those of the nationalist-communist Vietnamese movement of Ho Chi Minh. Both movements were reactions to French colonialism; both were founded by intellectuals who had spent time in France; and both wanted to emancipate their countries from French rule. But at the same time, they wanted to modernize their countries to resemble France.[7]

For Aflaq and al-Bitar, "disunity had to be overcome. Their answer was to try to bridge the gaps between rich and poor through a modified version of socialism, and between Muslims and minorities through a modified concept of Islam. Islam, in their view, needed to be considered politically not as a religion but as a manifestation of the Arab nation. Thus, the society they wished to create, they proclaimed, should be modern (with, among other things, equality for women), secular (with faith relegated to personal affairs), and defined by a culture of 'Arabism' overriding the traditional concepts of ethnicity."[8]

In the early 1950s, Aflaq and al-Bitar merged their Arab revival party (Ba'ath means 'revival' or 'resurrection') with Akram Hawrani's Arab Socialist Party. The result was the Ba'ath Arab Socialist Party, the party in whose Syrian branch Hafez al-Assad, and after him, his son, Bashar, would play important roles.

Ba'athism was guided by three values: unity of the Arab nation; freedom of the Arab nation from foreign domination; and Arab socialism. Arab socialism was defined as state planning, that is, direction and control of the economy in order to overcome the Arab world's colonial legacy of underdevelopment.

The party's commitment to unity was based on the view that all differences existing among Arabs ought to be considered "casual and fake"—in other words, of no political significance. This view was at variance with political Islam, which defined Islamic identity, rather than ethnicity, as the desired political organizing principle of the Arab world. For Ba'athists, the enemy was Western imperialism and its instruments, including Israel, the Jewish settler state in Palestine, and Washington's Arab client states, Saudi Arabia among the most important. The imperialist countries, in the Ba'athist view, had divided the Arab nation in order to dominate it economically and politically, and relied on Israel and the Arab monarchs as local instruments to help reinforce its hegemony.

Unity was the means by which the Ba'athists hoped to achieve the goal of political independence for the Arab nation. "Arabs," the party's constitution declared, "should struggle with all their power to raze the pillars of colonialism, occupation and every foreign political and economic influence in their countries." The reference to colonialism and occupation was understood to include Israel; therefore, Arabs should struggle to destroy Israel as a state for Jews implanted on Arab soil. Foreign political influences included such U.S. client states as Saudi Arabia and Egypt which collaborated with Washington and with other former colonial powers in the economic and political domination of the Arab world. "The Arab homeland," the Ba'athists insisted, "belongs to the Arabs. They alone"—not Jewish settlers and the Arab world's kings, emirs, sultans and dictators, who ruled at the pleasure of the West—"have the right to administer its affairs, wealth and [to realize] its potential." Indeed, colonialism "and anything relevant to it," from the Ba'athists' point of view, was "a criminal act that the Arab [nation must combat] by all possible means." Significantly, this meant that the Arab homeland, with its vast petroleum resources, was to be governed by Arabs for Arabs, not by collaborator monarchies installed by colonial powers and kept there by Washington in order to satisfy the profit-making objectives of corporate America.

The third pillar of Ba'athist ideology was socialism, conceived of as state-directed economic development. Specifically, Ba'athists prescribed public administration of the commanding heights of the economy, namely, natural resources, transportation and banking. They were also committed to incubating national industry by establishing a trade environment in which domestic enterprises could grow behind tariff walls, instead of being stifled by much larger foreign competitors, which had a hundred years or more head start.

The Ba'ath Party constitution declared that "The existing distribution of wealth in the Arab homeland is unjust and hence [it] must be reconsidered and distributed rightly among [its] citizens." In order to redress this unjust balance, the party's founders recommended profit-sharing and worker input into management decisions.

The party's central goal, then, was to uplift the Arab nation and to overcome its economic backwardness. This goal was to be accomplished by bringing Arabs together in order to overcome their domination by outside powers with a view to taking control of the resources and potential of the Arab homeland. Under Arab political control, the homeland's economy would grow behind tariff walls, assisted by government subsidies, and through state planning and ownership of the economy's commanding heights. In this manner, the Arab world would build a modern economy, uplifting itself and overcoming hundreds of years of foreign oppression.

Needless to say, the Ba'athists' program was the very antithesis of the model the United States favored for other countries, to wit, one of a U.S.-superintended global economy based on free trade, free enterprise, and open markets, overlaid with U.S. political leadership and military domination. It would be naive to think that Washington was prepared to tolerate an ideology which challenged this paradigm so fundamentally, especially in a region teeming with oil. A movement that declared that the world's richest oil-producing region belonged to the Arabs (and not to U.S. oil companies), and that the Arabs alone had the right to administer its affairs, free from foreign control, was not one that would muster much sympathy in a Washington in which Wall Street influences were strong and pervasive. Washington had declared its intention to "lead the global economy,"[9] proclaiming that history (no less) had "judged the market economy as the single most effective economic system,"[10] and had announced that it would induce "resource-rich countries to increase their openness" to U.S. investment.[11] This bold, globe-girding vision, clashed violently with the secular Arab nationalists' call for local control, guided by socialist principles.

Syria's 1973 Constitution

In 1973, Hafez al-Assad had been president of Syria for three years, and involved in the leadership of Syria for a decade. A Ba'ath Party activist in his youth, Assad was now leader of a Ba'ath Arab Socialist Party-headed state. Under his direction, a new constitution was drafted, which formalized the Ba'ath principles of unity, freedom, and socialism.

The constitution declared that the Syrian state would have a mission. The mission would be to foster the unity of the Arab nation, achieve its liberation from foreign domination, and overcome the underdevelopment of colonialism. The latter would be accomplished through planning and public ownership of the economy—that is, socialism. Assad identified three forces that would attempt to thwart the Syrian state from achieving its mission: imperialism, or foreign political and economic domination; Zionism, the colonization of Arab territory by Jewish settlers of mainly European origin; and exploitation.

The idea that the Syrian Arab Republic, under Ba'athist direction, would have a mission was signaled in the opening paragraphs of the constitution. Invoking the Arab nationalist thought of Sati al-Husri, the Syrian Arab Republic's founding political document declared that "The Arab nation managed to perform a great role in building human civilization when it was a united nation [but when] the ties of its national cohesion weakened, its civilized role receded and the waves of colonial conquest shattered the Arab nations' unity, occupied its territory, and plundered its resources."

Any doubt that the central political arrangements of Syria would be predicated on Ba'athist principles was dispelled when the framers of the constitution enshrined the Ba'athist motto, "unity, freedom, and socialism" in the document. The constitution declared that "The Arab masses did not regard independence as their goal and the end of their sacrifices, but as a means to consolidate their struggle, and as an advanced phase in their continuing battle against the forces of imperialism, Zionism, and exploitation under the leadership of their patriotic and progressive forces in order to achieve the Arab nation's goals of unity, freedom, and socialism."

The framers of the constitution saw their state as democratic. In articulating the state's political principles, their charter asserted that the "Syrian Arab Republic is a democratic, popular, socialist, and sovereign state." And while the Syrian democracy wasn't a replica of the U.S., British or French systems, the idea that the Republic could legitimately be called democratic was hardly without foundation. The constitution committed the state to "the principle of pluralism" and made provision for a legislature of elected members and multiple parties which would be allowed to contest legislative elections. After the outbreak of the Islamist insurrection in 2011, Western leaders spoke often of their vision of a political transition in Syria toward a pluralistic, democratic state, obfuscating the reality that pluralism and an elected legislature had been parts of Syrian political life for decades. Syria's political democracy would, however, depart from Western systems in two significant ways, both departures the products of the Ba'athists' mission to foster unity and lead the Arab nation toward freedom from foreign domination and economic development through state direction, planning and control of the economy.

The first was an explicit prohibition against establishing political parties on the basis of sub-national identities, as a means of overcoming the divisions which kept Arabs apart and which militated against Arab unity. Hence, carrying "out any political activity or forming any political parties or groupings on the basis of religious, tribal, regional, class-based, [or] professional [identity], or on discrimination based on gender, origin, race or color" was formally banned. Syrians were expected to identify as Arabs, not as women, workers, Sunnis, or members of an occupation, at least in so far as politics was concerned. While gender and class-based oppression existed, the Syrian state would prioritize emancipation from national oppression.

Adopting the ancient imperial practice the Romans called *divide et impera,* colonial powers had often sought to exploit divisions within the nations they dominated, turning politically insignificant disparities into significant ones which prevented oppressed communities from unifying to struggle against their common colonial oppressor. These were often divisions based on ethnicity or religion. One divide and rule practice was to transmute politically insignificant ethno-sectarian divisions within a community into significant ones by establishing quotas for political office based on ethno-sectarian identity. An egregious example of this practice was provided when, after invading Iraq in 2003 and toppling its secular Arab nationalist government, the United States, through its proconsul, Paul Bremer, established a governing council defined explicitly along ethno-sectarian and gender lines. "Whether you are a Shi'ite, Sunni, Arab or Kurd...man or woman," Bremer told Iraqis, "you will see yourself represented in the Council."[12] Some appointees were categorized on the basis of their religious identity, even if they didn't self-identify along religious lines. For example, one appointee, Hamid Moussa, was chosen as one of the council's Shi'a representatives, despite the fact that he self-identified as a communist.[13] This echoed the practice of the Nazi dictator Adolph Hitler, who, for the same reasons Bremer identified Moussa as a Shi'ite, identified Karl Marx as a Jew, though Marx was an atheist and self-identified as a communist. In both cases, religious labels were affixed to non-religious figures for political purposes. Bremer was resolved that Iraqis should not view the most significant opposition in their political lives as a conflict between nations, which is to say, between Iraqis and Americans, or the Arab world and the West, but in terms of conflicting polarities within Iraq: Arab versus Kurd, Sunni versus Shi'ite, female versus male. Hence, the conflicts that Bremer wanted Iraqis to focus on were differences within Iraq, and not differences between Iraq and its new imperial overlord.

This paralleled the Nazi's program of supplanting class divisions within German society as the chief way Germans were to think about politics, with a political ideology which priori-tized ethnic divisions, and pitted "Germans" against Jews and other peoples, such as Slavs, who the Nazis defined as sub-human. Because the Nazis were, in the first instance, implac-able foes of Marxism, their program could be defined as finding anything but class to form the basis of political mobilization in Germany. Rather than workers being mobilized to overthrow capitalist rule, the German "master" race would be mobilized to displace inferior peoples to win *lebensraum*, living space. This would profit Germany's industrialists and financiers, who would gain new markets and investment opportunities.

Because the United States had launched an unprovoked war of aggression on Iraq, had undertaken a military occupation of the country, and was remodeling Iraq's economy to suit the needs of U.S. investors—hence, was acting in a manner which could be expected to provoke Iraqi resistance—Bremer's task was to find alternatives to Iraqi identity to become the organ-izing principle of Iraq's political life. Iraq would be re-organized along ethno-sectarian lines to encourage its citizens to vie among themselves for the state's resources, rather than to unite in opposition to their U.S. and British occupiers. Under secular Arab nationalist rule, Iraq's politics were organized around Iraqi identity. Under U.S. domination, politics would be organized along Sunni vs. Shi'a, Arab vs. Kurd, and male vs. female lines. In other words, Bremer would implement in conquered Iraq exactly what Hafez al-Assad had proscribed in Syria: formal political divisions based on cleavages that would work against an oppressed people uniting against foreign domination.

A majority of Iraqis were opposed to Bremer's plan. A September 2003 poll found that only 29 percent of the coun-try's citizens agreed that it was important that their political leaders represent their sect.[14] They were more interested in politics based on ideas than politics based on competition with members of other ethnic and sectarian communities. The leader of the Association of Muslim Scholars, Harith al-Dahri, objected to Bremer's plan, condemning it as ploy to foment inter-communal hostility. "This council," he said, "has divided Iraq along communal and ethnic lines for the first time in history. It is the creation of the occupation forces. It is formed of parties that do not express the will of all Iraqis, whether Sunni or Shi'a." He said that "the divisions on which this council are based are unacceptable as they divide Iraq into communal and ethnic groups. It sows the seeds of hostility among the people of this society."[15]

Washington's publicly stated rationale for formalizing ethno-sectarian divisions in Iraq's new politics was to redress the ostensible Sunni domination of the country's Shi'a majority, which Washington alleged the Ba'athist government had enforced. This was a myth based on the fact that the country's leader, Saddam, was a Sunni Muslim, and that many of the people he appointed to key security positions in the state were also of the same sect. As it turned out, Saddam had appointed people he could trust, who happened to be intimates to whom he was connected by tribal and familial ties. Quite naturally, though not by design, these people also shared his religious beliefs. This, then, hardly constituted evidence of the Iraqi government pursuing a Sunni sectarian agenda. What's more, the Iraqi state had been headed by a Ba'athist party which was ideologically secular and non-sectarian. Indeed, consistent with its secular Arab nationalist ideology, Saddam's government deplored sectarian divisions as an impediment to unity. As scholars Samuel Helfont and Michael Brill put it, "Saddam plainly stated that his vision advanced a nationalistic and socialist state. He promoted the view that nationalism [would] alleviate divisiveness and sectarianism."[16] Furthermore, the party was introduced to Iraq by a Shi'ite, and a majority of its early leaders belonged to the same majority sect. In addition, of the "most wanted" members of Saddam's government, as identified by the deck of fifty-five playing cards issued by the Pentagon on the eve of the U.S. invasion of Iraq, two out of every three were Shi'a.[17] Whatever sectarian imbalances had arisen in Iraqi politics—and they were considerably exaggerated by Washington—were not the outcome of a deliberate design on the part of the Ba'athist government, but were an epiphenomenon of Saddam choosing to surround himself with people who were close enough to him that he could implicitly trust them.

Hence, to avoid division and infighting based on formal political divisions rooted in identities extraneous to Arab ethnicity, the Ba'athist framers of Syria's 1973 constitution introduced formal prohibitions against parties which challenged the primacy of Arab identity. This was internally consistent with the Ba'athist mission of fostering Arab unity as a necessary condition of overcoming foreign domination.

A second departure from Western political democracy was present in Syria's 1973 constitution, and it followed from the first. If Arab national identity had priority over all other political identities, then the political party which represented the aspirations of the Arab nation must also have priority. That party, at least according to the framers of the constitution, was their own, the Ba'ath Arab Socialist Party. Hence, Article 8 of the 1973 constitution decreed that the Ba'ath party would be the "leading party in the society and the state." What this meant was that the party would nominate a candidate for president, almost certainly a Ba'athist. The candidate would need to secure a majority of votes in a national referendum to take office. Candidates who failed to obtain a majority would be rejected, and the party would nominate another candidate, until one was found who was able to secure the consent of the majority. While different from the Western practice of elections contested by two or more candidates, this was hardly the dictatorship that Western propaganda alleged. Moreover, it was much closer to the multi-party electoral system favored by the West than the absolute monarchies which constituted Washington's key Arab allies. At least in Syria, there was a legislature in which multiple parties were represented and the population could exercise "consumer choice" if not "consumer sovereignty" over who their president was. (Consumer choice meant that Syrians had the choice of accepting or rejecting a candidate. Consumer sovereignty, had they had it, would have meant that Syrians could determine the candidates who would be presented to them as choices.)

Some critics of Western electoral democracy would argue that for all the surface distinctions between Syrian and U.S. democracy, the two systems were fundamentally alike. To be sure, in U.S. presidential contests, voters are presented with two or more alternatives, rather than being asked to approve or disapprove of a single candidate, as Syrians were. But for all intents and purposes, U.S. voters are typically presented with only two candidates, only one more than was allowed in the single candidate system of Syria under its 1973 constitution. The candidates on offer in U.S. presidential elections are effectively chosen by a tiny elite of wealthy investors based in the U.S. corporate community who presidential candidates must appeal to for campaign contributions. Alternatively, as in the case of Donald Trump, the candidates must be wealthy enough to finance their own campaigns. Candidates who espouse policies to promote the interests of ordinary U.S. citizens in competition with those who make up the top income stratum are at a serious disadvantage, since elite investors and business people—the biggest sources of campaign funds—will not provide them the money, resources, and connections they require to run competitive campaigns. The disproportionate ability of the wealthy to fund candidates who represent their own interests, or to self-fund campaigns, doesn't guarantee that candidates who appeal most to the wealthiest Americans will always prevail against a candidate who relies on small donations from many voters, but it does greatly enhance the chances they will.

In effect, then, the difference between presidential elections in Syria, under its 1973 constitution, and the United States today, is that presidential candidates in the former were chosen by Arab nationalists to carry out the country's Arab nationalist mission, while in the latter, the candidates are chosen by the U.S. capitalist class to carry out the country's capitalist-based imperialist mission. The Syrian system at least had the advantage of representing Syrians *en masse* as part of an oppressed Arab nation. By contrast, the U.S. system almost ineluctably leads to the selection of candidates who have a high probability of being committed to policies that favor their country's wealthiest citizens at the expense of the voters who elected them.

The elevation of the Ba'ath Party to the status of first party among equals originated in a recommendation the Ba'athists accepted from their Marxist allies. In Syria, Western-style parliamentary democracy, the Marxists argued, would be used as an instrument of urban landlords, industrialists and merchants for dominating Syrian society through their money power and command of key economic assets. The urban elite would use its wealth to shape the outcome of parliamentary contests and install its representatives and policies in the state. Western-style parliamentary democracy, therefore, would be a democracy for the few.

In Syria, religion and class intersected. Members of religious minorities—the people drawn to the Ba'ath Party's vision of a society free from sectarian discrimination—typically came from humble, rural, backgrounds. The urban elite, in contrast, was mainly Sunni. Although the Ba'ath Party's commitment to socialism was rooted in Arab nationalist objectives, the socialist pillar of Ba'athist doctrine also appealed to the party's members for a more immediate reason: it addressed the issue of their class oppression. Hence, the party appealed to religious minorities because they faced twin oppressions: one based on religion and one based on class. The material conditions of the Alawite community, for example, whose members were seen as the lowest caste of Syrian society, were greatly ameliorated as a result of the Ba'athists' socialist programs, a reality cited as evidence by the Arab nationalists' enemies that the Ba'athists, for all their talk about Arabism and socialism, were really just sectarians. After all, who benefited most from Ba'athist rule? What this criticism ignored was that all religious minority communities in Syria enjoyed improved standards of living under the Ba'athists, because members of these communities belonged to the class of poor, rural, laborers who the Ba'athists' socialist policies targeted for uplift. Alawites didn't benefit economically from Ba'athist rule as Alawites, but as members of an oppressed class.

A prerequisite of uplifting the rural poor was to prevent the Sunni urban elite from using its wealth and ownership of the economy to dominate electoral politics. To eclipse the influence of landlords and merchants, the Ba'athists would create, manage and defend a political system made up of popular organizations of peasants, workers, students, women, youth and intellectuals. It was in this sense that the Ba'athists proclaimed that their republic was a popular democracy.

Syria's 1973 constitution also declared that the Syrian Arab Republic would be socialist. The country's economy, the document proclaimed, "is a planned socialist economy which seeks to end all forms of exploitation." Natural resources and public utilities would be publicly owned, by law. Taxes would be progressive. The state would undertake "to provide work for all citizens" and would guarantee social security. All education was to be free and the state would guarantee health services.

These were not simply commitments made by a political party to win votes, which could later be ignored, or if implemented, easily reversed by a subsequent government. They were written into the foundational legal document of the republic. To be sure, enshrining socialist principles in a constitution does not mean necessarily that the principles will be adhered to in practice, but the very fact that they were deliberately embedded in the constitution was emblematic of the country's orientation under the leadership of a party which openly declared itself to be socialist. Not only did the Ba'athist leadership see itself as advancing a socialist agenda, so too did officials in Washington. Ba'ath Arab socialists "as far as the hawks were concerned," wrote CIA officer Robert Baer, "were Arab communists."[18] Baer himself referred to the country that Hafez al-Assad led as "socialist Syria."[19]

Socialism can be defined in many ways, but if it is defined as public-ownership of the commanding heights of the economy accompanied by economic planning, then Syria under its 1973 constitution clearly met the definition of socialism. However, the Syrian Arab Republic had never been a working-class social-ist state, of the category Marxists would recognize. It was, instead, an Arab socialist state inspired by the goal of achieving Arab political independence and overcoming the legacy of the Arab nation's underdevelopment. The framers of the 1973 con-stitution saw socialism as a means to achieve national liberation and economic development. "The march toward the establish-ment of a socialist order," the constitution's framers wrote, is a "fundamental necessity for mobilizing the potentialities of the Arab masses in their battle with Zionism and imperialism." Marxist socialism concerned itself with the struggle between an exploiting owning class and exploited working class, while Arab socialism addressed the struggle between exploiting and exploited nations. While these two different socialisms oper-ated at different levels of exploitation, the distinctions were of no moment for Westerns banks, corporations and major invest-ors as they cast their gaze across the globe in pursuit of profit. Socialism was against the profit-making interests of the U.S. industrial and financial elite, whether it was aimed at ending the exploitation of the working class or overcoming the imper-ialist oppression of national groups.

The Expedients of Political Survival

A country that rejected the leadership of the United States and sought to chart its own course in a world in which Washington demanded obedience, had to fight for its life. Washington would hardly allow foreign countries to exercise economic self-deter-mination, if it could stop them. In its 2015 U.S. National Security Strategy, the United States boldly proclaimed that it could and would "lead the world," recapitulating a goal which had guided its foreign policy since the end of World War II. Against such a declaration, the task of asserting authentic sovereignty for a small, underdeveloped country like Syria, would prove to be enormously challenging. Internal opposition would only add to the challenge, and, from the point of a view of a vanguard party, could not be tolerated. (Syria's Ba'ath Arab Socialist Party was nothing if not a party which regarded itself as being in the vanguard of a struggle; it had a mission.) All of the party's energies would have to be focused on asserting Syria's sovereignty. Dealing with internal opposition would distract from the main task of contending with formidable external opponents, namely, the United States, Israel and the hostile Arab potentates who ruled at Washington's pleasure. The external threat to independence posed by Washington's demand that all states fall in behind its leadership, would militate not only against a competitive multi-party state, but against an open society. By exploiting open society guarantees of civil and political liberties, such as freedom of speech, freedom of assembly, and freedom of the press, proxies of foreign countries, or indigenous forces which lacked commitment to the national independence project, would be able to organize opposition to the goal of asserting national self-determination. If so, the project of safeguarding the people from foreign domination and raising their material level would be undermined. Therefore, in the face of formidable obstacles to achieving freedom from foreign oppression, a party which abandoned its vanguard role before these tasks were complete, would fail. Democracy, in its original sense of rule by an oppressed people, would never be achieved. The theorist of democracy, C.B. Macpherson, made this point cogently.

> "The very enormity of the tasks confronting such a new state is apt to operate in two ways to reinforce the tendency to a non-liberal state. If the magnitude of the tasks captures the imagination of the whole people, or the whole active part of the people, they are likely to give full support to the leader and the movement which launched the new state, and are likely to see no point in competing parties.

"But equally, if the magnitude of the tasks fails to enlist the active support of the whole people, it works in the same direction. Suppose that there are sections of the population who do not share this zeal for modernization. Or suppose, as happens often enough, that there are sections who share the general purpose but who, because of tribal or religious or language difference, are reluctant to work under the leadership of the dominant party, and who consequently seek to establish or maintain opposition movements or parties. In such cases, their opposition is apt to be regarded as close to treason. For the newly-independent nation has to work, if not to fight, for its very life. It is bound to press on with the work of modernization at the risk of falling again under outside domination. The fear of falling into what they call neo-colonialism is always present. Hence, opposition to the dominant party appears to be, and sometimes actually is, destructive of the chances of nationhood. In such circumstances, opposition appears as treason against the nation. Matters are made worse if there is evidence, as there sometimes is, that the opposition has placed itself at the service of the foreigner, but this is not needed to make opposition appear as treason.

"Thus in a newly-independent underdeveloped country there are strong inherent pressures against a liberal-democratic system. The pressure militates not only against a competitive party system, but also against maintenance of realistic civil liberties. Freedom of speech and publication, and freedom from arbitrary arrest and detention, are under the same sort of pressure as is freedom of association."[20]

Politics is often reduced (unhelpfully) to the psychology of the men and women who assume leadership roles in political struggles. It is not unusual to hear of the non-liberal, single-party state of post-colonial societies as a form of government that springs from revolutionary leaders' lust for power, rather than from the logic of the circumstances in which revolutionaries find themselves. This fits an ubiquitous discourse which holds all revolutionaries to be dictators in embryo.

Another view is that some political arrangements are better adapted for some circumstances than are others. The Italian philosopher and historian Domenico Losurdo has argued that totalitarianism is the ideology of total war; in other words, that totalitarianism is not inherent in ideology but political circumstances.[21] Governments become totalitarian in times of grave crisis, no matter what their political stripe. However, totalitarianism has often been associated by liberal ideologues as the exclusive preserve of fascist and communist governments. But the exclusive association of totalitarianism with fascism and communism is an error. In times of danger, when strong leadership, unity of purpose and maintenance of the general will have been necessary, liberal democracies have become totalitarian. During the Second World War, the U.S. president and British prime minister assumed near dictatorial powers, presiding over virtual one-party states with national unity governments that took control of the economy, locked up suspected fifth columnists without trial, and, in the case of the United States, railroaded Japanese Americans into concentration camps.

In 1917, Bolshevik revolutionaries came to power in Russia, and created a multi-party political system based on councils. This turned out to be a short-lived experiment. By 1921, the Bolsheviks had abandoned their initial tolerance of a multi-party arrangement in favor of a one-party state. Why? Ideology was not the reason. The structural logic of the Bolshevik's situation was.

Lenin had embraced the idea of a decentralized workers' commune state in his *State and Revolution*, written shortly before the Bolshevik Revolution, and he initially set out to construct a decentralized model of socialism based on worker self-management and political power invested in soviets. The Bolsheviks quickly jettisoned this model as ill-suited to the circumstances in which Russia found itself at the time. The economy had virtually collapsed as a result of the pressures of the First World War. A civil war was in full swing. And over a dozen countries had invaded Russia to crush the nascent revolution. Lenin and his fellow revolutionaries faced a litany of Herculean problems whose solutions were not to be found in the works of Marx and Engels. Key elements of the 1917 revolu-

THE DEN OF ARABISM 57

tion—power to the Soviets, worker control of industry, abolition

tion—power to the Soviets, worker control of industry, abolition of the standing army—proved to be unworkable in the face of the redoubtable threats the country faced. Feeding the population, winning a civil war, and repelling the aggression of the Entente, demanded top down control and unity.[22] As it was once eloquently put, so many Bolshevik illusions were quickly ground away by the pumice stone of experience.

The Bolsheviks arrived at a conclusion that all other successful revolutionaries would arrive at in the twentieth century, namely, that multiple parties exacerbated divisions and antagonisms, as each party competed for electoral support, or squabbled over goals and pulled in different directions, at precisely the moment unity and cooperation were needed most.[23] Accordingly, a one-party state, or vanguard state, in which a single party existed with others but was *primus inter pares*, was a *sine qua non* of political survival under daunting circumstances.

U.S. propagandists have made careers of constructing panegyrics to the supposed American commitment to freedom and democracy, in contradistinction to the 'dictatorial' ways of communist and post-colonial states which had broken with capitalist exploitation or foreign domination or both. Their discourse encouraged the view that "freedom and democracy" were freely chosen, just as were restrictions on civil and political liberties, without regard to the structural logic of the circumstances in which countries found themselves. What the propagandists failed to mention was that non-liberal one-party states arose as adaptations to enormous political challenges which required strong leadership and unity of purpose; that communist and post-colonial states had to fight for their lives against the fierce opposition of the Great Powers; and that when Washington itself faced even less formidable dangers it regularly shed its liberal and democratic institutions. As Losurdo reminds us about the United States:

> "In reality, although protected by the Atlantic and Pacific, every time it has rightly or wrongly felt itself imperiled, the North American republic has preceded to more or less drastic reinforcement

of executive power and to more or less heavy restrictions on freedom of association and the press. This applies to the years immediately following the French Revolution (when its devotees on American soil where hit by the Alien and Sedition Act), to the Civil War, the First World War, the Great Depression, the Second World War and the Cold War. Even in our day, the sequel to the attack of 11 September 2001 was the opening of a concentration camp at Guantanamo, where detainees have been imprisoned without trial, and without even being informed of a specific charge, regardless of age. However terrible, the threat of terrorism is minor compared with that of invasion and military occupation, not to mention nuclear destruction."[24]

In regard to Syria, it should be noted that the threat of invasion from Israel was unremitting, and that part of Syria's territory, the Golan Heights, had been invaded in 1967 by Israel and was under Israeli military occupation. What's more, Israel, a hostile settler state with a long record of territorial expansion and aggression, was nuclear armed. The United States itself, the world's preeminent nuclear-weapons state (and one which refused to renounce the first strike use of nuclear arms) was openly committed to toppling the government in Damascus. The government of Bashar al-Assad was issued a virtual declaration of war on May 6, 2002 when Washington added Syria to its list of "Axis of Evil" states. Moreover, on two occasions, Syria was threatened with nuclear destruction—in 1970 by the United States and in 1973 by Israel.[25] In both world wars the United States faced neither the threat of nuclear annihilation nor a realistic threat of invasion, and certainly did not face the hostility of a country stronger than it militarily by many orders of magnitude. This remained the case after 9/11. In other words, the threats faced by the United States in two world wars and after 9/11, no matter how grave they were, were less minatory than the threats which Arab nationalist Syria faced. All the same, U.S. presidents assumed virtual dictatorial powers in both WWI and WWII, and strengthened the United States' police state powers in response to the 9/11 attacks. If it was acceptable, indeed, necessary for Washington to adopt totalitarian powers under conditions of total war, was it not also acceptable, or indeed, necessary, for Syria to do the same?

There was another reason why an illiberal, lead-party state was necessary in a post-colonial situation. As Macpherson explained, there is often a "need to create a pervasive loyalty to the nation rather than to the tribe, the ethnic community or the local community."[26] A single party was able to reach across the divisions of the nation, to bring people together and to fight against their common enemy.

To those of us who have grown up in liberal democratic societies, all of this is difficult to comprehend. How can a one-party, or lead-party, vanguard state be democratic, especially if it denies civil and political liberties to its opponents? Surely, a country is only democratic if its people can choose among two or more candidates in regularly scheduled elections. There are all kinds of ideas about what democracy is, and should be, but there are generally two kinds of ways in which democracy has been defined: as a set of procedures for electing candidates to public office, or as a type of society. The original definition of democracy hews closer to the second sense: as a type of society, specifically, one in which a formerly oppressed class or people rule.

A century and a half ago, aristocrats thought that democracy was a horrible idea, on par, if not synonymous with, kakistocracy, rule by the very worst people. (Aristocracy, by contrast, means rule by the "best" people.) The newly emergent capitalist class had its reservations about democracy, too. It was fine, but only if it was restricted to people of property and if elected chambers were held in check by the sober second thought of bodies of appointed representatives of the elite. It's only in the last 200 years that democracy has come to be almost universally lauded (though significantly not by Washington's allies in the war on Syria: the Arab monarchs and mujahedeen militants).

Today, democracy, as a set of procedures for electing people to public office, is lionized by the capitalist elite of the liberal democratic world, though it's very unlikely that capitalists would welcome democracy as real, genuine rule by the masses, in which decision-making is aimed at promoting and defending the interests of the rabble (employees or a formerly colonized people) against the elite (employers or imperialist powers). The capitalist elite embraces democracy in the first sense (a set of procedures), and deplores it in the second (a type of society).

Competitive multi-party elections haven't led to rule by elected representatives who represent the rabble in any meaningful sense, a reality that is obvious in examining who gets elected, and the kinds of policies elected representatives initiate and approve. Almost invariably, it is people with connections to the business community, or support from it, who win elections. Almost invariably, too, the policies elected politicians implement, favor business interests. As we've seen, Gilens and Page found that "economic elites and organized groups representing business interests have substantial impacts on government policy, while average citizens and mass-based interests groups have little or no independent influence."[27] The scholars' findings seriously challenge the idea that, as a type of society, the United States is democratic. Washington's ideologues might call the United States the world's premier democracy, but how can it be a democracy if average citizens and mass-based interest groups have little or no independent sway over the policies of the state? The fears that elites once had, when democracy was held in disrepute, that competitive multi-party elections would lead to socialist revolution through the ballot box and rule by the rabble, turned out to be baseless. Within a capitalist framework, democracy as a set of procedures for electing representatives does not translate into democracy as a type of society in which average citizens and mass-based interest groups have decisive influence over government policy.

There are a number of barriers which organically arise within a capitalist society which prevent democracy in the first sense from becoming democracy in the second. The most obvious barrier is that wealthy investors can shape electoral outcomes because they are the richest source of campaign contributions and are the most able to invest in the electoral process. But there are other mechanisms, as well, which allow the top income stratum to constrain the way in which representative democracies operate so that public policy regularly comports with its interests. These mechanisms will be explored more fully in a subsequent chapter, but for the moment, suffice to say, that liberal democracy has not led to a flowering of working class interests at the expense corporations, banks and wealthy investors. In political competitions within the framework of procedural electoral democracies in capitalist societies, the rabble rarely wins.

Still, however much business elite interests thrive, and the interests of the rabble are regularly ignored, Western-style multi-party elections elicit the consent of the ruled for their political rulers. As a consequence, democracy as a set of procedures for electing people to public office seems to produce legitimate outcomes. After all, who voted for the business-friendly candidates, if not the masses themselves?

However, equating democracy with a set of procedures for electing candidates to office confuses means and ends. The procedures are intended as a path to an end—the end being democracy as a type of society. But within capitalist societies the end is never reached. If a semblance of democracy is reached, it is usually because the rabble has exerted pressure on decision-makers through extra-electoral means—strikes, riots, demonstrations, civil disobedience, even insurgencies; in other words, because they've rejected the constraints of the electoral arena and moved the competition to the streets, where the constraints of procedural democracy no longer obtain. The rabble achieves full democracy when it rejects the top income stratum-connected decision-makers altogether, and replaces them with its own rule.

For oppressed people under the yoke of foreign domination, democracy is achieved the moment their oppression ends and they take control of their destiny—that is, the moment that rule by outside forces is replaced by a new type of society—one based on self-determination. Of course, liberation doesn't come all at once. It's a long term process, involving the smashing of thousands of chains of oppression, of resisting neo-colonialism, and overcoming the stilted development that foreign domination almost invariably produces. For these reasons, under its 1973 constitution, the Syrian Arab Republic proclaimed itself to be founded on the principle of popular democracy.

Syria's 2012 Constitution

If the structural logic of the Ba'athists' situation in 1973 favored a vanguard party and restrictions on civil liberties, the structural logic of Syria by 2011 favored the easing of restrictions to accommodate demands made throughout the Arab world for greater political openness. It was still necessary to guard against the risk that the country would fall under the sway of neo-colonial domination; to deter further encroachments on Syrian soil by the Zionist settler state; to recover the Syrian territory of the Golan Heights; to contribute to the Palestinian national liberation movement; to further the goals of Arab nationalism; and to discourage U.S. armed aggression. All of these goals could be served by maintaining the state as one led by a vanguard party, and by restricting the freedoms available to enemies to frustrate the party's achievement of these goals. The forces the Ba'athists were confronting—the U.S. compulsion to obtrude its political and economic agenda on other countries; the collusion of the former European colonial powers in the U.S. project of global domination; Israel's proclivity to expansionism; and the political reaction of the pro-imperialist Arab oil monarchies—were formidable, and much stronger than the Syrian state. Opening up Syrian society to unrestricted political opposition would imperil the Arab nationalist project. When the infant Bolshevik state was surrounded by enemies who were stronger than the Bolsheviks by many orders of magnitude, Lenin argued that allowing the revolution's enemies freedom of political organization would be self-defeating. "We do not wish to do away with ourselves by suicide and therefore will not do this," the Bolshevik leader averred.[28] However, by 2011, Lenin's logic as applied to Syria had to be moderated to fit new circumstances: protesters were demanding the lifting of restrictions on political opposition. The survival of Ba'athism as a movement of Arab national liberation now demanded flexibility. Accordingly, the Ba'athists made a number of concessions that were neither superficial nor partial.

First, they cancelled the long-standing abridgment of civil liberties that had been authorized by the emergency law. The law, invoked because Syria remained technically in a state of war with Israel, gave Damascus powers it needed to safeguard the security of the state in wartime, a measure states at war routinely take. Many Syrians, however, bristled under the law, and regarded it as unduly restrictive. Bowing to popular pressure, the government lifted the security measures.

Second, the government proposed a new constitution which would strip the Ba'ath Party of its special status. Additionally, the presidency would be open to anyone meeting basic residency, age and citizenship requirements, and would no longer be restricted to Ba'athists. Presidential elections would be held by secret vote every seven years under a system of universal suffrage.

By making these concessions, the Ba'athist government was delivering the multi-party democracy that Western state officials and media said (erroneously it turned out) protesters had clamored for. The constitution was put to a referendum and approved. New parliamentary multi-party elections were held. And a multi-candidate presidential election was set for 2014 (subsequently held and won handily by Assad).

Despite all of the preceding, the insurgency intensified, as outside powers—Saudi Arabia, Qatar and Turkey—poured money into it. The insurgents rejected the reforms, explaining that they had arrived too late. Yet the date the reforms were implemented hardly made them less desirable or significant. If single-payer health insurance comes to the United States, will U.S. citizens dismiss it on grounds that it should have come decades ago? Washington, London and Paris also dismissed the Syrian government's concessions. The concessions were "meaningless," they said, but did not explain why.[29] And yet the reforms were all that Western states said the opposition had asked for, inviting the question: Had they really asked for this? After all, if someone asks for A, and when A is granted, he dismisses it, did he really want A—or, had he even asked for it? If a methodical study had been carried out to document the aspirations of the people who participated in the uprising, I'm not aware of it. The only people who knew what had sparked the demonstrations were the demonstrators themselves. It was the Western media which gave the amorphous phenomenon of violent street demonstrations its form, declaring that protesters were demanding democracy and civil liberties. But if so, how could concessions of more democracy and more openness be meaningless? If the concessions were truly meaningless, as the West, by now the self-proclaimed champion of the "opposition," said they were, could the Ba'athist government be blamed for concluding that "democracy was not the driving force of the revolt"?[30]

Elaborating on this theme, the Syrian president noted:

> "It was seemingly apparent at the beginning that demands were for reforms. It was utilized to appear as if the crisis was a matter of political reform. Indeed, we pursued a policy of wide scale reforms from changing the constitution to many of the legislations and laws, including lifting the state of emergency law, and embarking on a national dialogue with all political opposition groups. It was striking that with every step we took in the reform process, the level of terrorism escalated."[31]

From Washington's perspective, the new constitution opened space for alternative political parties. Washington could exploit this new openness to gain leverage in Syria by quietly backing parties that favored pro-U.S. positions—a plus. But from the point of view of the Islamists, who were a major force in Syria, and had been for decades, there were only negatives. First, the constitution was secular, and not rooted in Islam. Second, it proposed to ban political parties or movements that were formed on the basis of religion, sect, tribe, or region, as well as on the basis of gender, origin, race or color. This would effectively ban any party whose aim was to establish an Islamic state.

There were negatives too for Washington, London, Paris and Tel Aviv.

First, the constitution's preamble sought continuity with the Arab nationalist mission of the 1973 constitution, defining Syria as "the beating heart of Arabism," and "the forefront of confrontation with the Zionist enemy and the bedrock of resistance against colonial hegemony on the Arab world and its capabilities and wealth." This hardly accorded with Washington's long held goal of turning Syria into a "peace-partner" with Israel and clashed with the Western project of spreading neo-colonial tentacles throughout the Arab world.

Second, the constitution formalized the political orientation of the Syrian Ba'athists. This had been summed up by Assad as "Syria is an independent state working for the interests of its people, rather than making the Syrian people work for the interests of the West."[32] Accordingly, the constitution mandated that important sectors of the Syrian economy would remain publicly owned and operated in the interests of Syrians as a whole. Western firms, then, were to be frozen out of profit-making opportunities in key sectors of the Syrian economy, a prospect hardly encouraging to the Wall Street financial interests that dominated decision-making in Washington.

Ba'ath socialism had long irritated Washington. The Ba'athist state had exercised considerable influence over the Syrian economy, through ownership of enterprises, subsidies to privately-owned domestic firms, limits on foreign investment, and restrictions on imports. The Ba'athists regarded these measures as necessary economic tools of a post-colonial state trying to wrest its economic life from the grips of former colonial powers and to chart a course of development free from the domination of foreign interests.

Washington's goals, however, were obviously antithetical to the Ba'athists' Arab nationalist mission. It didn't want Syria to nurture its industry and zealously guard its independence, but to serve the interests of the bankers and major investors who truly mattered in the United States, by opening Syrian labor to exploitation and Syria's land and natural resources to foreign ownership. "Our agenda," the Obama Administration had declared in 2015, recapitulating U.S. foreign policy strategy since the end of World War II, "is focused on lowering tariffs on American products, breaking down barriers to our goods and services, and setting higher standards to level the playing field for American...firms."[33] Damascus wasn't falling into line behind a Washington that insisted that it could and would "lead the global economy."[34]

If hardliners in Washington had considered Hafez al-Assad an Arab communist, U.S. officials considered his son, Bashar, an ideologue who couldn't bring himself to abandon the third pillar of the Ba'ath Arab Socialist Party's program: socialism (nor the party's pro-Palestinian and Arab nationalist positions). The U.S. State Department complained that Syria had "failed to join an increasingly interconnected global economy," which is to say, had failed to turn over its state-owned enterprises to private investors, among them Wall Street financial interests. The U.S. State Department also expressed dissatisfaction that "ideological reasons" had prevented Assad from liberalizing Syria's economy, that "privatization of government enterprises was still not widespread," and that the economy "remains highly controlled by the government."[35] Clearly, Assad hadn't learned what Washington had dubbed the "lessons of history," namely, that "market economies, not command-and-control economies with the heavy hand of government, are the best."[36] By drafting a constitution that mandated that the government maintain a role in guiding the economy on behalf of Syrian interests, and that the Syrian government would not

make Syrians work for the interests of Western banks, corporations, and investors, Assad was asserting Syrian independence
against Washington's agenda of "opening markets and leveling
the playing field for American...businesses abroad."[37]

On top of all this, Assad underscored his allegiance to socialist values against what Washington had once called the "moral
imperative" of "economic freedom,"[38] by writing certain social
rights into the constitution: security against sickness, disability and old age; access to health care; and free education at all
levels. These rights would continue to be placed beyond the
easy reach of legislators and politicians who could sacrifice
them on the altar of creating a low-tax, foreign-investment-
friendly climate. As a further affront against Washington's pro-
business orthodoxy, Assad retained the 1973 constitution's
commitment to progressive taxation.

Finally, the Ba'athist leader included in his updated constitution a provision that had been introduced by his father in
1973, a step toward real, genuine democracy—a provision which
decision-makers in Washington, with their myriad connections
to the banking and corporate worlds, could hardly tolerate: The
constitution would require that at minimum half the members
of the People's Assembly be drawn from the ranks of peasants
and workers.

Therein lay the real reasons Washington, London and Paris
rejected Assad's government. It championed the interests of
Syrians and Arabs rather than Wall Street and Jewish settlers
in historic Palestine. And nor was the difficulty that the
Ba'athists' reforms weren't democratic enough. It was that they
were too democratic, too focused on safeguarding and promoting the interests of Syrians, rather than making Syrians promote the interests of Wall Street, Washington and Tel Aviv.

Arab nationalist Libya

In 1969, a young Libyan military officer, Muammar Gaddafi,
led a successful *coup d'état* against the British-backed King

Idris I. Gaddafi was inspired by two figures. The first was Umar al-Mukhtar, an anti-imperialist patriot who was immortalized in the 1981 Hollywood film, "Lion of the Desert." He led his mujahedeen in opposition to Italian fascists enforcing colonial rule of Libya. The fascist leader Benito Mussolini dreamed of incorporating Libya into a new Roman Empire. The second figure who inspired Gaddafi was the great Arab nationalist leader, Gamal Abdel Nasser, the president of Egypt. "Qaddafi adored him. Indeed, in the first moments of the seizure of power, he and his colleagues wanted to turn Libya over to Egypt and themselves become Nasser's lieutenants."[39]

In the constitution Gaddafi wrote for the new state, the Arab nationalist identified the revolution's goals as freedom, socialism, and unity, the very same goals the Ba'ath Arab Socialist Party had proclaimed for itself in the 1940s, and that the Syrian Arab Republic had enshrined in its 1973 constitution. Gaddafi committed Libya to stand with "brothers from all parts of the Arab Nation in the struggle for the restoration of every inch of Arab land desecrated by imperialism and for the elimination of all obstacles which prevent Arab unity from the [Persian] Gulf to the [Atlantic] Ocean," the area historically inhabited by Arab speakers. This represented the Arab nationalist project of unity and freedom from foreign domination. As for the third goal, socialism, Gaddafi announced that the state would create "a system of national planning" and that its basis would be "public ownership." Private ownership would be allowed, but only if it was "not exploitative." Additionally, Libya would try to achieve "sufficiency in production," that is, wean itself as much as possible from dependence on industrialized countries, and march toward a just society marked by "equity in distribution." Finally, Gaddafi pledged solidarity with the Global South. Libya, he promised, would establish ties with all the people of the world who were struggling against imperialism and who understood "fully that the alliance of reaction and imperialism is responsible for their underdevelopment despite the abundance of their natural resources." This was hardly the kind of program that would appeal to the elites of the former European colonial powers, or of the United States, the new imperialist leviathan. Western powers abhorred both Marxist and Arab socialism, and didn't welcome the prospect of Arabs taking control of their own destinies, or, more to the point, their own oil.

After World War II, Libya was turned over to the United Nations, which arranged to install a man who had spent the war under the protection of the British. He would become King Idris I. The U.S. Air Force soon took over a British airbase near Tripoli. Pentagon planners coveted the base because it was close enough to the Soviet Union that its strategic bombers could easily reach Soviet targets. Gaddafi would later kick the Americans out.

In 1959, oil was discovered. King Idris I and his courtiers monopolized the oil money that flowed into Libya, infuriating Gaddafi. "For the poor tent-village-dwelling families like that of [Gaddafi's parents] this was rubbing silt into the wounds of poverty."[40]

After he seized power, Gaddafi arranged for Libya's oil wealth to be used to uplift Libyans, as the Arab socialist project enshrined in his constitution promised it would do. In 1963, "Tripoli was a city of slums with many of its houses made from scrap and most without running water or electricity," according to a former U.S. State Department official. Qaddafi's Arab socialist program "enormously improved the lives of the settled, coastal people." Under Gaddafi's government, they lived "beyond the dreams of their fathers and grandfathers."[41] Indeed, Arab nationalist Libya evinced "a remarkable record of development in almost every aspect—education, health care, infrastructure, job creation—and usually with a commendable sense of social justice."[42]

Gaddafi's Arab socialist record of human development was brought about by his "Libyanizing" the country's economy. This provoked the enmity of Washington, which preferred foreign governments which cooperated with U.S. banks, corporations and investors to "Americanize" their economies; accordingly,

Gaddafi became a favored target of U.S. regime change efforts. Those efforts came to fruition when in 2011, U.S.-led NATO forces intervened on the side of Islamist fighters who rejected Gaddafi's secular Arab nationalism, seeking to found an Islamic state in its place.

A year after Gaddafi was overthrown, *The Wall Street Journal* reported that private oil companies had been incensed at the pro-Libyan oil deals the Gaddafi government was negotiating and had "hoped regime change in Libya...would bring relief in some of the tough terms they had agreed to in partnership deals" with Libya's national oil company.[43] For decades, many European companies had enjoyed deals that granted them half of the high-quality oil produced in Libyan fields. But Gaddafi had renegotiated the companies' share of oil from each field to as low as twelve percent.[44] The Arab nationalist leader had also kept Libya's crown jewels off limits to foreigners. The huge onshore oil fields that accounted for the bulk of Libya's oil production remained the preserve of the country's state companies. Western oil companies were also frustrated that Libya's state-owned oil company "stipulated that foreign companies had to hire Libyans for top jobs."[45] A November 2007 U.S. State Department cable complained that those "who dominate Libya's political and economic leadership are pursuing increasingly nationalistic policies in the energy sector" and that there was "growing evidence of Libyan resource nationalism."[46] The cable cited a 2006 speech in which Gaddafi said: "Oil companies are controlled by foreigners who have made millions from them. Now, Libyans must take their place to profit from this money."[47] Gaddafi's government had also forced companies to give their local subsidiaries Libyan names. Worse, in the view of the oil companies, "labor laws were amended to 'Libyanize' the economy," that is, turn it to the advantage of Libyans. Oil firms "were pressed to hire Libyan managers, finance people and human resources directors." *The New York Times* summed up the West's objections. "Colonel Gaddafi," the U.S. newspaper said, "proved to be a problematic partner for international oil companies, frequently raising fees and taxes and making other demands."⁴⁸

After Gaddafi was ousted—murdered by NATO-backed Islamists—the United Nations lamented that Libya's "development has been handicapped by its command economy," and impeded by state "investments, price controls and subsidies."⁴⁹ And yet somehow Gaddafi, the Arab socialist inspired by Umar al-Mukhtar and Gamal Abdel Nasser, had transformed Libya from a country of slums and grinding poverty, where even the capital lacked running water and electricity, to a place where Libyans lived beyond the wildest imaginings of their forebears. Even a former U.S. State Department official would concede that under Gaddafi's Arab socialism, Libya had a remarkable record of development. Contrary to the UN's assessment, it wasn't Libya's development that was handicapped by Arab socialism—it was the profits of Western oil firms.

Today, the World Bank's vision for Libya is: "remove restrictions on foreign ownership of land and sectoral restrictions in banking, reform the labor code to provide necessary flexibility to business operations, and replace the progressive corporate tax with a low flat rate"⁵⁰—in other words, dismantle the Arab nationalist orientation of the Libyan state and return Libya to foreign domination.

Arab nationalist Iraq

Secular Arab nationalist Iraq was guided by the same Arab socialist principles that set the tone for the Syrian Arab Republic and Arab nationalist Libya. This was not by accident. Like the Assads in Syria, Saddam, Iraq's leader from 1979 to 2003, was a secular Arab nationalist, and partisan of the Ba'ath Party. Iraq's 1990 interim constitution sounds very much like Syria's 1973 constitution. The charter's orientation is summed up in the statement of the presidential oath: "I swear by God Almighty... to realize the objectives of the Arab Nation for unity, freedom and socialism." Here again is the tripartite commitment of the

Ba'ath Party to foster Arab unity in order to achieve freedom from foreign domination and to use state ownership, planning and intervention in the economy to overcome the colonial legacy of underdevelopment. The oath of Syria's 1973 constitution is almost identical: "I swear by God the Almighty to...work and struggle for the realization of the Arab nation's aims of unity, freedom, and socialism."

That Iraq under the leadership of the Ba'athist Saddam had an Arab nationalist mission is also evidenced in the educational goals the state set for itself in its constitution. These were to create "a national, liberal and progressive generation" which "struggles against...capitalistic ideology, exploitation, reaction, Zionism, and imperialism for the purpose of realizing Arab unity, liberty and socialism." The Syrian Arab Republic promoted similar values in its schools, inculcating students with "Syrian patriotism, Ba'athist socialism, anti-imperialism, and anti-Zionism," according to Moshe Ma'oz.[51] One can imagine the reaction in Washington to the promotion of such blatantly anti-imperialist, pro-Arab, and pro-socialist values. During the Vietnam War, then U.S. Secretary of State Dean Rusk asserted that the United States could not be secure until the total international environment was ideologically safe. Secular Arab nationalists in Iraq and Syria did not cooperate with the Rusk-defined project. Instead, they instilled in Arab children values which ran counter to the idea that a Washington-led global capitalist order was inevitable and desirable; that U.S. leadership was "indispensable."

The Arab nationalists' charter for Iraq set as a distant goal "the realization of one Arab State," following the thinking of Sati al-Husri. In the meantime, Saddam's government would focus on creating unity within Iraq. The Ba'athists encouraged citizens to identify as Iraqis, rather than as members of a clan, tribe or sect. To facilitate the achievement of this aim, clan and tribal names were banned. This explains why Saddam became know by a single name. Saddam's full name was Saddam Hussein al-Majid al-Tikriti, which comprised his first name, his father's first name, his clan name and his tribal name. With clan and tribal names proscribed, the remaining choices were Saddam, the man's first name, or Hussein, his father's first name. Contrary to a widely held misconception, Hussein was not Saddam's surname. Saddam called himself Saddam, and virtually everyone in Iraq knew him by this name.[52]

Socialism was also an important part of Arab nationalist Iraq, and it was prominently mentioned in the country's 1990 constitution, where its achievement was elevated to one of the principal goals of the Iraqi republic. The republic existed, in part, according to the constitution, to bring about the "build-up of the socialist system." According to the constitution, the commanding heights of the economy—Iraq's natural resources and "basic means of production"—were to be "owned by the People," and the state would assume "responsibility for planning, directing, and steering the national economy." While "private ownership and economic individual liberty" would be allowed, they would be subordinate to the public sector, which would be primary. Private sector activity would be exercised only in a manner compatible with "economic and general planning."

The Ba'athists defined work as a right, to be "ensured...for every citizen." Education would be "free of charge, in its primary, secondary and university stages, for all citizens," and the state would assume "the responsibility to safeguard the public by continually expanding free medical services, in protection, treatment, and medicine." In other words, Iraq's Arab socialists had written into their country's constitution pledges to provide full employment, free education and free health care, within an economy that was to be publicly owned and planned to serve the public interest, and which welcomed private enterprise so long as it remained subordinate to the public sector.

Iraqis loved their socialist system; U.S. officials did not.

For ordinary Iraqis, the country's public sector economy was one of Iraq's great achievements,[53] and the Ba'athists' nationalization of the Iraq Petroleum company "was perhaps the most popular move Saddam ever made."[54] The Ba'athists used Iraq's publicly-owned oil industry to remake Iraqi society, building vast new infrastructure. "A golden age seemed to have begun... Schools, universities, hospitals, factories, theaters and museums proliferated; employment became so universal that a labor shortage developed."[55]

While a boon for Iraqis, Iraq's booming public sector economy was a problem for Washington, for two reasons.

The first reason was that the Ba'athists' socialist policies removed Iraq from the geographic territory within which U.S. banks, corporations and investors could freely maneuver in search of profits. Since public ownership is exclusive of private ownership, whatever sectors of the Iraqi economy the Arab socialist state owned was a lost opportunity for U.S. businesses.

The second reason was that Ba'athist Iraq illustrated an Arab nationalist truth which Washington did not want publicized. The truth was that Arabs could thrive beyond their wildest imaginings if they united to free their homeland from foreign domination, and, by dint of public ownership and planning, used their vast resources, both natural and human, to overcome the colonial legacy of their underdevelopment.

Both Iraq and Syria were led by Arab nationalists committed to state ownership and planning of the economy, but Iraq had "programs in health, education and social affairs" which were "far in advance of other Arab countries," including Syria.[56] To be sure, Syria "had a remarkable social program including a more encompassing healthcare system than America's and free universal education,"[57] but Ba'athist "Iraq was socially and economically more progressive than Assad's Syria."[58] The reason for the difference was oil: Iraq had a lot of it, and Syria had hardly any.

So, if Ba'athist Iraq could create a new golden age, imagine what could be accomplished by harnessing the entire oil wealth of the Arab homeland, from Iraq to Arabia to North Africa. In his book *Devil's Game*, Robert Dreyfuss presented this as an inspiring vision for Arab nationalists, and a dire threat for the

United States and the kings, emirs and sultans of the Persian Gulf who relied on Washington to protect them from their subjects.

> "The oil monarchies are ruled by royal kleptocracies whose legitimacy is nil and whose existence depends on outside military protection. Most Arabs are aware that the monarchies were established by imperialists seeking to build fences around oil wells. Arabs would gain much by combining the sophistication and population of the Arab centers, including Iraq, with the oil wealth of the desert kingdoms. At the center lies Egypt, with its tens of millions of people and Saudi Arabia with its 200 billion barrels of oil. Uniting Cairo and Riyadh would create a vastly important Arab center of gravity with worldwide influence."[59]

Bernard Lewis, an intellectual attached to the enormously influential U.S. foreign policy think tank, the Council on Foreign Relations, outlined the reasons for the U.S. military intervention in the Persian Gulf in 1991 in the Council's magazine Foreign Affairs, with reference to the need to protect the security of a very large part of the world's oil supply:

> "If Saddam Hussein had been allowed to continue unchecked [following Iraq's 1990 invasion of Kuwait] he would have controlled the oil resources of both Iraq and Kuwait. If the rest of the region observed that he could act with impunity, the remaining Persian Gulf states would sooner rather than later have fallen into his lap, and even the Saudis would have had either to submit or be overthrown. The real danger was monopolistic control of oil—which is a very large portion of the world's oil."[60]

Dick Cheney, then the U.S. vice-president, invoked a similar rationale in August 2006 to explain the U.S. invasion of Iraq in 2003: "Armed with an arsenal of...weapons of mass destruction, and seated atop 10 percent of the world's oil reserves, Saddam Hussein could then be expected to seek domination of the entire Middle East [and] take control of the world's energy supplies."[61]

One cannot help but think that the motivation which drove Washington to attack Iraq in two wars, and to cripple it with sanctions in the interim, had little to do with safeguarding the security of the United States' oil supply. Canada is by far the largest foreign supplier of oil to the United States, accounting for 43 percent of all imports,[62] versus just 22 percent in 2012 from six Persian Gulf suppliers.[63] The United States itself, is a major producer of oil, third ranked in the world, behind only Saudi Arabia and Russia.[64] Moreover, "increasing production and declining consumption have unexpectedly brought the United States markedly closer to a goal that has tantalized presidents since Richard Nixon: independence from foreign energy sources."[65]

As a major producer of oil, the United States has never been as dependent on Persian Gulf oil as it is popularly believed—and indeed, has never been dependent on the Persian Gulf for supplies of oil to any significant degree. It wasn't until the mid-1970s, when consumption began to outstrip domestic supply that the United States began to import oil from the Persian Gulf. An observation made by the sociologist Albert Szymanski in 1983 is still relevant today. "Much has been made of supposed U.S. reliance on the Persian Gulf area for petroleum. But while tremendous profits are made by U.S.-based petroleum corporations that continue to dominate the petroleum industry in this region, the United States is not in fact especially reliant on petroleum imports from the Gulf."[66] Indeed,

> "until the mid-1970s, very little Middle Eastern petroleum was imported into the United States, even though U.S. transnational corporations had controlled the petroleum consortiums in the area for a generation. During this time, U.S. transnational corporations took the oil out of the ground and sold it to Europe and Japan (as well as to the less developed countries) making tremendous profits, which they in good measure repatriated to the United States.
>
> "In 1976...U.S. petroleum companies in the Middle East exported less than 7 percent of their output to the United States while selling 82 percent to third countries."[67]

The alarm raised by Cheney to justify the U.S. invasion of Iraq—that there was a risk that Arab nationalist Iraq would seize control of the world's energy supplies—is problematic in two ways. First, he falsely conflated Persian Gulf oil with "the world's" energy supplies. As we have seen, Persian Gulf oil makes up only a fraction of the world's oil supply, and the United States is not particularly dependent on it. Second, if the scenario Cheney envisaged were realized, it is very unlikely that the United States would have been cut off from the small proportion of its oil it derived from the Middle East. Since the golden age the Arab nationalists were building in Iraq depended crucially on oil sales, it would have remained in their interests to continue to provide oil to the world market. The problem, from Washington's perspective, was not that the Arab nationalists would cut the United States off from access to oil from the Middle East, but that they would cut U.S. oil companies off from the immense profits they derived from selling Arab oil to Western Europe and Japan.

The real danger from Washington's perspective was alluded to by Lewis. Had Arab nationalist Iraq been successful in conquering Kuwait, it may have achieved monopolistic control of the Arab homeland's oil in West Asia. This would have meant that Arab public sector control of oil would expand from Iraq to Kuwait to Saudi Arabia; that these new publicly-controlled resources would be used by ideologically-inspired Arab nationalists to provide full employment, free health care and free education, along with a vast expansion of infrastructure projects across the region; and that U.S. banks, corporations and investors would be largely cut out of the action. Washington's real concern, therefore, was not that Americans would be left to freeze in the dark and wait in queues at the gas pumps, but that U.S. oil firms would lose control of the Middle East's oil to Arabs who would use these resources for the uplift of the Arab nation, with the consequence that the lion's share of the benefit of Arab oil would flow to the resource's rightful owners, rather than to corporate America.

It could be said that Washington's long campaign against Ba'athist Iraq was precisely intended to crush the threat that the Arab nationalists in Baghdad would show the Arab street that substantial gains in living standards could be achieved if the Arab world followed the secular nationalists' program of unifying to bring the Arab nation's resources and destiny under its own control. At the same time, Washington's 2003 invasion of Iraq, subsequent occupation, and remaking of Iraqi economics and politics, was aimed at toppling Iraq's public sector economy to create new profit-making opportunities for U.S. businesses—ones they had been denied while the Arab nationalists were in power—while preventing a recrudescence of Arab nationalism by outlawing Ba'athism altogether.

U.S. proconsul Paul Bremer was no fan of Iraqi socialism, and anyone who doubts that Arab nationalist Iraq was socialist should not doubt that U.S. officials thought it was. Bremer complained that "Anybody who'd been in Iraq [under Ba'athist rule] had seen a totally socialist government-dominated economy."[68] He branded Iraq's public sector oil industry as a manifestation of the Ba'athists' "vicious brand of socialism."[69] Saddam, it seemed, was, like Assad, little more than an Arab communist, from the point of view of U.S. officials. At least, the consequences of his policies for U.S. business interests were the same as those that genuine communists would have implemented.

With Washington having dealt a crushing blow to secular Arab nationalism in Iraq with its 2003 invasion, there was a desire to prevent the ideology from ever again guiding the Iraqi state. Bremer's first order as the country's new military dictator was titled "De-Ba'athification of Iraqi Society." The edict ordered the disbanding of the Ba'ath Party and the purge of Ba'ath Arab nationalists from positions in the Iraqi state. Bremer's rationale, he explained, was to protect "the Iraqi people who have suffered large scale human rights abuses and deprivation over many years at the hands of the Ba'ath Party."[70] But Bremer's rationale was hardly convincing. The United States had long had an informal working relationship with the

Ba'athist government. It collaborated with the Arab nationalists to weaken Communist influence in Iraq, and to challenge
the Islamic Revolution in Iran. Washington had raised few
objections to Ba'athist Iraq carrying out large scale human
rights abuses against individuals, parties, and movements the
United States was hostile to. Nor did it object to Baghdad
waging war on Iran, at the point Iran had become an object of
U.S. hostility, following the country's Islamic revolution; on the
contrary, Washington helped Iraq prosecute the war. A more
convincing explanation of why Bremer ordered the anti-
Ba'athist purge was that Washington opposed most aspects of
the Ba'ath Party's ideological orientation: its commitment to
freedom from outside domination; its long-term goal of building a pan-Arabic super-state; and its embrace of socialism. It
could be said that the U.S. war on Syria, and Washington's
demand that "Assad step down," were simply Bremer's Coalition
Provisional Authority Number 1 applied to Syria. The object
was the De-Ba'athification of the Syrian state.

The post Arab nationalist, U.S. sanctioned, Iraqi constitution prohibited Ba'athism, banning any "entity or program"
which acted to "incite, glorify, promote, or justify" Arab nationalist ideology, "regardless of the name it adopts." Hence, promotion of unity, freedom and socialism was declared verboten.
Ba'athism, the constitution made clear, could "not be part of
political pluralism in Iraq." Only ideologies of subservience to
U.S. imperial power were permissible. If Lenin had decided that
opponents of the Bolshevik Revolution would not be allowed
to freely organize its demise, the United States decided that
opponents of U.S. imperialism would not be allowed to freely
organize anti-imperialist opposition within Iraq's political
arena. Thus, in post-Arab nationalist Iraq, pluralism had a special meaning: neither pro-Arab nor secular nationalist. Over
560 secular nationalist Iraqis were prevented from running as
candidates in Iraq's 2009 elections, under the provisions of the
de-Ba'athification articles of Iraq's Washington-approved constitution. This allowed the election to be monopolized by Shi'a

Muslim and Sunni Muslim sectarians.[71] If Westerners believed that the rise of sectarian parties in post-Ba'athist Iraq proved that the secular nationalists had no support, they were wrong. All it meant was that secular nationalism, with its emphasis on Arab unity, anti-imperialism, and socialism, had been permanently banned from Iraqi politics, leaving the field open to domination by sectarian parties and a future of religious division. How helpful for Washington.

Having eliminated secular nationalism *sine die* from Iraqi politics, the U.S. occupation authorities set out to reverse the sins the secular nationalists had committed against the profit-making interests of U.S. banks, corporations and investors.

> "At the center of the policy promulgated by Mr. Bremer and designed by the Bush administration was a series of moves that effectively 'denationalized' the Iraqi economy. This policy was directed toward not only privatizing state-owned enterprises but also allowing them to be purchased 100 percent by foreign interests. The intent of the Bush administration policy was to make Iraq the perfect example of what the Economist called 'a capitalist dream.' Actually, it was not only that but more pointedly a foreign capitalists' dream."[72]

In conjunction with transferring most of Iraq's economy to private sector control, Bremer promulgated policies to "lift all restrictions on the importation of goods. These edicts were effected when the Iraqi economy was shattered by the war and so placed local entrepreneurs and manufacturers at a severe disadvantage. They simply could not compete, often lacking adequate machinery and access to raw materials, with cheap imported goods."[73] At the same time, U.S. firms were "given the inside track on all major reconstruction contracts, while most Iraqi firms and firms from other countries" were excluded.[74] These policies demonstrated that Iraq, from the point of view of Washington, was simply an investment sphere for corporate America. Hillary Clinton underscored the point: "It's time for the United States to start thinking of Iraq as a business opportunity," she said.[75] It seemed to have escaped her notice that the

United States had never stopped thinking of Iraq as a business opportunity.

Oman

A secret war Britain waged against Arab nationalists in Oman to defend a despised puppet ruler illustrates the longstanding and continuing conflict between the West and its Arab proxies on one side and secular Arab nationalists on the other. The question was how the petroleum wealth lying beneath Arab soil would be used: for the benefit of investors who hold shares in Western oil companies or for the development needs of the indigenous Arab population?

For two centuries Britain controlled the sultans of Oman, a country situated on the southeastern tip of the Arabian Peninsula, overlooking the geo-strategically significant Strait of Hormuz, through which countless barrels of oil are shipped daily. London kept Omani rulers under its thumb by furnishing them with lucre and surrounding them with British advisers and cabinet ministers. In the mid-1960s, Sultan Said bin Taimur received over half of his income directly from Britain, a situation that was to change only when oil began to be pumped from the country in 1967, whereupon Oman's sultans no longer needed British subsidies to furnish their lavish lifestyles.[76]

While officially sovereign and independent, Oman was in reality a colony of the United Kingdom. The minister of defense and head of intelligence were British army officers. The government ministers were all British, but one. The Sultan's chief adviser worked for the British Foreign Office. The armed forces commander met every week with the British ambassador and every day with the British military attaché. And the Sultanate had a formal relationship with only one country: Britain. While in theory the Sultan had absolute authority, he was effectively a figurehead, an expedient to establish the illusion that the country was independent, and not simply what it was: a division of the British Foreign Office.[77]

Omanis were poor and ill-educated. In the mid-1960s, the country had only one hospital, three primary schools, no secondary schools, no telephones, and no infrastructure. Ninety-five percent of the population was illiterate and three-quarters died as infants. Oman was the only country in which slavery was still legal and London's man in Oman, the sultan, was a major slave owner.[78]

The sultan's rule was harsh and arbitrary. He banned radios, bicycles, soccer, sunglasses, shoes, trousers and electric pumps for wells. Offenders were publicly executed or shackled in dungeons. The Sultan owned 500 slaves, 150 of whom were women he kept at his palace, presumably for his licentious pleasure. The Sultan's subjects hated him, and hated the British who kept him in power.[79]

Conditions were not unlike those that prevailed in Libya and which had galvanized Gaddafi to launch his revolution—a British-backed monarch living in luxury in the midst of extreme poverty.

Omanis rose up against their Sultans numerous times, and each time the country's figurehead rulers relied upon British forces to quell the uprisings. By 1966, an Arab nationalist revolt broke out, backed by China. The revolutionaries threatened to seize control of Oman's new oil fields, and use them for the uplift of Omanis, rather than for the expansion of Western capital and enrichment of the Sultan and his retinue. In London, fears were raised about the Straits of Hormuz slipping from British control into the hands of the Arab nationalists, which is to say, into the hands of an indigenous force burning with aspirations for self-determination.

The British response to the revolt was swift and brutal. Villages were razed. Livestock was slaughtered. Everyone, insurgents and non-combatants, was treated as an enemy. The British journalist Ian Cobain wrote that "In their determination to put down a popular rebellion against the cruelty and neglect of a despot who was propped up and financed by Britain, British-led forces poisoned wells, torched villages, destroyed crops and shot livestock. During the interrogation of rebels they developed their torture techniques...Areas populated by civilians were turned into free-fire zones."[80]

By 1970, Britain's merciless efforts to crush the rebellion were faltering. The insurgency was growing stronger. To take the wind out of the rebellion's sails, London decided to try accommodation. MI6, the Foreign Office and Ministry of Defense plotted a palace coup. Sultan Said bin Taimur, the object of Omani animosity (along with the British) was deposed. His son, Qaboos bin Said, was installed. The new Sultan, at the behest of his British advisers, abolished slavery, and began to spend some the country's oil revenue on infrastructure development. At the same time, British SAS troops were dispatched to Oman to act as the new figurehead's palace guard.[81]

Into the second decade of the twenty-first century, Qaboos bin Said continued to rule as Oman's absolute monarch, issuing laws by decree. He maintained a ban on political parties, and acted as his own Armed Forces Chief of Staff, Minister of Defense, Minister of Foreign Affairs and head of the central bank. In theory, he formulated laws with reference to the Quran.

The Sultan was educated at Britain's Royal Military Academy, Sandhurst, training ground for various members of the British royal family, and the academy from which a number of Arab potentates working on behalf of Western interests graduated, including several Saudi princes, the Emir of Kuwait, the King of Jordan and the King of Bahrain.

Women occupied a legally subordinate position in the Sultanate and the use of torture in Omani prisons was reputed to be widespread. Oman hosted two U.S. Air Force bases, and in May 2016, Britain announced that it would establish a military base in the country.[82]

In contrast to Qaboos bin Said and his fellow Arab monarchs, Muammar Gaddafi and Saddam, men of humble origins, used their country's natural endowments to uplift their people, guided by secular Arab nationalist values. Neither, of course, was instilled with the imperialist values the Arab world's reigning potentates imbibed at Sandhurst. "When these post-colonial governments came into power, like Gaddafi or Saddam," remarked the veteran foreign correspondent Patrick Cockburn, "they were authoritarian but had a theory: they were under-developed nations so the leaders concentrated resources on regaining national sovereignty and controlling their own destiny. These had concrete aims, like in Libya or Iraq, to take control of oil and give the benefits to Libyans or Iraqis."[83]

Syria had fewer natural resources to exploit than did Libya and Iraq. Accordingly, the potential for uplift was more limited, but all the same, under the Ba'athists the rural poor made considerable advances and, as former U.S. State Department official William R. Polk observed, Ba'athist Syria "had a remarkable social program including a more encompassing healthcare system than America's and free universal education."[84] At the same time, the communist countries of Eastern Europe, despite having less material wealth than their capitalist counterparts in North America, Western Europe and Japan, produced outcomes in human development as favorable as those produced by their wealthier capitalist competitors.[85] This demonstrates the advantages that accrue in material terms to populations governed by revolutionaries who use planning and public ownership to organize their economies with explicit goals related to public welfare. The revolutionaries' goals were democratic in the sense of overcoming oppression and exploitation to uplift entire peoples and classes. Contrast the very real democratic outcomes in the Marxist and Arab socialist countries with the non-democratic outcomes in the United States, where, despite the apparatus of voting, health care and education at all levels are not free, and full-employment is not on the agenda. On the contrary, within countries which are firmly ensconced in the Washington-led global economic order, immigration, monetary and fiscal policy are deliberately formulated to avoid full employment, to ensure that an army of the unemployed is always present to keep labor in line and to maintain downward pressure on wages.

Secular Arab nationalist Syria, Libya and Iraq resisted demands from Washington that they integrate into the U.S.-superintended global economic order. Absorption into Washington's *de facto* empire would mean surrendering their development to Washington and its handmaidens, the World Bank and International Monetary Fund (IMF), which in turn would mean that the policies they were coerced into implementing would be designed to benefit Western banks, corporations and investors, not Arabs trying to break free from a legacy of colonial underdevelopment. Arab nationalists preferred to achieve political independence in order to develop their economies to deliver benefits to their populations as a whole; hence, they rejected U.S. economic prescriptions related to free-trade, free-enterprise, and open markets, and banned the U.S. military from their soil. "There were U.S. troops or other military personnel in about 160 foreign countries and territories,"[86] but none of them were in secular Arab nationalist Syria, and none were in Gaddafi's Libya or Saddam's Iraq.

The Arab socialist policies of Gaddafi and Saddam were an anathema to Washington. Socialist policies limited the space in which U.S. banks, corporations and investors could maneuver in their never ending quest for profits. Moreover, the success of Arab socialism in raising the living standards of Iraqis and Libyans—beyond the wildest dreams of their forebears—threatened to inspire people in other parts of the Arab world, who might be inclined to follow the lead of countries led by Arab nationalist ideologues. There was a danger for Washington that other Arabs would launch their own revolutions to overcome foreign domination, eject U.S. military bases from their soil, and further reduce the economic *lebensraum* of Western capitalism. The Arab nationalists' refusal to accept integration into a globe-girding U.S.-led economic order made Gaddafi and Saddam targets.

The Assads were targets too, and for precisely the same reasons. If one believed the views of U.S. officials, the United States' campaign to force Bashar al-Assad from power only began in

2011, and then only in connection with his government's response to the outbreak of unrest in March, 2011; on the contrary, Washington was motivated to eliminate Assad because he was an Arab nationalist threat to corporate America's pursuit of profits in the Arab world. Washington labored to have the world perceive the Syrian insurgency as the product of a vicious crackdown on pro-democracy dissent by a brutal dictator. Not only was this a misrepresentation (the insurgency was Islamist-inspired and what democratic content it had was meager at best), it was sheer hypocrisy and indicative of Washington's lack of sincerity. Washington had no particular dislike for vicious crackdowns on pro-democracy dissent; its Arab clients—all of them anti-democratic kings, emirs, sultans, and military leaders—were doing precisely what U.S. officials accused Assad of doing, except in their case, Washington averted its gaze. "We give a free pass to governments which cooperate and ream the others as best as we can," a U.S. official explained in a moment of candor.[87] The Saudis, Qataris, Bahrainis, Turks, Egyptians and Jordanians cooperated with Washington in protecting and promoting the interests of U.S. banks, investors and corporations in the Middle East; the Syrians did not. Accordingly, Washington's regional allies got a free pass to crack down on dissent without restraint, while the Syrian government was reamed for reacting to the eruption of violent unrest on the streets of Syrian towns in the same manner U.S. authorities would have reacted to violent unrest on U.S. streets.

Demonstrations against the absolutism of monarchy and for representative democracy in Saudi Arabia and Bahrain were paid far less attention to by the Western mass media than was the insurgency in Syria. The Saudi and Bahraini demonstrations were crushed violently, with tanks, by Washington's allies, and so Washington said nothing. By contrast, U.S. officials used febrile rhetoric to shape public understanding of Damascus's response to the insurgency in Syria. The words "brutal," "vicious," "crackdown," "dictator," and "strongman" were bandied about with little restraint. There were anti-government demonstrations in Syria, to be sure. But they were violent demonstrations. Police officers were killed. Government buildings were burned. The state reacted with force; but what state doesn't react with force to an insurrection? Nevertheless, what was a normal reaction of a government to violent unrest on its own streets was portrayed by Western officials, and in train, by the Western news media, as an illegitimate and brutal crackdown. Not only that, the crackdown, we were told, was ordered by a vicious "dictator," a description which elided the reality that the supposed dictator, having received a majority of votes in a referendum, ruled with the consent of the governed, unlike the kings, emirs, sultans and field marshals who made up Washington's roster of Arab allies. At any rate, Washington's effort to purge Damascus of its Ba'athists, with their offensive ideology of Arab unity, freedom from foreign domination, and Arab socialism, didn't begin in 2011, when U.S. president Barack Obama demanded that Assad step down. It began long before that.

CHAPTER TWO

REGIME CHANGE

Two forces sought to topple the secular Arab nationalists of Ba'athist Syria, each for its own, and separate reasons. Both forces were equally determined to end the influence of secular Arab nationalism in Syria. The common distaste of these forces for Ba'athism often led them into temporary alliances of convenience, but, apart from their shared dislike of their Ba'athist enemy, both forces were themselves mutually antagonistic.

The Ba'athists' rejection of U.S. domination of the Arab nation and their commitment to policies of economic independence provoked U.S. hostility. Ba'athist policies attenuated the profit-making *lebensraum* available to Western banks, corporations, and investors, leading Washington—heavily under the sway of Wall Street—to favor regime change in Damascus.

In the wake of the U.S.-British invasion of Iraq in 2003, the renowned Palestinian scholar Edward Said observed that "the role of American policy" is to install in Syria and Libya, regimes that are friendly to the United States, "so that [the Arab world] all becomes pro-American regimes" like the Gulf monarchies.[1] The Gulf monarchies—with their Sandhurst-educated rulers—were highly supportive of U.S. hegemony in the Arab world; their political survival in the face of their hostile subjects depended on the protection Washington provided them. In contrast, political analyst Moshe Ma'oz observed that from Washington's perspective, the roots of U.S. hostility to Ba'athist Syria could be found in the danger of its becoming "a focus of Arab nationalistic struggle against an American regional presence and interests."[2] U.S. efforts to purge Damascus of Ba'athist influence antedated the Arab Spring of 2011 by decades. In 1957, U.S. President Dwight Eisenhower and British Prime Minister Harold Macmillan approved a plan jointly formulated by their respective intelligence services to assassinate leading Ba'athists and Communists in the Syrian government. To the Washington-London axis, Abdel Hamid Sarraj, head of Syrian military intelligence, Afif al-Bizri, chief of the Syrian general staff, and Khalid Bakdash, leader of the Syrian Communist party, exercised decisive influence over the Syrian government. Washington and London believed the triumvirate was pushing Damascus toward a policy of fomenting revolts against Western-backed Arab governments which would see these governments replaced by secular Arab nationalist states aligned with the Soviet Union. This would, in the Western view, have regrettable consequences for the bottom lines of Western corporations with investments in the Middle East.

The CIA's Middle East chief Kermit Roosevelt, grandson of former president Theodore Roosevelt, masterminded the plot. He had spearheaded the *coup d'état* in Iran which overthrew the prime minister, Mohammed Mossadegh, in 1953. Mossadegh had provoked Washington's and London's animus by nationalizing Iran's petroleum industry. Roosevelt and others feared that Syria's Ba'athist-Communist alliance would encourage Mossadegh-like policies throughout the Middle East, and foster popularly-led regime change which would produce pro-independence policies.

Another of the West's concerns was that one of the main oil pipelines connecting Europe to Iraq ran through Syria. Control of the pipeline by Marxist and Arab socialists, in the view of the United States and Britain, would spell disaster for Western oil profits.[3]

Roosevelt planned to create internal uprisings in Syria, enlisting the aid of the country's Muslim Brotherhood, a principal rival to Ba'athist and Communist influence in Syria. He also plotted to create and arm paramilitary groups to wage a civil war within the country.

These features of Roosevelt's plan would show up later in Syria's 2011 uprising. The 1957 plan called for funding of a Free Syria Committee, adumbrating various Western-funded committees dedicated to regime change in Syria that sprang up circa 2011. The CIA and MI6 would also create paramilitary groups within Syria, calling to mind the CIA's covert, and Pentagon's overt, funding of anti-government fighters post 2011, as well as CIA coordination of arms deliveries from Turkey, Qatar and Saudi Arabia to jihadist paramilitary groups. The U.S. and British intelligence agencies would also "instigate internal uprisings" and "stir up the Muslim Brotherhood in Damascus."[4]

The Roosevelt plan was never carried out. Washington and London were unable to secure the support of Jordan and Iraq, both of which were expected, along with Turkey, to invade Syria and topple the Ba'athist-Communist-influenced government under the pretext of restoring order.[5]

The reasons Washington opposed secular Arab nationalism in Syria have already been explored. Washington insisted on U.S. leadership. Assad and other Arab nationalists rejected this view, resolved to follow a path that liberated the Arab world from foreign domination. Moreover, the path Syria's Arab nationalists were determined to follow—a socialist one—was at odds with U.S. demands that countries integrate into a U.S.-superintended global economy; that governments promote "economic freedom" and encourage free enterprise; and that all states stand aside to allow the United States to "lead the global economy." Rather than opening markets and leveling the playing field for U.S. businesses abroad, and dismantling "state capitalism," as Washington demanded, Arab nationalists insisted on doing the opposite—incubating domestic industry behind tariff walls, subsidizing local firms so that they could compete at home against much larger foreign competitors, and using state-owned enterprises and economic planning to overcome the colonial legacy of the Arab world's under-development. These policies put Arab industry, Arab businesses, and Arab citizens first, where Washington demanded that the interests of U.S. banks, U.S. corporations and U.S. investors be prioritized.

The second force which sought to expunge Ba'athist influence from Syrian politics was Sunni political Islam, of which the Syrian Muslim Brotherhood was emblematic. Founded in Egypt in 1928 by a young Islamic scholar named Hasan al-Banna, the Muslim Brotherhood began as a reaction against the diluting effects on the Islamic character of Egyptian society of the country's domination by Britain. Al-Banna was particularly concerned with the growing erosion of Islam as the basis for Egyptian law. Under British influence, the Islamic ethos of Egypt's jurisprudence was increasingly yielding to laws formulated without reference to the Quran, or the Sunna. Additionally, the British had narrowed the jurisdiction of Islamic religious courts, and overturned Islamic prohibitions against usury and the consumption of alcohol.

Political Islamists believed that for countries situated within the traditional domain of Islam, the Quran, the revealed word of God, and the example of Muhammad, ought to be the basis, not only of the Muslim world's moral and religious codes, but also its legal and political systems. Political Islamists followed an impeccable logic if one accepted their premise that God is perfect and had revealed a plan for humanity in the Quran. From this premise it followed that a Quran-based legal and political arrangement must be superior to systems and laws devised by mere mortals. Invoking this logic, the Muslim Brothers rejected secularism, Marxism, and nationalism as flawed (because their provenance was not God), un-Islamic (because they did not spring from the Quran), and foreign to the Muslim world (because they originated in the West).

All branches of political Islam rejected ideologies other than Islam as the basis for law. Accordingly, the Ba'ath Arab Socialist Party, with its emphasis on Arab identity rather than Islamic faith as the organizing principle of political mobilization against foreign domination, was abhorrent to the Muslim Brothers. More significantly, Ba'athism was reviled by the Brotherhood for its commitment to secularism and rejection of the Quran and Sunna as the bases for jurisprudence. Ba'athist Syria's alliance with the atheist Soviet Union during the Hafez al-Assad era, and the Brotherhood's belief that the Alawite faith, the Assads' religion, was heretical, only heightened the Brotherhood's animosity toward Syria's secular Arab nationalists.

In 1964, the Muslim Brothers led protests, strikes, demonstrations, and riots throughout Syria under the banner of "Islam or Ba'ath."[6] Brotherhood-led disturbances continued to erupt in major Syrian cities throughout the 1960s, rising to crescendos in 1965, 1967, and 1969, always in opposition to the secular government's "Godless character."[7] In 1967, in the wake of Syria's defeat by Israel in the Six Day War, the Brotherhood declared a jihad against the secular Ba'athists, denouncing them as infidels.[8]

The 1970s were marked by three significant events in the Muslim Brothers' war against the secular Syrian state.

The first of these was the outbreak of a series of violent eruptions in response to secular Arab nationalist plans to omit from the constitution a longstanding requirement that the Syrian president be a Muslim and that Islam form the basis of all jurisprudence. The plan to extirpate the historical influence of Islam on the politics of Syria and set the country's constitution on a firm secular footing was a direct affront against Muslim Brotherhood ideology, and it provoked a furious reaction. Hafez al-Assad was denounced as an enemy of Allah and jihad was declared against his "atheist" government.[9] In the face of Islamist fury, Assad eventually restored the Islamic clause to the constitution, but to no avail. Islamist hostility to his government continued unabated; indeed, it intensified.

By the mid-1970s the Muslim Brothers had moved to a new stage in their war against Syrian secularism. "Rioting would be succeeded by armed struggle with the aim of toppling Assad's secular government and supplanting it with an Islamic state under Sharia law."[10] The Brothers established an underground paramilitary group, the Combat Vanguard of Fighters. Trained and armed abroad—establishing a precedent that would be followed in 2011 when the United States and its allies armed Sunni Muslim militants to wage a guerilla war against the Syrian state—it launched a major campaign of urban guerilla warfare, assassinating Ba'ath Party leaders, state officials, army officers, and Soviet advisers, while at the same time carrying out bombings of military installations and government buildings.[11]

The guerilla campaign escalated throughout the latter half of the 1970s, culminating in the June 1979 slaughter of nearly three dozen cadets at a Syrian military school in Aleppo by a Muslim Brother who had secretly infiltrated the military. The assailant had separated the Alawite from non-Alawite cadets, locking the former in a building, where they were machine gunned and firebombed. Evincing the continuity of Islamist anger against the "infidel" Syrian state, in 2016 jihadists named an offensive in Aleppo after Ibrahim al-Yousef, the Muslim Brother who carried out the 1979 sectarian atrocity.[12]

Islamist armed struggle against Ba'athist secularism reached new heights in the 1980s. Robert Baer, a former CIA officer who spent decades in the Middle East, wrote that Syria "was the epicenter of Islamic terrorism. When I first set foot in Damascus in 1980, I estimated that Hafez al-Assad would have maybe three or four years before he went under. The Muslim Brothers owned the street. The mosque schools were teaching jihad...The mosque public-address system blared out a message of hate and revenge...I figured; the guy's going to get strung up on a light pole in downtown Damascus like a lot of other Syrians."[13]

The jihadists sought to plunge to country into a sectarian civil war to oust Assad. To bring their goal to fruition, they tried to provoke Assad's government through a campaign of growing violence, hoping that Assad would call out the army. The government's response to the violence would be labeled as an Alawite assault on the Sunni majority. It was hoped this would turn the population against the government. The same discourse about Alawites oppressing Sunnis would be used to encourage Sunni members of the Syrian Arab Army, who made up the majority of the recruits, to defect.[14]

This is evocative of the post-2011 Islamist war against the secular nationalist successors of Hafez al-Assad. Without the benefit of a historical perspective, the war in Syria appears to be a unique event, rather than what it is: a continuation of a longstanding struggle for power in Syria between secularists and Islamists.

In October 1980, the Brothers established an Islamic Front of Syria with the goal of gathering the Sunni opposition into a single anti-Ba'athist coalition. The jihadists' manifesto declared war without end until Ba'athism was eliminated in Syria.[15] Both Jordan and Israel provided support to the jihadists and training camps were established in Jordan, more or less openly,[16] adumbrating the role Jordan and Israel would play three decades later in supporting Jabhat al-Nusra, al-Qaeda's franchise in Syria.

In February 1982, the Muslim Brothers seized control of Hama, Syria's fourth largest city. Hama was the epicenter of Sunni fundamentalism in Syria, and a major base of operations for the jihadist fighters. Galvanized by a false report that Assad had been overthrown, Muslim Brothers went on a gleeful blood-soaked rampage throughout the city, attacking police stations and murdering Ba'ath Party leaders and their families, along with government officials and soldiers. In some cases, victims were decapitated,[17] a practice which would be resurrected decades later by Islamic State fighters. Every Ba'athist official in Hama was murdered.[18]

The Hama events of 1982 are usually remembered in the West (if they're remembered at all), not for the atrocities carried out by the Islamists, but for the Syrian army's response, which, as would be expected of any army, involved the use of force to restore sovereign control over the territory seized by the insurrectionists. Thousands of troops were dispatched to take Hama back from the Muslim Brothers. Former U.S. State Department official William R. Polk described the aftermath of the Syrian army assault on Hama as resembling that of the U.S. assault on the Iraqi city of Fallujah in 2004,[19] (the difference, of course, being that the Syrian army was acting legitimately within its own sovereign territory, while the U.S. military was acting illegitimately as an occupying force to quell opposition to its occupation). How many died in the Hama assault, however, remains a matter of dispute. The figures vary. "An early report in *Time* said that 1,000 were killed. Most observers estimated that 5,000 people died. Israeli sources and the Muslim Brotherhood"—sworn enemies of the secular Arab nationalists who therefore had an interest in exaggerating the casualty toll—"both charged that the death toll passed 20,000."[20] Robert Dreyfus, who has written about the West's collaboration with political Islam to undermine secular nationalists and communists in the Muslim world, argues that Western sources deliberately exaggerated the death toll in order to demonize the Ba'athists as ruthless killers, and that the Ba'athists went along with the deception in order to intimidate the Muslim Brotherhood.[21]

As the Syrian army sorted through the rubble of Hama in the aftermath of the assault, evidence was uncovered that foreign governments had provided Hama's insurrectionists with money, arms, and communications equipment. Polk writes that:

"Assad saw foreign troublemakers at work among his people. This, after all, was the emotional and political legacy of colonial rule—a legacy painfully evident in most of the post-colonial world, but one that is almost unnoticed in the Western world. And the legacy is not a myth. It is a reality that, often years after events occur, we can verify with official papers. Hafez al-Assad did not need to wait for leaks of documents: his intelligence services and international journalists turned up dozens of attempts by conservative, oil-rich Arab countries, the United States, and Israel to subvert his government. Most engaged in 'dirty tricks,' propaganda, or infusions of money, but it was noteworthy that in the 1982 Hama uprising, more than 15,000 foreign-supplied machine guns were captured, along with prisoners including Jordanian- and CIA-trained paramilitary forces (much like the jihadists who appear so much in media accounts of 2013 Syria). And what he saw in Syria was confirmed by what he learned about Western regime-changing elsewhere. He certainly knew of the CIA attempt to murder President Nasser of Egypt and the Anglo-American overthrow of the government of Iranian Prime Minister Mohammad Mossadegh."[22]

In his book *From Beirut to Jerusalem, New York Times* columnist Thomas Friedman wrote that "the Hama massacre could be understood as, 'The natural reaction of a modernizing politician in a relatively new nation state trying to stave off retrogressive—in this case, Islamic fundamentalists—elements aiming to undermine everything he has achieved in the way of building Syria into a twentieth century secular republic. That is also why," continued Friedman, that "if someone had been able to take an objective opinion poll in Syria after the Hama massacre, Assad's treatment of the rebellion probably would have won substantial approval, even among Sunni Muslims."[23]

The outbreak of a Sunni Islamist jihad against the Syrian government in the 1980s challenges the view that militant Sunni Islam in the Levant is an outcome of the 2003 U.S. invasion of Iraq and the pro-Shi'a sectarian policies of the U.S. occupation authorities. This view is historically myopic, blind to the decades-long existence of Sunni political Islam as a significant force in Levantine politics. From the moment Syria achieved formal independence from France after World War II, through the decades that followed in the twentieth century, and into the next century, the main contending forces in Syria were secular Arab nationalism and political Islam. As journalist Patrick Cockburn wrote in 2016, "the Syrian armed opposition is dominated by Isis, al-Nusra and Ahrar al-Sham." The "only alternative to [secular Arab nationalist] rule is the Islamists."[24] This has long been the case.

Following their defeat at Hama, the Muslim Brothers established an alliance with other Islamist groups opposed to the Syrian government to form the National Alliance for the Liberation of Syria, which in 1990 became the National Front for the Salvation of Syria. The Front had two goals. First, to assassinate Hafez al-Assad, in revenge for the killing of Islamist militants in the Hama uprising. And second, to overturn the secular character of the state, establishing Islam as the state religion and the Quran and Sunna as the bases of jurisprudence.[25]

The Muslim Brotherhood's efforts to establish alliances hostile to Syria's secular Arab nationalists continued into this century, observed the scholar Liad Porat.[26] The Islamists played a lead role in drafting the Damascus Declaration in the mid-2000s, which demanded regime change.[27] In 2007, the Brothers teamed up with a former Syrian vice-president to found the National Salvation Front. The front met frequently with the U.S. State Department and the U.S. National Security Council, as well as with the U.S. government-funded Middle East Partnership Initiative,[28] which did openly what the CIA once did covertly, namely, funnel money and expertise to fifth columnists in countries whose governments Washington opposed.

By 2009, just two years before the eruption of unrest throughout the Arab world, the Syrian Muslim Brotherhood denounced the Arab nationalist government of Bashar al-Assad as a foreign and hostile element in Syrian society which needed to be eliminated. According to the group's thinking, the Alawite community, which the Brothers regarded as heretics, used Ba'athism as a cover to furtively advance a sectarian agenda to destroy Syria from within by oppressing "true" (i.e., Sunni) Muslims. In the name of Islam, the heretical regime would have to be overthrown.[29]

A mere three months before the 2011 outbreak of violence in Syria, Porat wrote a brief for the Crown Center for Middle East Studies, based at Brandeis University. "The movement's leaders," the scholar concluded, "continue to voice their hope for a civil revolt in Syria, wherein 'the Syrian people will perform its duty and liberate Syria from the tyrannical and corrupt regime.'" The Brotherhood stressed that it was engaged in a fight to the death with the secular Arab nationalist government of Bashar al-Assad. A political accommodation with the government was impossible because its leaders were not part of the Sunni Muslim Syrian nation. Membership in the Syrian nation was limited to true Muslims, the Brothers contended, and not Alawite heretics who embraced such foreign un-Islamic creeds as secular Arab nationalism. [30]

That the Syrian Muslim Brotherhood played a key role in the uprising that erupted three months later was confirmed in 2012 by the U.S. Defense Intelligence Agency. A leaked report from the agency said that the insurgency was sectarian and led by the Muslim Brotherhood and al-Qaeda in Iraq, the forerunner of Islamic State. The report went on to say that the insurgents were supported by the West, Arab Gulf oil monarchies and Turkey. The analysis correctly predicted the establishment of a "Salafist principality," an Islamic state, in Eastern Syria, noting that this was desired by the insurgency's foreign backers, who wanted to see the secular Arab nationalists isolated and cut off from Iran.[31]

Documents prepared by U.S. Congress researchers in 2005 revealed that the U.S. government was actively weighing regime change in Syria long before the Arab Spring uprisings of 2011, challenging the view that U.S. support for the Syrian rebels was based on allegiance to a "democratic uprising" and showing that it was simply an extension of a long-standing policy of seeking to topple the government in Damascus. Indeed, the researchers acknowledged that the U.S. government's motivation to overthrow the secular Arab nationalist government in Damascus was unrelated to democracy promotion in the Middle East. In point of fact, they noted that Washington's preference was for secular dictatorships (Egypt) and monarchies (Jordan and Saudi Arabia). The impetus for pursuing regime change, according to the researchers, was a desire to sweep away an impediment to the achievement of U.S. goals in the Middle East related to strengthening Israel, consolidating U.S. domination of Iraq, and fostering open market, free enterprise economies. Democracy was never a consideration.[32]

Indeed, the idea that U.S. foreign policy had much of anything to do with democracy promotion had even been met with skepticism by the normally chauvinistic U.S. press. Commenting on U.S. policy toward communist North Korea—a state which, like Arab nationalist Syria, had no intention of being integrated into the Washington-led global economic order—*The Wall Street Journal*'s Andrew Browne noted that in East Asia "Washington supported a procession of strongmen from Park Chung-hee in Korea to Chiang Ching-kuo in Taiwan and Ferdinand Marcos in the Philippines."[33] The implication was that Washington's hostility to North Korea was unrelated to the communists' rejection of a plural, multi-party democratic state, since Washington had nurtured relationships with autocratic leaders in the Asia-Pacific region. The point could have been made just as cogently by reference to Washington's penchant for supporting the Sandhurst-educated kings, emirs, and princes of the Arab world, none of whom had the slightest intention of yielding to the democratic aspirations of their own subjects.

Washington, however, had long fostered a myth that U.S. foreign policy is "an intrinsic force for good in the world" and that U.S. power is "inherently virtuous."[34] "American leadership," declared the 2015 U.S. National Security Strategy, "is a global force for good." Obama, in his final address as U.S. president to the United Nations General Assembly in 2016 reiterated the point, adding that he believed that the United States had "been a rare superpower in human history insofar as it has been willing to think beyond narrow self-interest."[35] The problem was that no one, except U.S. citizens who had been continually bombarded with this bilge, believed it. Jeremy Shapiro, the research director at the European Council on Foreign Relations, branded the idea "something of a fallacy" which "only Americans believe." Elsewhere in the world, he told *The New York Times*, "people see this idea as not only false, but dangerous."[36] An American, Shapiro explained that the myth developed as a way of mobilizing support for aggressive U.S. foreign policy interventions abroad. "This self-conception developed over the past century as a way to overcome the country's physical isolation. As American presidents sought domestic support to intervene in faraway crises...they have 'always had to infuse foreign policy with a much stronger moral tint than do other countries.'"[37] In Syria, the accustomed pretext of intervening for moral reasons—in this case, to unseat "a strongman"—was once again invoked.

Congress's researchers revealed that an invasion of Syria by U.S. forces was contemplated following the U.S.-led aggression against Iraq in 2003, but that the unanticipated heavy burden of pacifying Iraq militated against an additional expenditure of blood and treasure in Syria. As an alternative, the United States chose to pressure Damascus through sanctions and support for groups opposed to the secular Arab nationalist government.[38]

The researchers also revealed that nearly a decade before the rise of Islamic State and Jabhat al-Nusra that the U.S. government recognized that Islamic fundamentalists were the main opposition to the secular Assad government and worried about the re-emergence of an Islamist insurgency that could lead Sunni fundamentalists to power in Damascus. The researchers described a U.S. strategy that sought to eclipse an Islamist take-over by forcing a negotiated settlement to the Islamist vs. secularist war in Syria in which the policing, military, judicial and administrative functions of the Syrian state would be preserved, while the secular Arab nationalists would be forced to step down. While Congress's researchers didn't speculate on what would transpire if and when Assad and his Arab nationalist associates were forced to yield power, it seemed fairly certain that a de-Ba'athification program would be carried out along the lines of the Iraq model. This would open space for the replacement of pro-independence Ba'athists, with their commitment to Arab unity, freedom from foreign domination, and Arab socialism, with biddable U.S. surrogates willing to facilitate the achievement of U.S. goals.

In 2005, Congress's researchers reported that a consensus had developed in Washington that change in Syria needed to be brought about, but that there remained divisions on the means by which change could be effected. "Some call for a process of internal reform in Syria or alternatively for the replacement of the current Syrian regime," the report said.[39] Whichever course Washington would settle on, it was clear that the U.S. government was determined—six years prior to the 2011 insurrection and President Obama's call for Assad to step down—to bring about a change in either the policies or key personnel of the Syrian government, or both.

The document described the Assad government as an impediment "to the achievement of U.S. goals in the region."[40] These goals were listed as: resolving "the Arab-Israeli conflict;" fighting "international terrorism;" reducing "weapons proliferation;" inaugurating "a peaceful, democratic and prosperous Iraqi state;" and fostering market-based, free enterprise economies.[41]

Stripped of their elegant words, the U.S. objectives for the Middle East amounted to a demand that Damascus capitulate to the military hegemony of Israel and the economic hegemony of Wall Street. To be clear, this meant that in order to remove itself as an impediment to the achievement of U.S. goals—and hence to escape U.S. hostility—Syria would have to:

- Accept Israel's right to exist as a Jewish state on territory seized from the Palestinians and carved out of the Arab homeland. Damascus might also have to accept Israel's conquest of Syria's Golan Heights, annexed by Israel in 1987 and occupied since 1967, as a *fait accompli*, never to be reversed.
- End its support for militant groups seeking Palestinian self-determination and sever its connections with the Lebanese

national resistance organization Hezbollah, the main bulwark against Israeli expansion into Lebanon.

- Leave itself effectively defenseless against the aggressions
  of the United States and its Middle East allies, including
  Israel, by abandoning even the capability of producing chemical, biological and nuclear weapons (while conceding a right
  to Israel and the United States to maintain vast arsenals of
  these weapons).
- Terminate its opposition to U.S. domination of neighboring
  Iraq.
- Transform what the U.S. Congress's researchers called
  Syria's mainly publicly-owned economy, "still based largely
  on Soviet models,"[42] into a sphere of exploitation for U.S. corporations and investors.

In other words, the Ba'athists would have to overturn their
Arab nationalist ideology, performing a *volte-face* to become
non-Ba'athists and pro-imperialists. They would have to
renounce their commitment to emancipating the Arab world
from foreign domination and would have to abandon Arab
socialism. In order to avoid forced regime change, they would
have to undergo their own voluntarily regime change, adopting
the pro-West, pro-foreign investment, pro-Israel practices a
regime installed by Washington would follow. The words Unity,
Freedom, and Socialism would be effaced from their banner to
be replaced by Division, Subordination, and Free Enterprise.

U.S. government objections to Syrian policy were organized
under three U.S.-defined headings: terrorism; WMD; and economic reform. These headings translated respectively into:
principled support for Palestinian and Lebanese resistance
against Zionist conquest of Arab territory; self-defense; and
economic sovereignty.

The researchers noted that while Syria had "not been impli-
cated directly in an act of terrorism since 1986" that Syria had
"continued to provide support and safe haven for Palestinian
groups" seeking self-determination, allowing "them to maintain

offices in Damascus." This was enough for the U.S. government to label Syria a state sponsor of terrorism. The researchers went on to note that on top of supporting Palestinian "terrorists" that Damascus also supported Lebanese "terrorists" by permitting "Iranian resupply via Damascus of the Lebanese Shi'ite Muslim militia Hezbollah in Lebanon."[43]

U.S. Secretary of State Colin Powell travelled to Damascus on May 3, 2003 to personally demand that Damascus sever its connections to militant organizations pursuing Palestinian self-determination and to stop providing them offices in Damascus from which to operate. In testimony before the Senate Foreign Relations Committee on February 12, 2004, Powell complained that "Syria has not done what we demanded of it with respect to closing permanently of these offices and getting these individuals out of Damascus."[44]

The Syrian government rejected the characterization of Hezbollah and Palestinian militants as "terrorists," noting that the actions of these groups represented legitimate resistance.[45] Clearly, Washington had attempted to discredit the pursuit of Palestinian self-determination and Lebanese sovereignty by labeling the champions of these causes as terrorists.

"In a speech to the Heritage Foundation on May 6, 2002, then U.S. Under Secretary [of State John] Bolton grouped Syria with Libya and Cuba as rogue states that...are pursuing the development of WMD."[46] Later that year, Bolton told the U.S. Senate Foreign Relations Committee that the Bush administration was very concerned about Syrian nuclear and missile programs. By September 2003, Bolton was warning of a "range of Syrian WMD programs."[47]

Syria clearly had chemical weapons (later destroyed), though hardly in the same quantities as contained in the much larger arsenals of the United States, Russia, and (likely) its regional nemesis, Israel. (Israel signed the global treaty banning the production and use of chemical weapons, but never ratified it.) Citing *The Washington Post*, Congress's researchers noted that Syria had "sought to build up its CW and missile capabilities as a 'force equalizer' to counter Israeli nuclear capabilities.'[48] However, the idea that chemical weapons could act as a force equalizer to nuclear weapons was not only untenable, but risible.

U.S. president George H.W. Bush was responsible for rendering the concept of WMD meaningless by expanding it to include chemical agents. Before Bush, WMD was a term used to denote nuclear weapons or weapons of similar destructive capacity that might be developed in the future. Bush debased the definition in order to go to war with Iraq. He needed to transform the oil-rich Arab nationalist republic which challenged U.S. domination of the Arab world from being seen accurately as a comparatively weak military power to being seen inaccurately as a significant threat.

In 1989, Bush pledged to eliminate the United States' chemical weapons by 1999. In 2016, the Pentagon still had the world's largest stockpile of militarized chemical agents. U.S. allies Israel and Egypt also had chemical weapons. In 2003, Syria proposed to the United Nations Security Council that the Middle East become a chemical weapons-free zone. The proposal was blocked by the United States, likely in order to shelter Israel from having to relinquish its store of chemical arms. Numerous calls to declare the Middle East a nuclear weapons-free zone were also blocked by Washington, again presumably to shelter Israel from having to dismantle its nuclear arsenal. Israel's role in the United States' informal empire was to act as an extension of the Pentagon, a virtual U.S. aircraft carrier in the middle of the oil-rich Arab world. Washington negotiated long-term military aid packages with the settler state, financing the Israeli military to the tune of $3 billion per annum through the first decade and a half of the twenty-first century. The Obama administration re-negotiated a ten-year package in 2016, hiking subventions to the Israeli military to $3.8 billion per year. On top of bankrolling the Israeli Defense Forces, Washington also furnished it with the Pentagon's most advanced weapons. For example, in 2016, Israel was scheduled to be the first country outside the United States to receive the F-35 jetfighter. Washington invested in the Israeli military as a proxy military that could be wielded against pro-independence forces in the Arab and Muslim worlds.

Bolton was among the velociraptors of the Bush administration to infamously and falsely accuse secular Arab nationalist Iraq of covertly holding on to weapons the UN Security Council had demanded it destroy. In effect, Iraq was ordered to disarm, and when it did, was falsely accused by the United States of still being armed. This was used as a pretext for U.S. forces to invade the now virtually defenseless country. Bolton may have chosen to play the same WMD card against Syria for the same reason: to manufacture consent for an invasion. But as Congress's researchers pointed out, "Although some officials...advocated a 'regime change strategy' in Syria" through military means, "military operations in Iraq...forced U.S. policy makers to explore additional options,"[49] rendering Bolton's accusations academic.

Since the only legitimate WMD are nuclear weapons, and since there is no evidence that Syria had even the untapped capability of producing them, much less possessed them, Syria had never been a true WMD-state or a threat to the U.S. goal of limiting nuclear weapons to a small circle of allies. What's more, the claim that Washington saw non-proliferation as a genuine goal is contestable, since it blocked efforts to make the Middle East a chemical- and nuclear-weapons-free zone, in order to spare its fixed aircraft carrier in the Middle East, Israel, from relinquishing its most menacing weapons. It would be more accurate to say that Washington's goal was to discourage nuclear weapons proliferation among countries the United States might one day invade, as a means of facilitating their invasion. Moreover, there was an egregious U.S. double-standard. Washington maintained the world's largest stockpiles of nuclear, chemical and biological weapons, but demanded that countries which refused to accept its self-declared global leadership role abandon their own arsenals, or foreswear their development. This was obviously self-serving and had nothing whatever to do with fostering peace and everything to do with promoting U.S. world domination. One U.S. grievance with secular Arab nationalist Syria, then, was that it refused to accept the international dictatorship of the United States.

In connection with Syria impeding the achievement of U.S. goals in the Middle East, the Congressional Research Service made the following observations in 2005 about the Syrian economy: it was "largely state-controlled;" it was "dominated by...[the] public sector, which employ[ed] 73% of the labor force;" and it was "based largely on Soviet models."[50] These departures from the preferred Wall Street paradigm of open markets and free enterprise appeared, from the perspective of Congress's researchers, to be valid reasons for the U.S. government to attempt to bring about "reform" in Syria. But then, why wouldn't the goal of bringing about a change in Syria's economic policies appear to be wholly justified to U.S. government researchers? After all, the United States had been clear in its official policy documents, including its 2015 National Security Strategy, that sustaining U.S. leadership meant "shaping an emerging global economic order" that reflected U.S. "interests and values" and that these interests and values were at odds with "alternative, less open-models," such as the "Soviet models" on which the Syrian economy was based. Indeed, it would be naive to believe that the U.S. government was prepared to allow foreign governments to exercise sovereignty in setting their own directions economically if they could be made to do otherwise. Washington was implacably opposed to foreign states implementing economic policies which failed to mesh with Washington's preferred free enterprise plus open markets paradigm. That this was the case was evidenced by the existence of a raft of U.S. sanctions legislation against "non-market states." For example, the Congressional Research Service's 2016 report, "North Korea: Economic Sanctions," contained a detailed list of sanctions imposed on North Korea for having a "Marxist-Leninist" economy; in other words, Washington was in the business of waging economic warfare against people in other lands because it didn't like the decisions they made about how to organize their own economic lives. What could be more hostile to democracy—and more imperialist—than that?

And Washington's intolerance of economic *dirigisme* was additionally evidenced in U.S. policy documents which asserted that Washington looked askance on states which held "fast to the false comforts of subsidies and trade barriers"[51] and that U.S. determination to lead the global economy meant promoting "economic freedom beyond America' shores."[52]

To recapitulate the respective positions of Syria and the United States on issues of bilateral concern to the two countries:

On Israel. To accept Israel's right to exist as a settler state on land illegitimately acquired through violence from its Arab inhabitants would be to collude in the denial of the fundamental right of Palestinian self-determination. Damascus refused to collude in the negation of this right. Washington demanded it.

On Hezbollah. Hezbollah was the principal deterrent against Israeli territorial expansion into Lebanon and Israeli aspirations to turn Lebanon into a client state. Damascus's support for the Lebanese national resistance organization, and Washington's opposition to it, placed the Assad government on the right side of the principle of self-determination and successive U.S. governments on the wrong side.

On WMD. Syria had a right to self-defense through means of its own choosing; the demand that it abandon its right was not worthy of discussion. The right to self-defense was a principle the United States and its allies accepted as self-evident and non-negotiable. It was not a principle that was valid only for the United States and its satellites.

On opposition to the U.S. invasion of Iraq. The 2003 U.S.-led aggression against Iraq was an international crime on a colossal scale, based on an illegitimate *casus belli*, and a fabricated one at that, and which engendered massive destruction and loss of life. It was the supreme international crime by the standards of the Nuremberg trials. Were the perpetrators of the aggression arraigned before an international tribunal and the Nuremberg principles applied, they would be hanged. U.S. aggression against secular Arab nationalist Iraq, including the deployment of "sanctions of mass destruction" through the 1990s, which led to hundreds of thousands of Iraqi deaths, and was accepted by then U.S. Secretary of State Madeleine Albright as "worth it," was undertaken despite the absence of any physical threat to the United States. It would be disingenuous to say that Iraq's Arab nationalists did not pose *some* threat to *some* section of U.S. society. There was a perceived danger in Washington, as we've already seen, that Saddam, pursuing Arab nationalist goals, would attempt to conquer the Arabian Peninsula militarily, in order to recover the territory, with its rich bounty of oil, for the Arab nation as a whole. The threat Saddam's Iraq posed, then, was to the bottom lines of U.S. oil companies, not to the physical safety of the U.S. homeland. The deliberate creation of humanitarian calamities in the absence of a physical threat to the United States, as a matter of choice and not necessity, in pursuit of profits, is an iniquity on a signal scale. What, then, are we to think of a government in Damascus that opposed this iniquity, and a government in Washington that demanded that Damascus reverse its opposition and accept the crime as legitimate?

Syria's ruling Arab nationalists unambiguously adopted positions that had traditionally been understood to be concerns of the political left: support for self-determination; public ownership and planning of the economy; opposition to wars of aggression; and anti-imperialism. This is not to say that on a political spectrum from right to left that the Ba'athists occupied a position near the left extreme. Notwithstanding the rhetoric of U.S. hardliners, Ba'ath Arab Socialists were not communists. But from Washington's point of view, Assad and his fellow Arab nationalist ideologues were far enough to the left to be unacceptable. Indeed, it was the Syrian government's embrace of traditional leftist positions—expressed in the Ba'athists' Unity, Freedom, and Socialism slogan—that accounted for why it had long been in the cross-hairs of the United States. On December 12, 2003, U.S. president George W. Bush signed the Syria Accountability Act, which imposed sanctions on Syria unless, among other things, Damascus halted its support for Hezbollah and Palestinian resistance groups and ceased "development of weapons of mass destruction." The sanctions included bans on exports of military equipment and civilian goods that could be used for military purposes (in other words, practically anything). This was reinforced with an additional (and largely superfluous) ban on U.S. exports to Syria other than food and medicine, as well as a prohibition against Syrian aircraft landing in or overflying the United States.[53]

On top of these sanctions, Bush imposed two more. Under the USA Patriot Act, the U.S. Treasury Department ordered U.S. financial institutions to sever connections with the Commercial Bank of Syria.[54] And under the International Emergency Economic Powers Act, the U.S. president froze the assets of Syrians involved in supporting policies hostile to the United States, which is to say, supporting Hezbollah and groups fighting for Palestinian self-determination, refusing to accept as valid the territorial gains which Israel had made through its wars of aggression, and operating a largely publicly-owned, state-planned economy, based on Soviet models.[55]

The sanctions devastated Syria. In October 2011, *The New York Times* reported that the Syrian economy "was buckling under the pressure of sanctions by the West."[56] By the spring of 2012, sanctions-induced financial hemorrhaging had "forced Syrian officials to stop providing education, health care and other essential services in some parts of the country."[57] By 2016, "U.S. and E.U. economic sanctions on Syria" were "causing huge suffering among ordinary Syrians and preventing the delivery of humanitarian aid, according to a leaked UN internal report."[58] The report revealed that aid agencies were unable to obtain drugs and equipment for hospitals because sanctions prevented foreign firms from conducting commerce with Syria. The sanctions resembled the economic warfare Washington had waged on Arab nationalist Iraq in the 1990s. Those sanctions, as we've seen, destroyed the "golden age" the Arab nationalists had brought to the country. Patrick Cockburn wrote that "the U.S. and E.U. sanctions" resembled the Iraqi sanctions regime, and were "an economic siege on Syria." He surmised that the siege was killing numberless Syrians through illness and malnutrition.[59] Certainly, the siege of Iraq had led to the hunger- and disease-related deaths of hundreds of thousands of Iraqis, if not more. Sanctions of mass destruction were now being visited on Syria with grim humanitarian consequences.

In order to strengthen internal opposition to the Syrian government, Bush signed the Foreign Operations Appropriation Act. This act required that a minimum of $6.6 million "be made available for programs supporting" anti-government groups in Syria "as well as unspecified amounts of additional funds."[60]

By 2006, the Bush administration had "been quietly nurturing individuals and parties opposed to the Syrian government in an effort to undermine the" government of President Bashar al-Assad. Part of the effort was being run through the National Salvation Front. The Front included the Muslim Brotherhood. Front representatives "were accorded at least two meetings" at the White House in 2006.[61] Another Muslim Brotherhood front organization that received U.S. funding was the Movement for Justice and Development. Founded by former members of the Syrian Muslim Brotherhood, the group openly advocated regime change. Washington gave the Islamists money to set up a satellite TV channel to broadcast anti-government news into Syria.[62] Hence, from 2005, the U.S. government was secretly financing "Syrian political opposition groups and related projects" to topple the Syrian government, reported *The Washington Post*.[63]

The U.S. government, then, at its highest level, was colluding with Islamists to bring down the Syrian government at least six years before the recrudescence in 2011 of the long-running Islamist insurgency, challenging the myth that Washington's demand that Assad step down was related to his response to the spring 2011 uprisings. In fact, Washington had been conspiring with Islamists to oust Syria's secular Arab nationalist leader from power, and had contemplated a military intervention in 2003 to topple his government.

After 2011 a discourse emerged which made no reference to the decades-long struggle of Sunni political Islam to depose the secular Arab nationalist leadership in Damascus. Neither did it acknowledge the Muslim Brotherhood's vow to wage unending jihad against what it termed the "infidel" Ba'athists. Nor did it acknowledge Washington's collusion with the Muslim Brotherhood prior to 2011 to destabilize secular Syria. Other facts, similarly ignored, in favor of a narrative that the United States' involvement in the Syrian conflict was motivated by the loftiest of motives, and that the uprising was driven by a thirst for democracy, rather than an appetite for an Islamic state, revealed that regime change in Syria was a long-standing foreign policy goal of the United States. Washington "always wanted to get rid of Assad," observed veteran foreign correspondent Patrick Cockburn.[64]

In March 2007, Democracy Now's Amy Goodman interviewed retired four star U.S. Army General Wesley Clark, who had commanded NATO forces during the alliance's 1999 unprovoked air war on Yugoslavia. Clark revealed that in the days following the 9/11 al-Qaeda attacks on New York and Washington of September 2001, the Bush administration developed plans to wage war on seven countries, one of which was Syria. Recalling a visit to the Pentagon he made in late September 2001, Clark said:

"About ten days after 9/11, I went through the Pentagon and I saw Secretary Rumsfeld and Deputy Secretary Wolfowitz. I went downstairs just to say hello to some of the people on the Joint Staff who used to work for me, and one of the generals called me in. He said, "Sir, you've got to come in and talk to me a second." I said, 'Well, you're too busy.' He said, 'No, no.' He says, 'We've made the decision we're going to war with Iraq.' This was on or about the 20th of September. I said, 'We're going to war with Iraq? Why?' He said, 'I don't know.' He said, 'I guess they don't know what else to do.' So I said, 'Well, did they find some information connecting Saddam to al-Qaeda?' He said, 'No, no.' He says, 'There's nothing new that way. They just made the decision to go to war with Iraq.' He said, 'I guess it's like we don't know what to do about terrorists, but we've got a good military and we can take down governments.' And he said, 'I guess if the only tool you have is a hammer, every problem has to look like a nail.'"[65]

A few weeks later, Clark returned to the Pentagon, and talked to the same general. By this point, the United States had launched a war on Afghanistan.

"I said, 'Are we still going to war with Iraq?' And he said, 'Oh, it's worse than that.' He reached over on his desk. He picked up a piece of paper. And he said, 'I just got this down from upstairs' —meaning the Secretary of Defense's office—'today.' And he said, 'This is a memo that describes how we're going to take out seven countries in five years, starting with Iraq, and then Syria, Lebanon, Libya, Somalia, Sudan and, finishing off, Iran.'"[6]

Clark's revelations indicate that Washington had contemplated regime change in Syria since at least 2001, a full decade before the Islamist insurgency re-erupted in Syria in March 2011. The addition of Syria to the "Axis of Evil" on May 6, 2002 by then U.S. Undersecretary of State John Bolton underscores the point that Washington wanted to take down the Assad government a full decade before the Arab Spring upheavals. Two of the six Axis of Evil countries, Iraq and Libya, both Arab nationalist states, and both with strong public-sector economies, were regime changed by U.S.-led military interventions subsequent to their designation as Axis of Evil countries. It would not have been unreasonable for Damascus to draw the conclusion that it was next, and as we've seen, it may well have been next had it not been for the reality that the difficulties the

United States encountered in pacifying Iraq and Afghanistan militated against the Pentagon taking on an invasion of Syria.

As to the other countries on the list, North Korea and Cuba had long been subjected to U.S.-led economic warfare, undertaken with the unconcealed goal of bringing about the demise of their communist governments. Since its 1979 Islamic Revolution, Iran had been the target of an unending campaign of U.S.-orchestrated low-level warfare intended to overthrow the pro-independence, pro-Palestinian Iranian state. Every one of the Axis countries rejected the United States' self-declared global leadership role, refused to be integrated into the U.S.-led global economic order, and had what U.S. strategists called "economies [featuring] the heavy hand of government."[67] That Washington labeled these countries as "evil" followed from the view, unapologetically expressed by the George W. Bush administration, that "economic freedom," defined as "free and fair trade, open markets... [and]...the integration of the global economy" is "a moral imperative."[68] By rejecting "economic freedom" in favor of state ownership, planning and direction of their economies, these countries had marked themselves as immoral, and therefore evil. As for the Obama administration, it eschewed references to moral principles in promoting a global economic order based on Wall Street's interests, preferring instead to invoke what it called "facts." U.S. President Barack Obama told the United Nations General Assembly in 2016 that it was a matter of fact, and not "theory or ideology," that "the principles of open markets... remain the firmest foundation for human progress." Fact, in Obama's view, also demonstrated that "central, planned control of the economy is a dead end," and that "the answer" to overcoming underdevelopment "cannot be a simple rejection of global integration."[69]

Washington's assigning Syria to the company of countries in which it sought regime change, a full decade before the Arab Spring uprising, is evidence that the March 2011 disturbances, or more precisely, Damascus's response to them, did not precipitate Washington's decision to topple the Syrian government. This conclusion is strengthened by the facts that Washington contemplated military intervention in Syria in 2003 (if not as early as 2001, according to Wesley Clark) and began funding Syrian opposition groups, including the Muslim Brotherhood, in 2005. That the Syrian government's values of Arab unity, freedom from foreign domination, and Arab socialism, were inimical to Wall Street's interests—and given the enormous influence Wall Street exercised in Washington—suggests very strongly that the U.S. government had a compelling reason to topple the Ba'athist government in Damascus. Washington's long record of overthrowing foreign governments which had undertaken acts hostile to Western business interests—for example, the ousting of Mossadegh for nationalizing Iran's petroleum industry—only strengthens the conclusion.

U.S. citizens may have been sympathetic to the values embraced by Syria's ruling Arab nationalists and, as a consequence, opposed the U.S. campaign to compel Assad to step down. For this reason, Washington was motivated to conceal its authentic economics-related regime change reasons behind contrived concerns. Western propagandists would additionally ensure that the ideology of Syria's ruling secular Arab nationalists would remain concealed. Hence, in order to justify a hostile stance toward Syria, Washington drew attention to Syria's chemical weapons arsenal, insinuated that Damascus was covertly developing nuclear weapons, and branded the Syrian government as a state sponsor of terrorism. So demonized, Washington's hostility to Damascus could be presented as an inherently benevolent opposition to evil.

Later, U.S. officials drew attention to the 2011 use of force by Syrian security services to contain violent unrest on Syrian streets, presenting a normal security response as a vicious crackdown on legitimate dissent by a brutal dictator, a more apt description of what was going on in Saudi Arabia and Bahrain, than in Syria. The Syrian president, as we've seen, obtained a majority of votes in a referendum and therefore governed with the consent of the governed, unlike the kings of Saudi Arabia and Bahrain, both U.S. allies, who presided over monarchical states. And while demonstrators in Saudi Arabia and Bahrain called for a transition from monarchy to democracy, unrest on Syrian streets was largely Islamist-inspired. Washington ignored uprisings in Saudi Arabia and Bahrain, where royal dictatorships cracked down on pro-democracy dissent with tanks, and presented attempts to contain violent demonstrations in Syria as illegitimate repression. U.S. hostility was veiled behind an insincere solidarity with expressions of what Washington would misleadingly term "legitimate" dissent. At the same time, U.S. foreign policy was presented as inherently virtuous in order to conceal its aim of securing economic advantages abroad for corporate America. If the true aim were revealed, it is unlikely that U.S. officials would be able to rally popular support to their anti-Syria policy. U.S. propagandists seemed to recognize, as Hitler had asserted, that people will support war waged for an ideal, but not for profits. (In *Mein Kampf,* Hitler had written that "Men do not sacrifice themselves for material interests. They will die for an ideal, not a business.")

CHAPTER THREE

THE 2011 DISTEMPER

There are three views on the origins of the 2011 uprising in Syria whose wide circulation is inversely proportional to the degree to which the views have been critically examined. All are highly contestable.

The first contestable view is that the demonstrations against the Assad government that erupted in the spring of 2011 were disconnected from the main force of opposition within Syria to the secular Arab nationalist state, namely Sunni political Islam. The evidence, however, shows that the demands of the protesters had an Islamist content. It reveals that jihadist groups at the fore of the insurrection had begun operations in early 2011, before the violent protests erupted, not after, challenging the view that Islamists 'hijacked' a popular uprising (and the evidence challenges the view that the uprising was "popular"). The evidence also demonstrates that the Sunni Islamist character of the protests was reflected in the unqualified support that heterodox Muslim, and Christian, communities gave the government. Minority religious communities recognized that the insurrectionists, if successful, would implement a sectarian Sunni Islamic state, which would treat them harshly as infidels and apostates. Those who argued that the protests were inspired by a thirst for democracy were on shaky ground. If Syrians had a thirst for democracy, one would have expected the thirst to have been universal, and distributed across all sects, rather than concentrated in the Sunni Muslim community. More significantly, the demands of the protesters had very little to do with democracy and more to do with freeing Islamists from jail and lifting restrictions which limited their legal room for maneuver to organize Islamist opposition to the secular state.

The second view, which is clearly untenable, is that the protests were non-violent. They were, on the contrary, violent from the beginning, a reality that was acknowledged by the U.S. government early on, but later obfuscated by U.S. state officials who preferred to speak of the violent eruptions as "largely" peaceful. There were, doubtlessly, protesters who did not resort to violence, and they may have been in the majority. But this did not negate the reality that a minority that set fire to buildings and cars and clashed with police, eventually killing large numbers of them, were engaged in violence, and that the character of a protest movement containing even a minority of violent participants is still violent.

The third contestable view is that the uprising had broad popular support, that the Assad government was widely reviled, and that Assad himself had lost legitimacy among Syrians. Western mainstream media reports in the months immediately preceding the mid-March 2011 eruption of anti-government violence said the very opposite. These reports indicated that Assad was widely viewed by Syrians as a legitimate leader and that there was little chance that the popular uprisings that swept through Egypt, Tunisia and elsewhere in the Arab world would spread to Syria. (That, however, didn't mean that there was little chance of an Islamist guerilla war re-erupting, of the kind that had frequently plunged Syria into chaos). Washington had been holding meetings with Sunni Islamists and funding their front organizations from 2005. An alternative view can be advanced that Washington had recycled parts of Kermit Roosevelt's plan to topple the Ba'athist-Communist triumvirate that ruled in Damascus in 1956; that is, it enlisted the aid of Sunni Islamists to create internal uprisings in Syria, as Roosevelt had planned to do in the mid-1950s. Washington would portray the uprisings as popularly based, and declare that this demonstrated the president had lost legitimacy and must therefore step down. As such, Washington could justify its almost immediate overt support of the armed insurrectionists as an exercise in democracy promotion.

In late January 2011, a page was created on Facebook called The Syrian Revolution 2011. It announced that a "Day of Rage" would be held on February fourth and fifth.[1] The protests "fizzled," reported *Time*. The Day of Rage amounted to a Day of Indifference. Moreover, the connection to Syria was tenuous. Most of the chants shouted by the few protesters who attended were about Libya, demanding that Muammar Gaddafi—whose government was under siege by Islamist insurrectionists—step down. Plans were set for new protests on March fourth and March fifth, but they too garnered little support.[2]

Time's correspondent Rania Abouzeid attributed the failure of the protest organizers to draw significant support to the fact that most Syrians were not opposed to their government. Assad had a favorable reputation, especially among the two-thirds of the population under thirty, and his government's policies were widely supported. "Even critics concede that Assad is popular and considered close to the country's huge youth cohort, both emotionally, ideologically and, of course, chronologically," Abouzeid reported, adding that unlike "the ousted pro-American leaders of Tunisia and Egypt, Assad's hostile foreign policy toward Israel, strident support for Palestinians and the militant groups Hamas and Hezbollah are in line with popular Syrian sentiment." Assad, in other words, had legitimacy. The *Time* correspondent added that Assad's "driving himself to the Umayyad Mosque in February to take part in prayers to mark the Prophet Muhammad's birthday, and strolling through the crowded Souq Al-Hamidiyah marketplace with a low security profile" had "helped to endear him, personally, to the public."[3]

This depiction of the Syrian president—a leader endeared to the public, ideologically in sync with popular Syrian sentiment—clashed starkly with the discourse that would emerge shortly after the eruption of violent protests in the Syrian city of Daraa less than two weeks later. But on the eve of the signal Daraa events Syria was being remarked upon for its quietude. No one "expects mass uprisings in Syria," Abouzeid reported, "and, despite a show of dissent every now and then, very few want to participate."⁴ A Syrian youth told *Time*: "There is a lot of government help for the youth. They give us free books, free schools, free universities. Why should there be a revolution? There's maybe a one percent chance."⁵ *The New York Times* shared this view. Syria, the newspaper reported, "seemed immune to the wave of uprisings sweeping the Arab world."⁶ Syria was distemper-free.

But on March 17, there was a violent uprising in Daraa. Accounts conflict as to who or what sparked it. *Time* reported that the "rebellion in Daraa was provoked by the arrest of a handful of youths for daubing a wall with anti-regime graffiti."⁷ *The Independent*'s Robert Fisk offered a slightly different version. He reported that "government intelligence officers beat and killed several boys who had scrawled anti-government graffiti on the walls of the city."⁸ Another account holds that the factor that sparked the uprising in Daraa that day was extreme and disproportionate use of force by Syrian authorities in response to demonstrations against the boys' arrest. There "were some youngsters printing some graffiti on the wall, and they were imprisoned, and as their parents wanted them back, the security forces really struck back very, very tough."⁹ Another account, from the Syrian government, denies that any of this happened. Five years after the event, Assad told an interviewer that it "didn't happen. It was only propaganda. I mean, we heard about them, we never saw those children that have been taken to prison that time. So, it was only a fallacious narrative."¹⁰

But if there was disagreement about what sparked the uprising, there was little disagreement that the uprising was violent.

The New York Times reported that "Protesters set fire to the ruling Ba'ath Party's headquarters and other government buildings...and clashed with police...In addition to the party headquarters, protesters burned the town's main courthouse and a branch of the SyriaTel phone company."[11] *Time* added that protesters set fire to the governor's office, as well as to a branch office of a second cellphone company.[12] The Syrian government's news agency, SANA, posted photographs of burning vehicles on its Web site.[13] Clearly, this wasn't a peaceful demonstration, as it would be later depicted. Nor was it a mass uprising. *Time* reported that the demonstrators numbered in the hundreds, not thousands or tens of thousands.[14]

Assad reacted immediately to the Daraa ructions, announcing "a series of reforms, including a salary increase for public workers, greater freedom for the news media and political parties, and a reconsideration of the emergency rule,"[15] a war-time restriction on political and civil liberties, invoked because Syria was officially at war with Israel. Before the end of April, the government would rescind "the country's 48-year-old emergency law" and abolish "the Supreme State Security Court."[16]

Why did the government make these concessions? Because that's what the Daraa protesters demanded. Protesters "gathered in and around Omari mosque in Daraa, chanting their demands: the release of all political prisoners...the abolition of Syria's 48-year emergency law; more freedoms; and an end to pervasive corruption."[17] These demands were consistent with the call, articulated in early February on The Syrian Revolution 2011 Facebook page "to end the state of emergency in Syria and end corruption."[18] A demand to release all political prisoners was also made in a letter signed by clerics posted on Facebook. The clerics' demands included lifting the "state of emergency law, releasing all political detainees, halting harassment by the security forces and combating corruption."[19] Releasing political detainees would—in a Syria in which jihadists made up the principal section of oppositionists likely to be incarcerated—amount to releasing jihadists, or, to use a designation current in the West, "terrorists." Clerics demanding that Damascus release all political prisoners was equal in effect to the Islamic State demanding that Washington, Paris, and London release all Islamists detained in U.S., French, and British prisons on terrorism charges. This wasn't a demand for greater democracy, but a demand for the release from prison of activists inspired by the goal of bringing about an Islamic state in Syria. The call to lift the emergency law, similarly, appeared to have little to do with fostering democracy and more to do with expanding the room for jihadists and their collaborators to organize opposition to the secular state.

A week after the outbreak of violence in Daraa, *Time*'s Rania Abouzeid reported that "there do not appear to be widespread calls for the fall of the regime or the removal of the relatively popular President."[20] Indeed, the demands issued by the protesters and clerics had not included calls for Assad to step down. And Syrians were rallying to Assad. "There were counterdemonstrations in the capital in support of the President,"[21] reportedly far exceeding in number the hundreds of protesters who turned out in Daraa to burn buildings and cars and clash with police.[22]

By April 9—less than a month after the Daraa events—*Time* reported that a string of protests had broken out and that Islam was playing a prominent role in them. For anyone who was conversant with the decades-long succession of strikes, demonstrations, riots, and insurrections the Muslim Brotherhood had organized against what it deemed the "infidel" Ba'athist government, this looked like history repeating itself. The protests weren't reaching a critical mass. On the contrary, the government continued to enjoy "the loyalty" of "a large part of the population," reported *Time*.[23] Assad's broad support, the protesters' failure to reach critical mass, and the Islamic content of the protests, clashed heavily with the way events would later be depicted in Western mass media. This was not a broad-based popular uprising for democracy against an unpopular government; it was a jihadist uprising for an Islamic state.

To underscore the point that the protests lacked broad popular support, two weeks later, on April 22, *The New York Times'* Anthony Shadid reported that "the protests, so far, seemed to fall short of the popular upheaval of revolutions in Egypt and Tunisia." In other words, more than a month after only hundreds—and not thousands or tens of thousands—of protesters rioted in Daraa, there was still no sign in Syria of a popular Arab Spring upheaval. The uprising remained a limited, prominently, Islamist affair. By contrast, there had been huge demonstrations in Damascus in support of—not against—the government, Assad remained popular, and, according to Shadid, the government commanded the loyalty of "Christian and heterodox Muslim sects."[24] Shadid wasn't the only Western journalist who reported that Alawites, Ismailis, Druze and Christians were strongly backing the government. *Times'* Rania Abouzeid observed that the Ba'athists "could claim the backing of Syria's substantial minority groups."[25]

One can speculate on why the Western press drew attention to the strong support religious minority communities accorded the government, when Assad was acknowledged to be popular among Syrians as a whole. Why not point out that he was popular with Sunnis, as well? It could be that Western journalists accepted the Sunni Islamist discourse that Ba'athism was a cover for the pursuit of a sectarian agenda against the Sunni Muslim majority. Certainly, the Western media would, in subsequent years, adopt an analysis which was consonant with the Syrian Muslim Brotherhood view that the struggle for power in Syria between secular Arab nationalists and Sunni political Islam was really a sectarian conflict between the "ruling" Alawite minority and "oppressed" Sunni Muslim majority. In this vein, U.S. newspapers would often point out that Assad was Alawite and the jihadists were Sunni, even though the Syrian Arab Army, the largest fighting force in Syria, was predominantly made up of Sunni recruits. Assad, himself, the great sectarian Alawite, according to Sunni Islamists, had a Sunni wife. Calling the Ba'athist government an "Alawite regime," a misrepresentation as favored by Western journalists as by militant sectarian Sunni Muslims, served a political purpose: to discredit secular Arab nationalist ideology by insinuating that it was really a cover for the sectarian agenda of a religious minority. Judeophobes did the same when, in the 1930s, they labeled the major program of the U.S. Roosevelt administration the "Jew Deal," and dubbed the president "Rosenfeld" owing to the "very visible presence of so many Jews among Roosevelt's closest aides."[26] True, Assad counted Alawites among his closest colleagues, but Ba'athists were staunchly anti-sectarian and the Assad government was no more Alawite than the Roosevelt administration was Jewish. While the uprising was driven by Sunni Islamists, it did not follow that the Sunni community as a whole supported the Islamists' jihad, for a simple reason—not all Sunnis, or even most of them, were Islamists. The "notion that everyone in Syria despises [Assad], all these things you hear, that's not true," remarked Seymour Hersh, the renowned investigative journalist who revealed the My Lai massacre, for which he received the Pulitzer Prize for International Reporting. Assad "has a lot of native support," Hersh told *Democracy Now!*, "and even from [Sunni] Muslims, because every [Sunni] Muslim in Syria is not a Wahhabi or a Salafist, an extremist. Many are very moderate people who believe they would be in trouble if the Islamic force, the Islamic groups, came into power, because they would go and seek out those fellow Muslims that don't agree with their extreme views. So he does have an awful lot of support, more than most people think."[27]

The reality that the Syrian government commanded the loyalty of Christian and heterodox Muslim sects, as *The New York Times'* Shadid reported, suggests that Syria's religious minorities recognized something about the uprising that the Western press under-reported, namely, that it was driven by a sectarian Sunni Islamist agenda which, if brought to fruition, would have unpleasant consequences for anyone who wasn't considered a "true" Muslim. For this reason, Alawites, Ismailis, Druze, and Christians lined up with the Ba'athists whom, it will be recalled, sought to bridge sectarian divisions as part of their programmatic commitment to fostering Arab unity. The slogan "Alawites to the grave and Christians to Beirut!" chanted during demonstrations in those early days"[28] only confirmed the point that the uprising was a continuation of the death feud that Sunni political Islam had vowed to wage against the secular Arab nationalist government, and was not a mass upheaval for democracy. The uprising was a fight for an Islamic, not a democratic, state. Indeed, a largely democratic state, as we have seen, already existed.

"From the very beginning the Assad government said it was engaged in a fight with militant Islamists."[29] The long history of Islamist uprisings against Ba'athism prior to 2011 certainly suggested this was very likely the case, and the way in which the uprising subsequently unfolded, as an Islamist-led war against the secular state, only strengthened the view. Other evidence, both positive and negative, corroborated Assad's contention that the Syrian state was under attack by jihadists (just as it had been many other times in the past). The negative evidence, that the uprising wasn't a popular upheaval against an unpopular government, was inhered in Western media reports that showed that Syria's Arab nationalist government was popular and commanded the loyalty of the population. By contrast, anti-government demonstrations, riots and protests were small-scale, attracting far fewer people than did a mass demonstration in Damascus in support of the government, and certainly not on the order of the popular upheavals in Egypt and Tunisia. What's more, the protesters' demands centered on the release of political prisoners (mainly jihadists) and the lifting of war-time restrictions on the expression of political dissent, not calls for Assad to step down or to open presidential elections to multiple candidates. The positive evidence came from Western news media accounts showing that Islam played a prominent role in the riots. Also, while it was widely believed that armed Islamist groups only entered the fray subsequent to the initial spring 2011 riots—and in doing so "hijacked" a "popular uprising"—in point of fact, two jihadist groups which played a prominent role in the post-2011 armed revolt against secular Arab nationalism, Ahrar-al-Sham and Jabhat al-Nusra, were both active at the beginning of 2011. Ahrar al-Sham "started working on forming brigades...well before mid-March, 2011, when the" Daraa riot occurred, according to *Time*.[30] Jabhat al-Nusra, the al-Qaeda affiliate in Syria, "was unknown until late January 2012, when it announced its formation...[but] it was active for months before then."[31]

Another piece of evidence that is consistent with the view that militant Islam played a role in the uprisings very early on—or, at the very least, that the protests were violent from the beginning—is that '"there were signs from the very start that armed groups were involved." The journalist and author Robert Fisk recalled seeing a video from "the very early days of the 'rising' showing men with pistols and Kalashnikovs in a Daraa demonstration." He recalls another event, in May 2011, when "an Al Jazeera crew filmed armed men shooting at Syrian troops a few hundred metres from the northern border with Lebanon but the channel declined to air the footage, which their reporter later showed to me."[32] Even U.S. officials, who were hostile to the Syrian government and might be expected to challenge Damascus's view that it was embroiled in a fight with armed rebels, "acknowledged that the demonstrations weren't peaceful and that some protesters were armed."[33] By September, Syrian authorities were reporting that they had lost more than 500 police officers and soldiers, killed by guerillas.[34] By late October, the number had more than doubled.[35] In less than a year, the uprising had gone from the burning of Ba'ath Party buildings and government offices and clashes with police, to guerilla warfare, involving methods that would be labeled "terrorist" were they undertaken against Western targets.

Assad would later complain that:

> "Everything we said in Syria at the beginning of the crisis they say later. They said it's peaceful, we said it's not peaceful, they're

killing – these demonstrators, that they called them peaceful demonstrators – have killed policemen. Then it became militants.
They said yes, it's militants. We said it's militants, it's terrorism.
They said no, it's not terrorism. Then when they say it's terrorism,
we say it's al-Qaeda, they say no, it's not al-Qaeda. So, whatever
we said, they say later."[36]

One reason a violent uprising with a predominantly Islamist
content led by armed jihadists against a popular government
could be presented as a popular upheaval against an unpopular government was that "the opposition movements during
2011 had well-developed PR operations," according to Patrick
Cockburn,[37] funded largely by the U.S. government and its
anti-democratic Arab monarch allies. It was in the interests
of the U.S. government, which was leading the charge to de-
Ba'athify the Syrian state, to ensure that a discourse of popular
upheaval against an unpopular government prevail, in order
to enlist the support of U.S. citizens, or at least their passive
acceptance, of Washington's championing of the campaign to
force Assad to step down. When it became evident that the
most prominent of the armed rebel groups were dyed-in-the-
wool, head-chopping jihadists who sought to replicate in Syria
the medieval Muslim society of Medina established by the
Prophet Muhammad, U.S. propagandists created the concept
of the "moderate" rebel to assuage concerns that Washington
was backing al-Qaeda and its clones. Now it was said that the
United States supported only moderates, without actually
defining what a "moderate" was. In practice, a "moderate,"
according to the head of U.S. Intelligence, James Clapper,
was any rebel who didn't belong to Islamic State,[38] a group
Washington opposed because it threatened to take control of
lucrative oil fields in Iraq, and sought the overthrow of the
Saudi monarchy. All other groups, irrespective of their methods, aims, ideology or orientation toward democracy, were
sanitized as "moderates." Jabhat al-Nusra remained an ogre
in the U.S. bestiary by virtue of the fact that it was al-Qaeda's
affiliate in Syria and Washington could not be seen to be

supporting an affiliate of an organization that was held culpable of the 9/11 attacks. All of this was of little moment, however, since U.S.-backed "moderates" were enmeshed with al-Nusra, coordinating with the al-Qaeda affiliate on the battlefield, and sharing with it their U.S. supplied weapons. In other words, Washington was using "moderate" jihadists who, despite the label, were ideologically and methodologically indistinguishable from al-Nusra, as a conduit to funnel arms and other support to al-Qaeda's Syria operation. Hence, while Assad was dismissed by U.S. officials and media pundits when he said that his government was engaged in a fight with militant al-Qaeda-linked Islamists, he was right all along. Al-Qaeda—the offspring of the Muslim Brotherhood, the secular Arab nationalists' decades-long antagonist—was Washington's vehicle for ousting Assad.

A final set of points should be made about the Syrian government's response to the Daraa riot and its aftermath. Some have argued that the uprising was sparked by the disproportionate use of force by Syrian authorities, either in their dealings with the youths who had painted anti-government graffiti on a wall, or in their response to the violent protests that ensued. Assuming that the graffiti incident actually occurred, and that the government's response to it and to the subsequent protests to the youths' treatment was disproportionate, we can ask two questions:

1. Is it reasonable to believe that the disproportionate use of force sparked the war that broke out soon after?
2. Was it predictable that the Syrian government would react strongly to challenges to its authority?

Concerning the first point, it strains belief that an overreaction by security forces to a challenge to government authority in the Syrian town of Daraa could spark a major war, involving scores of states, and mobilizing jihadists from scores of countries. A slew of discordant facts would have to be ignored to begin to give this theory even a soupcon of credibility.

First, we would have to overlook the reality that the Assad government was popular and viewed as legitimate. A case might be made that an overbearing response by a highly unpopular government to a trivial challenge to its authority might have provided the spark that was needed to ignite a popular insurrection, but notwithstanding U.S. president Barack Obama's insistence that Assad lacked legitimacy, there's no evidence that Syria, in March 2011, was a powder keg of popular antigovernment resentment ready to explode. As *Time*'s Rania Abouzeid reported on the eve of the Daraa riot, "Even critics concede that Assad is popular"[39] and "no one expects mass uprisings in Syria and, despite a show of dissent every now and then, very few want to participate."[40]

Second, we would have to discount the fact that the Daraa riot involved only hundreds of participants, hardly a mass uprising, and the protests that followed similarly failed to garner a critical mass, as *Time*'s Nicholas Blanford reported.[41] Similarly, *The New York Times*' Anthony Shadid found no evidence that there was a popular upheaval in Syria, even more than a month after the Daraa riot.[42] What was going on, contrary to Washington-propagated rhetoric about the Arab Spring breaking out in Syria, was that jihadists were engaged in a campaign of guerilla warfare against Syrian security forces, and had, by October, taken the lives of more than a thousand police officers and soldiers.

Third, we would have to close our eyes to the fact that the U.S. government, with its British ally, had drawn up plans in 1957 to provoke a war in Syria by enlisting the Muslim Brotherhood to instigate internal uprisings. The Daraa riot and subsequent armed clashes with police and soldiers resembled the plan which regime change specialist Kermit Roosevelt had prepared. That's not to say that the CIA dusted off Roosevelt's proposal and recycled it for use in 2011; only that the plot showed that Washington and London were capable of planning a destabilization operation involving a Muslim Brotherhood-led insurrection to bring about regime change in Syria. We would also have to ignore the fact that U.S. strategists had planned since 2003, and possibly as early as 2001, to force Assad and his secular Arab nationalist ideology from power, and was funding the Syrian opposition, including Muslim Brotherhood-linked groups, from 2005. Accordingly, Washington had been driving toward the overthrow of the Assad government with the goal of de-Ba'athifying Syria. An Islamist-led guerilla struggle against Syria's secular Arab nationalists would have unfolded, regardless of whether the Syrian government's response at Daraa was excessive or not. The game was already in play, and a pretext was being sought. Daraa provided it. Thus, the idea that the arrest of two boys in Daraa for painting anti-government graffiti on a wall could provoke a major conflict is a believable as the notion that WWI was caused by nothing more than the assassination of Archduke Franz Ferdinand.

Syria was often denounced in journalism that was more jingoistic propaganda than dispassionate reportage as a police state. To be sure, Syria was, indeed, a police state. But all states are police states to one degree or another, a reality that Western chauvinism elides. Every state has a political policing function. The United States has the FBI, which has a long history of policing political dissidents, mainly communists, socialists, anarchists, civil rights and black power activists, and trade union activists, and these days, Islamists. Britain has Special Branch. Canada has the Mounties and CSIS. Devil's Island, until 1953, was used by France to incarcerate political prisoners. After 9/11, the United States, Britain, France and many other countries increased their police state powers in response to "terrorist" threats, leading some critics to say that these states have become "like" police states, rather than what they were: longstanding police states whose political policing powers grew or receded depending on the intensity of internal and external challenges to their authority.

When dissidents pose a growing threat, a country's police state powers are increased. When external threats are few in number, and internal dissent is inappreciable, the police state is scaled back. Countries that contend with few threats and therefore are able to minimize their police state powers have been inclined to denounce, where they can, the stronger police states of governments they're hostile to. The point of the propaganda is to misattribute the openness of a society to ideology rather that to the comparatively strong security environments these states enjoy, in order to score propaganda points.

The United States, for example, is protected from the external threat of military invasion by two vast oceans, and by its formidable military. It is therefore in a position to maintain police state powers at a level far below those of many other countries that exist within very precarious security environments. Arab nationalist Syria, for reasons already mentioned, was emblematic of an objectively insecure state. U.S. officials attributed their own country's comparatively low level of police state powers to a supposed ideological commitment to openness and civil liberties, rather than to the comparative absence of threat. U.S. officials also attributed Arab nationalist Syria's comparatively high level of police state powers to a supposed ideological attachment to repression rather than to a precarious security environment.

The precarious security environment with which Arab nationalist Syria had to contend, as did other targets of U.S. hostility, were to a large degree the creations of the United States itself. Washington threatened states that refused to be integrated into its empire by establishing military bases on their peripheries, arming their enemies, and fomenting strife within their countries. The number of *coups d'état,* assassinations and covert interventions the United States engineered around the world was ample evidence of Washington's ability to significantly threaten the political survival of governments that failed to fall into line behind its leadership. William Blum calculated that since the end of WWII alone, the United States government had attempted to overthrow more than 50 foreign governments, attempted to assassinate more than 50 foreign leaders, and grossly interfered in the elections of at least 30 foreign countries.[43]

In reaction to U.S.-instigated threats, targeted states strengthened their political policing powers. While this increased their probability of survival, it also handed Washington a propaganda victory. The threatened states could be portrayed as inherently repressive. Just as the comparative openness of the United States could be misattributed to ideology rather than to a comparatively strong security environment, so too could the strong police state powers of countries which were the targets of U.S. hostility be misattributed to the ideology of the countries' leadership, rather than to the precarious security environments which Washington had a hand in creating. This had two benefits for Washington.

First, by misattributing strong police state powers to the ideological orientation of a target country's leadership the challenging ideology could be discredited as inherently authoritarian and repressive, as against U.S. ideology, which could be presented as valuing openness.

Second, by labeling a targeted country's leadership as authoritarian, headed by a "strongman" who was declared to be contemptuous of human rights and guided by an inherently repressive ideology, Washington could establish a humanitarian pretext to escalate the level of threat it could bring to bear on the target country. Sanctions could be made more onerous, ostensibly to punish the target country's leadership for its "bad" behavior, while funding to opponents of the government could be increased, to do the same. At the same time, Washington might let it be known that in its deliberations on how to deal with the new "strongman" it was leaving all options on the table. These actions simply escalated the level of threat, making the target country's security environment even more precarious, and making strong police state powers even more exigent. The more the United States threatened its target, the more the target reacted by strengthening its police state powers, and the more strongly Washington issued threats.

There is a rhetoric and a reality of police states. The reality is that every state is a police state; the rhetoric is that we acknowledge only the police states of our enemies, whose strong police state powers are often a reaction to the threats we create. To reinforce the point: Through most of its history the United States hasn't had to create a strong police state apparatus because it has found itself protected from external threats by two vast oceans. All the same, on the few occasions it has faced threats of any significance—during two world wars and the Cold War—it has greatly strengthened its police state powers. Even in response to 9/11, a minor threat in comparison to the threats many other states have faced, Washington scaled back civil liberties, carried out extra-judicial assassinations by drone of U.S. citizens abroad, tortured suspected terrorists, locked up suspected militants without charge at Guantanamo Bay, and, as Edward Snowden has revealed, carried out history's most extensive program of government eavesdropping.

On top of Islamist insurrection and terrorism, Syria faced the threat of invasion, military occupation and on two occasions was threatened with nuclear destruction—in 1970 by the United States, and in 1973 by Israel.[44] Arab nationalist Syria faced three major opposition forces, corresponding to its three major Ba'athist values: its secularism was opposed by political Islam, its Arab nationalism by Israel and the United States, and its Arab socialism by Wall Street. As we've seen, Sunni political Islam—which was able to draw on the financial support of the Arab Gulf states—posed a major threat to the viability of the Ba'athist state since the secular Arab nationalists' rise to power in 1963. On top of the danger posed by Sunni political Islam, Syria was in a state of war with Israel since 1948. And Israel—with its military funding from the United States of $3 billion per year, renegotiated in 2016 to rise to $3.8 billion annually—was a military powerhouse in comparison to Syria. The two countries had fought three major wars, and Israel occupied the Golan Heights, part of Syria's territory. Finally, the United States, history's most formidable military power, had a long record of colluding with political Islam against Syria's Arab nationalist state. Washington also issued a virtual declaration of war when it declared Syria part of the Axis of Evil in 2002 and openly contemplated an invasion in the wake of the 2003 war on Iraq. In addition, it funded the Syrian opposition beginning in 2005. Had the United States, itself, been faced with threats of this magnitude, it is fairly certain that it would have increased its police state powers to a level equal, if not beyond, those which the threatened and beleaguered Syrian state was forced, by the structural logic of its circumstances, to adopt.

In light of the multiple threats Syria faced, and considering the Muslim Brotherhood's vow of war to the death with Ba'athism, it is predictable that Syrian authorities would have reacted strongly to any challenge to their authority. This conclusion is strengthened by two other considerations. U.S. diplomatic documents placed on the public record by WikiLeaks revealed that Syrian security agents knew that Washington was providing funding to the opposition.[45] Additionally, in early 2011, Islamists had launched a war to the death with Libya's secular Arab nationalist government—a war which would soon be backed by NATO. This was a campaign to eliminate secular Arab nationalism from Libya, and it was likely to have been regarded by Syria's secular Arab nationalists as a model the United States would try to implement in Syria. Under circumstances of escalating threat, it is reasonable to assume that Damascus would intensify its repression of dissent. As Lenin had said in a similar context, "We do not wish to do away with ourselves by suicide and therefore will not" offer an open society in which our political opponents, much more powerful than us, can freely organize our demise.[46] The journalist Patrick Seale, who specialized in the Middle East, wrote that the Syrian government's use of force "can be explained, if not condoned, by the fact that it" believed it was "fighting for its life—not only against local opponents but also against an external conspiracy led by the United States (egged on by Israel) and including Saudi Arabia, Qatar, Britain and France."[47]

We can also ask whether the Syrian government's use of force to quell the violent uprising at Daraa was at all illegitimate and whether it was typical of other state's security services to react under similar circumstances in a forceful manner. What "countermeasures would you resort to when you have people killing in the street and attacking property?" asked Assad.

> "To tell them do whatever you want, I'm open, I'm not going to respond? That's not correct. We have only one option; it is to stop them and to prevent them from continuing the killing, at the same time they have machineguns, we cannot throw balloons at them, we have to use our guns, because they are militants. This is the only option that we had that time."[48]

How were Washington's Arab allies reacting to upheavals in their own countries? The question is important for two reasons. First, the answer illuminates whether Damascus's response to the violent uprising in Syria was excessive by the standards of its neighbors. Second, it indicates whether Washington had established a double standard by which it accepted the use of force by allies to put down violent dissent but established a higher, and impossible, standard, by which Damascus was to be judged. Did Washington expect Syrian authorities to throw balloons at armed insurrectionists?

A day before protesters in Syria shot at police and set fire to buildings, Bahrain's royal dictatorship violently suppressed a popular uprising with the assistance of Saudi tanks and U.S. equipment. *New York Times*' columnist Nicholas D. Kristof lamented that "America's ally, Bahrain" used "American tanks, guns and tear gas as well as foreign mercenaries to crush a prodemocracy movement" as Washington remained "mostly silent."[49] Kristof said he had "seen corpses of protesters who were shot at close range, seen a teenage girl writhing in pain after being clubbed, seen ambulance workers beaten for trying to rescue protesters." He didn't explain why the United States— the world's self-proclaimed champion of democracy—would have a dictator as an ally, much less one who crushed a prodemocracy movement. All he could offer was the weak excuse that the United States was "in a vice—caught between its allies and its values," as if Washington didn't chose its allies, and that they were a force of nature, like an earthquake or a hurricane, that you had to live with and endure

Meanwhile, the Yemeni government was using "excessive and deadly force against peaceful demonstrators, killing hundreds and wounding thousands." A United Nations report found "an overall situation where many Yemenis peacefully calling for greater freedoms, an end to corruption and respect for rule of law were met with excessive and disproportionate use of lethal force by the state."[50]

In February 2011, unrest erupted in Saudi Arabia's Eastern Province. Protesters demanded political reforms and the release of political prisoners. The unrest continued throughout the year. In October, it turned violent. Protesters attacked a police station with guns and Molotov cocktails, injuring eleven police officers.[51] To quell the unrest, Saudi security forces used tanks and mass arrests, sentencing many of the protesters to death.[52] Saudi human rights activists circulated videos on social media showing armored vehicles firing on protesters and photos of protesters killed by Saudi authorities.[53]

Three factors set U.S. allies' use of force to suppress internal disturbances apart from the Syrian government's use of force to do the same.

First, the response of the U.S. allies was unequivocally harsh. More than a thousand Saudi troops put down the uprising in Bahrain and remained in the country afterward to deter more unrest.[54] Three dozen protesters were killed and nearly 3,000 were arrested.[55] A UN report called out the U.S.-supported government in Yemen for its excessive and disproportionate use of lethal force. And the Saudi National Guard, expressly formed to protect the Saudi royal family from internal uprisings, used armored vehicles to shoot at protesters. At the same time, thousands of protesters were arrested and sentenced to death, including the cleric Nimr al-Nimr, who was beheaded for his role in the protests, and his nephew, who was sentenced to death by crucifixion.

Second, there are no indications that the Saudis made any concessions to the protesters, while the Assad government almost immediately lifted the security law, as protesters had demanded, and amended the constitution to allow more political openness.

Third, the U.S. government expressed no meaningful opposition to its allies' draconian use of lethal force. Nor did it send aid to the protesters and the armed groups that rose up against its client states. Conversely, Washington condemned the Assad government unreservedly, declared that Assad had lost legitimacy, and ordered him to step down. When he didn't, U.S. officials stepped up their aid to the opposition. By 2015, the CIA had trained and equipped nearly 10,000 fighters and was spending "approaching $1 billion a year" to support anti-government combatants. Between itself and its allies, Saudi Arabia, Qatar and Turkey, Washington had armed and trained 50,000 insurgents.[56] On the other hand, Washington was spending nothing on support to opponents of the Bahraini and Saudi monarchies but was spending a king's ransom to prop up its client government in Afghanistan—a government which had no legitimacy. As *The Wall Street Journal* put it, "the Afghan government and security forces rely on the largess of the U.S. and its allies to survive."[57] Hence, the U.S. president was describing his Syrian counterpart as having lost legitimacy, when, according to *Time* and *The New York Times*, Assad was popular and commanded the loyalty of most of the Syrian population. At the same time, Obama was using the U.S. military to prop up a government in Kabul which had so little popular support it was unable stand on its own and required massive U.S. support to survive.

A final point on the origins of the violent uprising in 2011: Some social scientists and analysts have drawn on a study published in *The Proceedings of the National Academy of Sciences* to suggest that "drought played a role in the Syrian unrest." According to this view, drought "caused crop failures that led to the migration of as many as 1.5 million people from rural to urban areas." This, in combination with an influx of refugees from Iraq, intensified competition for scarce jobs in urban areas, making Syria a cauldron of social and economic tension ready to boil over.[58] The argument sounds reasonable, even "scientific," but the phenomenon it seeks to explain—mass upheaval in Syria—never existed. As we've already seen, a review of Western press coverage found no reference to mass upheaval. On the contrary, reporters expected to encounter the phenomenon, and were surprised when they didn't. Instead, Western journalists found Syria to be surprisingly quiet. Demonstrations called by organizers of the Syrian Revolution 2011 Facebook page fizzled. Critics conceded that Assad was popular. Reporters could find no one who believed a revolt was imminent. Even a month after the Daraa incident—which involved only hundreds of protesters, dwarfed by the tens of thousands of Syrians who demonstrated in Damascus in support of the government—*The New York Times* reporter on the ground, Anthony Shadid, could find no sign in Syria of the mass upheavals of Tunisia and Egypt. In early February 2011, "Omar Nashabe, a long-time Syria watcher and correspondent for the Beirut-based Arabic daily Al-Ahkbar" told *Time* that "Syrians may be afflicted by poverty that stalks 14% of its population combined with an estimated 20% unemployment rate, but Assad still has his credibility."[59]

So, yes, internal migration from the drought-afflicted countryside to the cities, in combination with an inward migration of refugees from Iraq, may have created severe economic stress within the country, but there's no evidence that it touched off a mass upheaval, because there's no evidence that there ever was one. What there was, instead, was an insurrection, with a predominantly Islamist content, led by armed groups, affiliated with the Syrian Muslim Brotherhood, which was colluding with Washington. We know from a leaked U.S.

Defense Intelligence Agency document that by 2012 "the major forces driving the insurgency" were "the Salafist, Muslim Brotherhood, and AQI [al-Qaeda in Iraq]."[60] And we also know that the leading rebel groups were "Brotherhood-affiliated," as *The Wall Street Journal's* Middle East specialist, Yaroslav Trofimov, termed them.[61] We also know that the Brothers had vowed an unending jihad against the secular government in Damascus and had been supported since 2005 by Washington. The U.S. government, furthermore, had been openly calling for regime change in Syria since 2002, when it added Syria to the Axis of Evil. Hence, the phenomenon that needs to be explained is not a popular upheaval against an unpopular government, but an armed rebellion with an Islamist character supported by Washington against a popular government.

People are sometimes cautioned to seek explanations of complex social phenomena, like mass upheavals, in anonymous social and economic forces, rather than in the machinations of the U.S. (or some other) government. Good advice. Except in this case, there is no evidence that the uprising was either popular or that the government was unpopular. The evidence, instead, appears to accord more congenially with the following scenario: The U.S. government enlisted the aid of political Islamists to prosecute a guerilla war against a government it was inimical to because it pursued an Arab nationalist agenda which was an ideological threat to U.S. domination of the oil-rich Arab world. Washington chose to ally with Sunni political Islam because it was the major opposition to Syria's secular Arab nationalist government. Washington had a history of teaming up with mujahedeen to topple secular leftist governments. It had done so in Afghanistan, where it joined with Saudi Arabia and Pakistan—and infamously with Osama bin Laden—to fund, arm and organize a jihad against the "atheist" Soviet communists and their 'infidel' secular leftist allies who formed the Afghan government. CIA-backed jihadists would do the same in Syria to topple the "infidel" secular Arab nationalists who were led by the Alawite "heretic" Bashar al-Assad.

One might object to Washington's fanning the flames of the Muslim Brotherhood's animus toward the secularist Arab nationalists; it touched off a conflagration which would create a holocaust of ruined lives. An interviewer for *Le Nouvel Observateur* once asked the former U.S. National Security Adviser Zbigniew Brzezinski if he regretted U.S. support to the mujahedeen in Afghanistan. Brzezinski replied, "What is more important in world history?...Some agitated Moslems or the liberation of Central Europe and the end of the cold war?"[62] One suspects that Brzezinski's successors might have had a similar attitude to Washington's agitating some Muslims in Syria. What is more important in world history? they might have asked: Millions of refugees and hundreds of thousands of lives lost (infinitesimally few of them American) or eliminating a movement that challenged U.S. leadership of the Arab world? When she served as U.S. Secretary of State, Madeleine Albright thought the U.S.-led sanctions-related deaths of a half a million Iraqi children were "worth it." It was the price to be paid to eliminate the Arab nationalist threat to U.S. hegemony in the Middle East presented by Iraq's Ba'athists. If some "agitated Muslims" and 500,000 sanctions-related deaths are worth it, what's to prevent us from thinking that, in the view of U.S. officials, the loss of a few hundred thousand Syrian lives wasn't also worth it?

CHAPTER FOUR

THE MYTH OF THE MODERATE REBEL

Islamists seeking to establish an Islamic state in Syria based on the Quran were the chief domestic rival of secular Arab nationalists for control of the Syrian state ever since the country achieved independence from France in 1945. As we've seen, in 1980, the main Islamist group, the Syrian Muslim Brotherhood, declared a war without end against the secular Ba'athist government. The Muslim Brothers viewed the Syrian government as an infidel regime led by an Alawite heretic. None of this was lost on the U.S. government. "Sunni Islamic fundamentalists," a U.S. State Department study concluded, "have posed the most sustained and serious threat to the Ba'ath regime."[1]

By 2009, just two years before the Arab Spring upheavals, the Muslim Brotherhood denounced Syria's secular state as a foreign and hostile element which needed to be eliminated.[2] A mere three months before the 2011 outbreak of violence in Syria, "the movement's leaders" continued "to voice their hope for a civil revolt in Syria, wherein "the Syrian people" would "perform its duty and liberate Syria from the tyrannical and corrupt regime.""[3]

When the Daraa riot broke out in mid-March, 2011, two armed Islamist groups, which would play a lead role in the war against the Syrian government, Jabhat al-Nusra and Ahrar al-Sham, had already been formed. As violence began to spread, at least one Western news report noted that Islam was playing a prominent role."[4] Within a year, the U.S. Defense Intelligence Agency reported that Salafists, the Muslim Brotherhood, and Islamic State's predecessor, al-Qaeda in Iraq, were the driving forces of the insurgency.

Despite evidence that the rebellion was driven by Islamists seeking an Islamic state, a myth was insinuated into public discourse that there existed an armed secular opposition to the Ba'athist government, the "moderate" rebels. This fit with the rhetoric of the Arab Spring, which misrepresented an Islamist-led urban guerilla uprising against a secular government as a popular upheaval against an unpopular government, animated by a hunger for democracy. That the revolt was driven, in point of fact, by hunger for an Islamic state which would be guided by the Quran and which anathematized democratic decision-making, was a reality to be marginalized. It challenged the script. How could Washington openly support the rebels, if the rebellion was seen correctly as an Islamist assault on a secular state whose leader governed with the consent of the governed?

The Syrian Muslim Brotherhood played a lead role in the revolt from the very first moment, dominating the Syrian National Council, formed in early October, 2011, which the United States and its Western allies immediately apotheosized as "the leading interlocutor of the opposition with the international community." The Syrian National Council, proclaimed the West, would be "a legitimate representative of all Syrians"—a potential government-in-exile.[5]

The Free Syrian Army was the SNC's military wing. "What we are aiming for is a revolution with a political wing, represented by the SNC, and a military wing, represented by the FSA," Col. Aref Hammoud, a Turkey-based commander with the FSA, told *The Wall Street Journal*.[6]

Funding for Syria's Muslim Brotherhood was pouring in "from wealthy private individuals and money from Gulf states, including Saudi Arabia and Qatar."[7] "Qatar, host to the largest American military base in the Middle East," was eagerly financing the Muslim Brotherhood, in Syria and elsewhere, and doling out wads of cash to other Islamist groups, as well.[8] Much of the funding, as then Syrian National Council president Burhan Ghalioun told *The Wall Street Journal*, was being used "to help equip the Free Syrian Army."[9]

Funding for the Free Syrian Army was also coming directly from the Syrian National Council, which was "dominated by the Muslim Brotherhood,"[10] and had "a significant contingent of Islamists."[11] Indeed, so strongly was the Brotherhood represented in the new "government-in-waiting" that Western officials became concerned that the opposition was "at risk of becoming dominated by Islamists pushing for a Muslim Brotherhood government after Assad."[12] "Molham al-Drobi, a senior council member and a representative of the Syrian Muslim Brotherhood on the council," told *The Wall Street Journal* that Saudi Arabia, Qatar, Kuwait and the United Arab Emirates were funding the council to the tune of $40 million per month.[13] Weren't all of these states presided over by princes, emirs, and kings, who preferred to govern by decree, eschewing any form of democratic input? What a curious set of allies for a so-called pro-democracy movement.

As the military vehicle of the SNC, the Free Syrian Army bore a name which had been carefully crafted to imply that it was free from the ostensible tyranny of the government in Damascus, though, once the rhetoric was stripped away, it was clear that the Free Syrian Army wasn't free of the anti-democratic Gulf Arab monarchies—the protégés of the United States—who provided their arms and salaries. The SNC and its military wing, the Free Syrian Army, depended on the Gulf anti-democracies to fund a fight many in the West were led to believe was a quest for democracy, not a journey whose destination was a Muslim Brotherhood-led government in Damascus. As Zbigniew Brzezinski tartly observed, "You know, we started helping the rebels, whatever they are, and they're certainly not fighting for democracy, given their sponsorship, Qatar and Saudi Arabia."[14]

Not only was the Free Syrian Army not fighting for democracy, it wasn't secular, either. According to the myth of the
Syrian uprising, the FSA represented the early secular phase
of the revolt, before it was 'hijacked' by Jabhat al-Nusra and
Islamic State. But the FSA was always largely Islamist, and the
uprising was never hijacked. It was Islamist from day one.

The FSA began as a broad umbrella of urban guerilla groups,
most of which were Islamist. It was "an entirely Sunni Arab
phenomenon,"[15] challenging the idea that it represented the
democratic aspirations of Syrians. If the FSA were truly a pro-
democratic army, why did it have virtually no representation
among the roughly 30 percent of Syria's population that wasn't
Sunni? Was democracy a strictly Sunni-aspiration? What's
more, democracy wasn't listed among the FSA's goals—an odd
omission for a group that was supposed to be fighting for rule
by the people. The FSA's stated purpose was entirely negative:
to overthrow the Assad government, not to create a democratic
state. Moreover, "Most FSA brigades used religious rhetoric
and were named after heroic figures or events in Sunni Islamic
history."[16] *The Associated Press* reported that many of the participating groups had strong Islamist agendas,[17] and *The New
York Times* noted that "some groups in the Free Syrian Army
have similar ideologies [as Jabhat al-Nusra], [and] follow the
strict Salafist interpretation of Islam."[18] Among the FSA's
Islamist members was the Muslim Brotherhood itself, which,
according to one Brother, existed "on the ground" working
"under the FSA umbrella."[19] One of the Brotherhood-affiliated
guerilla groups was the Tawid Brigade, or Tawheed Division,
which led the fight against the Syrian government in Aleppo.[20]
The New York Times pointed to one Free Syrian Army commander who told recruits: "Those whose intentions are not for
God, they had better stay home, whereas if your intention is for
God, then you go for jihad and you gain an afterlife and
heaven."[21] This was hardly the exhortation of a secularist.

Not only was the Free Syrian Army "dominated by Islamist
groups" as Brig. Gen. Mithkal Albtaish, an FSA leader, told *The*

Wall Street Journal, it was also, said the General, "in close coordination with al-Nusra,"[22] Al-Qaeda's affiliate in Syria. Indeed, *Time* had reported that "rebel offensives are joint operations between groups of FSA fighters, Islamists, Salafists and even the extremist Jabhat al-Nusra group."[23] A number of reports from other mainstream Western media sources echoed *Time*. *The Wall Street Journal* reported that "The Free Syrian Army...had some of its members fighting alongside the Nusra Front. Some of the same groups being backed by Washington are liaising and cooperating with the Nusra Front."[24] On other occasions, the newspaper noted that "Nusra is cooperating with...the Western-backed Free Syrian Army;"[25] "CIA-backed Free Syrian Army factions and extremist elements such as Nusra Front and Ahrar al Sham...have been collaborating;"[26] and "the Nusra Front and the FSA, which receives Western aid" are cooperating.[27] *Time* observed that the cooperation between the FSA and al-Nusra extended to sharing arms and ammunition and that the two groups were so close that it would be impossible to keep arms the CIA supplied to the FSA out of al-Nusra's hands.[28]

Not only was the FSA largely Islamist, it was hardly moderate. *The Associated Press* reported that some FSA brigades "fought in ways that could scare away Western backers."[29] One way in which they fought would hardly earn the approbation of Western populations: they used suicide bombers. This led *Time* reporter Rania Abouzeid to refer to the FSA groups which adhered to this practice as "so-called moderates."[30] She also noted that FSA units that professed to be secular spoke "in ugly sectarian terms that demonize minorities, particularly members of Assad's Alawite sect,"[31] inviting the question of whether the labels "moderate" and "secular" were deliberately chosen as misrepresentations to disguise the Islamist orientation of the insurgency, which few in the West would support. The truth of the matter was that the FSA was not a secular guerilla army which eschewed the barbarities the Islamic State would become notorious for. This became clear when a U.N.-appointed

commission documented cases of the Free Syrian Army practicing torture and summary executions.[32]

The pseudo-secularist army "largely collapsed at the end of
2013," and was taken over by the CIA, which directed its units.[33]
The Syrian National Council collapsed too, as non-Islamists
accused the council of being an "autocratic" organization "dominated by the Muslim Brotherhood,"[34] which sought to use the
council as vehicle for a Muslim Brotherhood government in
waiting.[35] From that point forward, the Islamist rebellion
would no longer be dominated by the Syrian Muslim
Brotherhood, but by its ideological progeny, Jabhat al-Nusra,
with which the Free Syrian Army had, from the beginning,
worked hand in glove, as well as by Islamic State. Both organizations were al-Qaeda derivatives, and al-Qaeda derived much
of its inspiration and personnel from the Muslim Brotherhood.

The Nusra Front was created as an offshoot of al-Qaeda in
Iraq, which, according to the U.S. Defense Intelligence Agency,
was one of the driving forces early in the rebellion, along with
the Muslim Brotherhood. Al-Nusra's principal goal was the
same as the FSA's (and Washington's, the Saudi's, the Turk's,
the Qatari's, the Jordanian's and the Israeli's): to force the
secular Arab nationalists from power in Damascus. But
al-Nusra had another explicit goal, shared with the FSA's
Islamists—to establish "a Salafist-oriented Sunni Islamist
state in Syria."[36]

Al-Qaeda is often understood to recapitulate the Wahhabist
ideology which underlies Saudi Arabia's state religion. To be
sure, al-Qaeda and Wahhabism are Salafist and anti-Shi'a. But
al-Qaeda's thinking more closely resembles that of the Muslim
Brotherhood, especially in incorporating innovations introduced by the movement's chief ideologue in the 1960s and
1970s, Sayyid Qutb. Wahhabism is "a tribal, desert Islam...
hugely different from the cosmopolitan Islam of diverse trading cities like Baghdad and Cairo," observed *The New York
Times'* Scott Shane.[37] The political Islam that arose in the
Arabian Desert was partly born of a need to legitimize the rule

of the Saud family. By contrast, the political Islam that arose in Egypt sprang from Islam's encounter with European colonialism. Al-Qaeda's ideology is directly related to the question of Western domination of the Muslim world, and so followed the Muslim Brotherhood's concerns. Qutb argued that Muslims had an obligation to wage jihad against all governments within the Islamic domain which were un-Islamic, including those that were nominally Muslim, but were proxies of the West, helping to keep the Muslim world under the ascendancy of foreign interests and creeds. Al-Qaeda's innovation was to direct the attack of Muslims seeking to free their homeland against the "far enemy," namely, the United States and its Western satellites which "divided the (Muslim world) into small and little countries...[T]here is no more important duty than purging the American enemy out of the holy land," declared Osama bin Laden.[38]

The slogan devised for the Muslim Brotherhood by its founder Hasan al-Banna was: God is our purpose, the Prophet our leader, the Quran our constitution, jihad our way and dying for God's cause our supreme objective. This "was, in effect, the motto by which the 9/11 hijackers lived and died," CIA officer Robert Baer argued.[39] Baer went further, insisting that while the "press kept calling the [9/11] attackers al-Qaeda" that, in effect, 9/11 was a Muslim Brotherhood operation "through and through," at least in its inspiration. The Brothers cum al-Qaeda, he added, were the "same crew" the United States used to do its "dirty work in Yemen, Afghanistan, and plenty of other places," countering secular leftist movements and governments.[40] *The Wall Street Journal* noted in 2007 that "Osama bin Laden and other al-Qaeda leaders cite the works of the Brotherhood's late intellectual, Sayyid Qutb, as an inspiration for their crusade against the West and Arab dictators. Members of the Egyptian and Syrian Brotherhood have also gone on to take senior roles in Mr. bin Laden's movement," the newspaper noted.[41] This included bin Laden's immediate successor, Ayman al-Zawahiri, who joined the Muslim Brotherhood at the age of 14.

The point is that al-Qaeda, and its derivatives, al-Nusra and The Islamic State, flowed seamlessly from the Muslim Brotherhood, and that the Sunni Islamist ideology expressed concretely in the political programs of the Free Syrian Army, al-Qaeda, al-Nusra and Islamic State represented the program of the Muslim Brotherhood at its core.

The goal of Sunni political Islam was to defend and promote Sunni Islam as the central organizing principle of society and government in the traditional Muslim world. It was, therefore, opposed to rule by non-Muslims, Muslims deemed to be infidels or apostates (including Shi'ites), and un-Islamic ideologies. Sunni political Islam was against the existence in traditional Muslim territory of: foreign occupations; nominally Muslim governments which were local proxies of non-Muslim imperialist powers; nominally Muslim governments which practiced un-Islamic ways; secular governments; governments led by non-Muslims or self-identified Muslims deemed to be apostates; and communism, socialism, and secular nationalism. Many Islamists rejected democracy as un-Islamic. Islamists advocated "replacing existing political systems based on the 'laws of men' with a system based, in theory, on the 'laws of God'."[42]

There were differences within Sunni political Islam. Al-Nusra was content to limit its aspirations to forming an Islamic state within the borders of Syria, while AQI under the leadership of Abu Bakr al-Baghdadi decided to declare an Islamic State without borders but based in the broader Levant.[43] When AQI demanded that al-Nusra fold itself into the Islamic State, the latter balked, pledging allegiance to al-Qaeda, and became al-Qaeda's Syrian affiliate. Later, it would formally sever its connection to al-Qaeda, in a vain attempt to encourage Washington to remove it from the U.S. terrorism list, but the demarche was dismissed by Washington as a vacuous exercise in re-branding. At the same time, the leadership of al-Qaeda disavowed the Islamic State and deplored al-Baghdadi's passion for attacking heterodox Muslims.

Al-Nusra was largely tolerated by Washington, and Washington actively collaborated with the organization, funding groups it labeled as "moderate" who were in reality auxiliaries of the al-Qaeda affiliate. Already we've seen that the Free Syrian Army was enmeshed with al-Nusra, sharing arms and coordinating with it on the battlefield, a level of cooperation doubtlessly facilitated by their shared Muslim Brotherhood ideology. The cooperation of CIA-armed and trained rebel groups with al-Nusra was noted repeatedly in the Western press.

The Wall Street Journal reported that some "of the same groups being backed by Washington are liaising and cooperating with the Nusra Front"[44] and that many "U.S.-backed moderate rebels are allied with Nusra. Most ground commanders backed by the U.S. coordinate operations with Nusra Front."[45] The newspaper also noted that "Nusra Front...fights alongside... Western-backed...rebels;"[46] and "al-Nusra has fought alongside rebel units which the U.S. and its regional allies have backed;"[47] and "CIA-backed Free Syrian army factions and extremist elements such as Nusra Front and Ahrar al Sham...have been collaborating."[48]

The New York Times revealed that the al-Qaeda affiliate "coordinates closely with (groups that receive Western aid)"[49] and that many "of the anti-Assad groups aligned with the United States fight alongside the Nusra Front."[50] *New York Times* reporters also explained that "insurgents who have been trained covertly by the Central Intelligence Agency...are enmeshed with or fighting alongside more hard-line Islamist groups, including the Nusra Front, al-Qaeda's Syria affiliate"[51] and that the "rebel groups that the West considers relatively moderate are...intertwined in places with the Nusra Front.[52]

The Washington Post reported that Jabhat al-Nusra's "forces are intermingled with moderate rebels,"[53] and *The Independent's* Patrick Cockburn wrote that "smaller armed groups, which sometimes have good weapons supplied by the Americans, had acted as auxiliaries to Nusra and Ahrar al-Sham" (another Muslim Brotherhood-related group).[54]

The Nusra Front led a rebel coalition named Jaish al Fatah, which included Ahrar al-Sham, and—as *New York Times* reporter Ben Hubbard put it—"more moderate rebel factions that... received covert arms support from the intelligence services of the United States and its allies."[55] When Russian air strikes hit the coalition's fighters, Washington complained that the Russians were targeting groups "that have received covert American aid."[56] But the Russians were also targeting the U.S.-backed fighters' comrades in arms, al-Nusra, which had been designated as a foreign terrorist organization by the U.S. Treasury Department.[57] Al-Nusra had been condemned, along with Islamic State, by the United Nations Security Council, as well. The United States fit al-Nusra with the terrorist label "to signal to the opposition coalition and Middle East governments that Washington" wouldn't "accept radical Islamist forces playing a central role in any government after Mr. Assad's expected fall."[58] Al-Nusra's designation by Washington and the Security Council as an outcast organization rankled the al-Qaeda affiliate's CIA-backed comrades who staged protests in several Syrian cities, raising banners which declared "we are all Jabhat al-Nusra."[59] Later, when Washington arrived at an accord with Russia to coordinate air strikes against al-Nusra targets, soon after rejected and sabotaged by the Pentagon, the group's U.S.-backed auxiliaries objected, letting it be known that "they did not think al-Nusra should be singled out as a target for air strikes."[60]

That Washington regarded the Nusra Front in a different light than Islamic State, was evidenced, in the first instance, in the reality that CIA-armed and trained rebels were embedded with al-Nusra, but not, it seemed, with Islamic State. One could search far and wide through press reports for mention of insurgents on the Western payroll who were cooperating with the Islamic State and turn up nothing. In contrast, references to U.S.-backed rebels operating conjointly with al-Nusra were legion. Islamic State appeared to be a true anathema as far as Washington was concerned, while it was clear that U.S. officials regarded al-Qaeda's official affiliate in Syria on altogether different terms. This became clear when Russia entered the fray in Syria with the stated goal of destroying terrorist groups, and Washington acted as if it had forgotten that it had tarred Jabhat al-Nusra with the terrorist brush. Russia can't be targeting terrorists, Washington complained. If that were its true goal, it would only be attacking Islamic State. It seemed that, unofficially at least, the United States preferred that Jabhat al-Nusra be viewed as part of the agglomeration of "moderate" rebel groups. So it is that when the U.S. Director of Intelligence James Clapper was asked exactly who the much-talked-about moderates were, he replied: "Moderate these days is increasingly becoming anyone who's not affiliated with Islamic State."[61] Hence, as far as Washington was concerned, every non-Islamic State armed group was moderate, including al-Nusra, even though the al-Qaeda affiliate had been designated a terrorist organization by the United States itself, and despite the fact that it was part of an organization—indeed, the largest part— which attacked New York and Washington on September 11, 2001.

The reason for separating Islamic State from the Islamist insurgency against the Syrian Ba'athists, and regarding it as immoderate, was that, unlike al-Nusra and the al-Qaeda affiliate's CIA-armed auxiliaries, Islamic State aspired to replace more governments than Washington cared to see replaced. The U.S. government was willing to work with any group which shared its goal of de-Ba'athifying Syria, as long as it limited its aims to that end. But it was not willing to work with an organization which also wanted to oust the government in Baghdad— which Washington had installed—or the monarchy in Riyadh, which Islamic State condemned as un-Islamic, but which Washington considered an important ally.

What recommended Jabhat al-Nusra to Washington was that it was a useful instrument in the campaign to efface Arab nationalist ideology from the Syrian state. The U.S. strategy was to afford the al-Nusra coalition enough support for it to wear down the Syrian government sufficiently enough that the Ba'athists would acquiesce to a political transition, but never so much support that they would be forced to yield power to the Islamists. In other words, Washington had no intention of seeing either of the participants in the decades-long battle between secular Arab nationalism and Sunni political Islam prevail. Washington would let the two sides bleed each other dry, and when they were exhausted, interpose itself with a "compromise" candidate who would cater to U.S. business interests.

Washington played a similar game with Islamic State, though not by calibrating its level of support, which it wasn't providing anyway, but by calibrating its military campaign against the group. The Pentagon struck Islamic State hard in Iraq, but barely at all in Syria. U.S. airstrikes were concentrated in Iraq, reported *The Wall Street Journal*, because "in Syria, U.S. strikes against the Islamic State would inadvertently help the regime of President Bashar al-Assad militarily."[62] Likewise, France "refrained from bombing the group in Syria for fear of bolstering" the Syrian government.[63] The British, too, focused their air war overwhelmingly on Islamic State targets in Iraq, conducting less than 10 percent of their airstrikes on the Islamist organization's positions in Syria.[64] *The New York Times* reported that "United States-led airstrikes in Syria... largely focused on areas far outside government control, to avoid...aiding a leader whose ouster President Obama has called for."[65] Hence, U.S.-coalition "airstrikes against the Islamic State in Syria...were so limited as to make it little more than a symbolic gesture."[66] Robert Fisk summed up the phony war against Islamic State in Syria with a sarcastic quip: "And so we went to war against Isis in Syria—unless, of course, Isis was attacking Assad's regime, in which case we did nothing at all."[67]

Who was backing al-Qaeda's Syrian branch? The organization's main sources of direct funding were Saudi Arabia, Turkey and Qatar. Patrick Cockburn reported that "Saudi Arabia and Turkey had backed Jabhat al-Nusra,"[68] while the *The Wall Street Journal* revealed that Turkey and Qatar "reached out directly to al-Nusra, believing that the rebel group would be useful in achieving [their] ultimate goal: the overthrow of Assad."[69] U.S. Vice President Joe Biden corroborated these assessments. Speaking at Harvard's Kennedy School in October 2014, Biden told students that "the Saudis, the emirates, etc. were so determined to take down Assad and essentially have a proxy Sunni-Shi'a war [that] they poured hundreds of millions of dollars and tens of thousands of tons of military weapons into anyone who would fight against Assad, except the people who were being supplied were al-Nusra and al-Qaeda."[70] Biden didn't, however, refer to the indirect funding the al-Qaeda affiliate was getting from its CIA-backed auxiliaries, the famed "moderates," who were sharing U.S.-supplied weapons with al-Nusra and filling out the ranks of the group's Jaish al Fatah coalition.

Apart from Clapper's negative definition of "moderate" as any insurgent who wasn't affiliated with Islamic State, the term was so vague as to be virtually meaningless. *New York Times* reporter David Sanger, a member of the highly influential Wall Street-connected foreign policy body, the Council on Foreign Relations, acknowledged that "no one can agree who, exactly, is a 'moderate.'"[71] The Turkish definition of "moderate," according to Patrick Cockburn, included "extreme jihadis such as Ahrar al-Sham that usually fight in alliance with the al-Qaeda affiliate, Jabhat al-Nusra."[72] He also noted that Turkey regarded al-Nusra as a moderate faction.[73] *The Guardian's* Ewen MacAskill, perhaps operating on the not unreasonable assumption that the designation "moderate" ought to be based on a group's methods and ideology, noted that some of the groups the United States and its Western allies had labeled "moderates" were far from moderate, sharing the ideology of al-Qaida."[74] The British Ministry of Defense admitted that groups deemed moderate "can commit unpalatable acts or ally with groups considered unacceptably extremist."[75]

When Washington said "moderate," we were supposed to hear "secularists with a pluralist and democratic agenda," and not what the word actually denoted, which was a fighter engaged in a holy war against Syria's secular government who received arms from a program coordinated by the CIA. There wasn't anything close to a significant number of "moderates" in the sense in which we were supposed to understand the word. Ben Hubbard, reporting for *The New York Times* in 2013, wrote that nowhere "in rebel-controlled Syria is there a secular fighting force to speak of. The Islamist character of the opposition reflects the main constituency of the rebellion, which has been led since its start by Syria's Sunni Muslim majority, mostly in conservative, marginalized areas."[76] Hubbard quoted Elizabeth O'Bagy, who had made numerous trips to Syria to interview insurgent commanders for the Institute for the Study of War. O'Bagy told Hubbard that my "sense is that there are no seculars."[77] Islamists interviewed by *The Wall Street Journal* found the Western concept of a secularist Syrian rebel in a Muslim society to be incomprehensible,[78] perhaps seeing the idea as a product of the West's ignorance of the role political Islam played in the Arab world, to say nothing of failing to recognize the strong position of Sunni political Islam as the major opposition within Syria to the Ba'athist government.

"Moderates," if there were any in the sense of secular pro-democrats, were few in number, despite the extravagant claim of British Prime Minister David Cameron that there were 70,000 of them. Certainly, their ranks were so limited that arming them, in the view of U.S. President Barack Obama, would have made little difference. Obama told *New York Times* columnist Thomas Friedman that his administration had "difficulty finding, training and arming a sufficient cadre of secular Syrian rebels: 'There's not as much capacity as you would hope,'" Obama confessed.[79] Obama's assessment was underscored when "a U.S. general admitted that it had just four such 'moderate' fighters in Syria after spending $500 million on training them."[80] Robert Fisk dismissed the idea of the "moderates" as little more than a fantasy. "I doubt if there are 700 active 'moderate' foot soldiers in Syria," he wrote. And "I am being very generous, for the figure may be nearer 70."[81]

A multinational coalition funded, armed and coordinated the Islamist insurgency, with Washington in the lead. Here's how it worked. Washington assumed a supervisory role. It coordinated the provision of arms, decided which weapons would be distributed and which groups would receive them. The Saudis foot the lion's share of the bill, with the Qataris, Turks and Jordanians kicking in, as well. The United States also covered part of the cost of running the insurgency. Additionally, Washington, along with selected Western allies, provided training to Islamist fighters, at bases in Jordan and Qatar. Turkey allowed Islamists to flow freely over its border with Syria, and in the early days of the insurgency allowed the Free Syrian Army to operate from Turkish soil.

Regarding the specifics, the United States coordinated, assigning various insurgency-support roles to its allies, most of them authoritarian anti-democracies.[82] In addition, Washington worked through the CIA in collaboration with "British, French and Jordanian intelligence services to train rebels on the use of various kinds of weapons[83] at bases in Jordan and Qatar, with the Saudis bankrolling much of the operation."[84]

In 2013, the CIA launched a covert program to train and equip insurgents, with an annual U.S. budget of nearly $1 billion.[85] The Saudis, Qataris, Jordanians and Turks also contributed funding, with the Saudi contribution estimated to be several billions of dollars.[86] By mid-2015, "the CIA has trained and equipped nearly 10,000 fighters sent into Syria."[87] Together, the United States, Saudi Arabia, Qatar, and Turkey had fielded an insurgent army of 50,000 fighters.

The Saudis, who for several years had funded al-Nusra's Jaish al-Fatah coalition,[88] kicked in much of the money to fund the program, reprising the Kingdom's accustomed role of bankrolling guerillas to counter leftist movements and governments Washington opposed.

Qatar, which hosted the largest U.S. military base in the Middle East, also contributed significantly to bankrolling the armed opposition to Syria's Arab nationalists. The Emirate had "eagerly financed Islamists in Tunisia, Libya, Syria and Egypt, often siding with the Muslim Brotherhood or its affiliates."[89] Along with the Saudi monarchy, the Qatari monarchy poured money into al-Qaeda's Syrian affiliate, and the affiliate's Jaish al-Fatah coalition. Additionally, it set up bases on Qatari soil to train Syrian insurgents.[90]

Turkey's role in supporting the Islamist insurgency against Syria's secular Arab nationalist state was the most multifaceted. Not only did the government of Recep Tayyip Erdogan, himself an Islamist with ties to the Muslim Brotherhood, open its borders to allow insurgents to freely flow into Syria, it also provided funding and weapons to the insurgency, as well as hosting a U.S. superintended command and control center from which the insurgency was coordinated.

In 2011, Turkey began hosting the Free Syrian Army, allowing it "to orchestrate attacks across the border from inside a camp guarded by the Turkish military."[91] From that point until mid-2014, Ankara's policy was that "anyone and everyone who wanted to fight Assad was welcome to go to Syria and do so."[92] By mid-2014, Washington decided that Islamic State was becoming too strong, and that Turkey's border controls would have to be tightened to cut off the flow of recruits to the Islamist group.

As it was providing the Free Syrian Army shelter behind the Turkish military, and facilitating the flow of mujahedeen into Syria, Ankara "reached out directly to al-Nusra."[93] According to Seymour Hersh, "American intelligence had accumulated intercept and human intelligence demonstrating that the Erdogan government had [not only] been supporting Jabhat al-Nusra for years, [but] was...doing the same for Islamic State."[94]

Ankara didn't play favorites, spreading its lucre around to other Islamist insurgents, as well. Ahrar al Sham received weapons[95] and Erdogan contributed funding to the CIA's covert train and equip program.[96]

So extensive was Turkish support to Islamist rebels that when Erdogan's Muslim Brotherhood-connected Justice and

Development Party won elections in November 2015, the victory was "welcomed with effusive messages by no fewer than 15 different non-Isis armed opposition groups in Syria. Prominent among those congratulating President Erdogan" was the Jaish al-Fatah coalition of al-Qaeda's affiliate, the Nusra Front.[97]

Jordan, by comparison, played a less significant role, but it nevertheless made important contributions to the Islamists' fight to upend secular Arab nationalism in Syria, providing "a staging ground for rebels and their foreign backers on Syria's southern front,"[98] furnishing a base to train and equip jihadists under the CIA's covert program, and also contributing funding to the CIA program.[99]

In addition, Syria's Muslim Brotherhood "opened its own supply channel to the rebels, using resources from wealthy private individuals and money from Gulf states, including Saudi Arabia and Qatar."[100]

Washington presented itself as limiting its role in the insurgency to backing armed groups other than al-Nusra and Islamic State, which it had officially designated as terrorist groups. Islamic State's goals were too far out of line with U.S. foreign policy objectives to make it a useful ally of convenience. Al-Nusra's ambitions, on the other hand, were limited to overthrowing Syria's secular Arab nationalists, making the group's agenda more simpatico with Washington's aims. But once these groups were branded as terrorists, it became impossible to openly back them, not least of all because they were linked to al-Qaeda, a group which had been presented in the United States as the epitome of evil.

The methods the al-Qaeda derivatives used were not germane to their designation as "terrorists." U.S. officials had made this clear in the case of al-Nusra when they said that they officially sanctioned the Nusra Front to send a signal that the United States would not tolerate a radical Islamist government in Damascus, not that they would not tolerate politically-inspired violence against civilians. Hence, the terrorist designation was extraneous to the methods Jabhat al-Nusra used in its fight against the Syrian government. Designating the Nusra Front a terrorist group was, then, a politically expedient demarche which Washington used in an effort to shape events to its purposes. Moreover, Washington had not designated the Free Syrian Army as terrorists, even though the mock secularists used suicide bombings and operated on the battlefield with Jabhat al-Nusra, a reality suggesting that the two organizations shared the same methods.

But while Washington wouldn't openly support al-Nusra and Islamic State, its allies did, and Washington appeared to have no objections. James Stavridis, who had been NATO's supreme allied commander, told *The Wall Street Journal's* Yaroslav Trofimov that he didn't think Saudi, Qatari and Turkish funding of Jabhat al-Nusra was "a showstopper for the U.S." Indeed, Stavridis said, "It is unlikely we are going to operate side by side with cadres from Nusra, but if our allies are working with them, that is acceptable."[101]

Perhaps the biggest funder of al-Nusra was the Saudi royal family. Washington had long relied on the Saudi dynasty to step in when U.S. law or other circumstances prevented the United States from acting itself. For example, in the late 1970s, the CIA found itself increasingly fettered as oversight of the agency's activities was stepped up following revelations of years of abuses. The CIA turned to the Saudi royal family to organize a coalition of countries called the Safari Club, comprising Morocco, Egypt and France, to run undercover operations in Africa on Washington's behalf.[102] Relying on the Saudis to bankroll al-Qaeda's affiliate in Syria to bring down a leftist nationalist government was a continuation of a longstanding relationship that existed between Washington and Riyadh, in which Riyadh picked up the tab for campaigns that Washington found it expedient not to be directly associated with.

Not only did Washington back al-Nusra through its Saudi intermediary but it did the same by training and equipping rebel groups which fought under Nusra command but maintained a separate identity. CIA-trained and equipped groups coordinated with Nusra on the battlefield and shared arms. They were so thoroughly intertwined with the al-Qaeda franchise that they could act as arms conduits to al-Nusra, as well as operate as Nusra Front auxiliaries. In other words, the rebels the CIA trained and armed were *de facto* Nusra fighters who maintained a nominal independence to conjure the illusion that Washington wasn't backing a group it had officially sanctioned.

The "Syrian uprising," wrote Patrick Seale, "should be seen as only the latest, if by far the most violent, episode in the long war between Islamists and Ba'athists, which dates back to the founding of the secular Ba'ath Party in the 1940s. The struggle between them is by now little short of a death-feud."[103] "It is striking," Seale continued, citing Aron Lund, who had written a report for the Swedish Institute of International Affairs on Syrian Jihadism, "that virtually all the members of the various armed insurgent groups are Sunni Arabs; that the fighting has been largely restricted to Sunni Arab areas only, whereas areas inhabited by Alawis, Druze or Christians have remained passive or supportive of the regime; that defections from the regime are nearly 100 per cent Sunni; that money, arms and volunteers are pouring in from Islamic states or from pro-Islamic organisations and individuals; and that religion is the insurgent movement's most important common denominator."[104]

The moderate rebel was a myth. The insurgency was continuous with an Islamist rebellion that had broken out the moment secular Arab nationalists came to power in Damascus in 1963. That rebellion, in turn, was continuous with a war which had raged between the two movements after 1945, when French colonial forces quit the country, and indigenous forces mounted their first bids for control of the state. By 2005, Washington had struck an alliance of convenience with the Syrian Muslim Brotherhood to topple a common enemy, Syria's secular Arab nationalists. But U.S. strategists faced a public relations problem. Washington couldn't be seen to openly back militant Islamists, not in light of the 9/11 attacks and Washington's declared war on terrorism, which was effectively a war on people who shared the same ideology as the jihadists who were seeking to topple the secular Syrian government. The terrorists who Washington had declared war on were Islamists who used terrorist methods. The insurgents who were battling the Syrian government were also Islamists who used terrorist methods. To resolve the dilemma, Washington organized a deception: If it was inexpedient to directly funnel arms to al-Qaeda-affiliated fighters in Syria, it would have its allies take on the task. In addition, it would provide training, arms and money to other jihadists who fought alongside al-Qaeda, but would label these mujahedeen "moderates," to create the illusion that U.S. support was limited to a secular fighting force with a democratic and pluralist agenda. This accorded with the larger myth that the foreign policy of the United States was inherently virtuous, and motivated solely by Olympian aims—in this case, the realization of the Arab Spring goal of a creating democracy in the Middle East and North Africa. But as we've seen, Syria was closer to the Western model of a pluralist, multi-party democratic state than were any of Washington's Arab allies, and had moved even closer to that model by 2012, when the secular Arab nationalists amended the country's constitution to allow multiple candidates in presidential elections. There were great ironies here. If the uprising truly represented an outcry for democracy, it was happening in an Arab country in which democracy, at least by Western standards, had already sunk roots. In point of fact, the insurgency was animated by the goal of *reversing* Syria's democracy, and replacing it with an anti-democratic Islamic state. Among the major backers of the insurgency were the Arab world's anti-democratic monarchies. And while Washington professed to be on the side of democracy in Syria, it backed jihadists who scorned democracy and drew their support from the Arab world's kings, princes, emirs and sultans, all of whom held democracy in contempt.

CHAPTER FIVE

THE BA'ATHISTS' ISLAMIC ALLY

There were two officially recognized Islamic states in the Middle East which played key roles in the conflict in Syria. One, Saudi Arabia, an important regional satellite of the United States, was an absolute monarchy. The other, Iran, to which the United States was hostile, was an anti-monarchical state, in which political rule was based on clerical supervision of a representative democracy.

Saudi Arabia, whose royal family was virtually integrated into the U.S. financial elite, cooperated with Washington in defending and promoting the United States' informal empire. The Islamic Republic of Iran, which was born in opposition to Mohammad Reza Shah Pahlavi, a U.S.-installed monarch who governed Iran on behalf of U.S. interests, was committed through its constitution to "the complete elimination of imperialism and the prevention of foreign influence."

The Saudis, who reigned over the holy Muslim sites of Mecca and Medina, had aspirations to lead Sunni Islam, which they pursued in ways that benefited their protector, the United States. In contrast, the constitution of the Islamic Republic of Iran committed Tehran to "constantly strive to bring about the political, economic and cultural unity of the Islamic world" in order to shed "all forms of domination" by "hegemonist superpowers."

The Saudis followed a Salafist form of Islam, which pro-hibited women from driving, sequestered the sexes, and pre-scribed decapitation, crucifixion, and lapidation as punishment for crime, and recognized such medieval transgressions as sor-cery. In Iran, by contrast, women wore chador, but drove and worked with men.

The Saudis were vehemently anti-Shi'a and encouraged anti-Shi'a sentiment, while Iran's leadership, predominantly Shi'a, was studiously non-sectarian, aiding both Shi'ite and Sunni groups, and also supporting secular movements within the Arab world which opposed foreign domination, such as Syria's secular Arab nationalists and the Palestinian Marxist organ-ization, the Popular Front for the Liberation of Palestine.

The Saudis spent billions of dollars to arm and train Sunni jihadists to overthrow the Ba'athist government in Damascus, while the Iranians provided the Syrian government funds, weapons, military advisors, militia fighters and even some regular army special forces personnel to help repel the U.S.-led war on independent Syria. Staffan de Mistura, the U.N. Special Envoy to Syria, estimated that Iran provided $6 billion per year in military and economic aid to the Syrian republic.[1]

Among the objectives of the Iranian state, promulgated in its constitution, were "the complete elimination of imperialism and the prevention of foreign influence;" "the attainment of self-sufficiency in scientific, technological, industrial, agricul-tural and military domains;" and "the planning of a correct and just economic order...in order to create welfare, eliminate poverty, and abolish all forms of deprivation with respect to food, housing, work, health care, and the provision of social insurance for all." How many constitutions in the world had set the elimination of imperialism as an objective, much less mentioned it? How many committed the state to abolish poverty, food scarcity, inadequate housing, and deprivation in respect of health care? And how many states which officially opposed imperialism and designated the food security, shelter and health care needs of its population as responsibilities of the state, were likely to evade the hostility of Washington, where imperialism and abhorrence of the welfare state were worshipped as virtues?

While Iran was an Islamic republic, and Arab nationalist Syria, Libya, and Iraq were secular, they were all alike in having constitutions which committed their respective states to act in three broad areas: promoting unity; achieving independence from foreign influence; and using the levers of the state to direct economic development to overcome the colonial legacy of underdevelopment and provide for the common welfare of their citizens. These commonalities originated in the countries' shared histories of domination by foreign powers, their struggles to manumit themselves from that domination, and their efforts to prevent backsliding into neo-colonialism. The Ba'athist motto of unity, freedom and socialism, while not proclaimed explicitly in the Iranian constitution, was implicitly present in it.

The Arab nationalist states emphasized the goal of promoting the unity of the Arab nation, both as an end in itself, and also as a means to fully mobilize all the resources of the Arab world, from the Atlantic to the Gulf, to maximize the chances that the project of Arab self-determination would be successfully carried through. Islamic Iran also emphasized the promotion of unity, but as an Islamic state its focus was on the unity of the Muslim world rather than on the integration of an ethno-linguistic subset of it. Hence, whereas Syria's Ba'athist constitution committed Damascus to "support Arab cooperation in order to promote integration and achieve the unity of the Arab nation," the Iranian constitution committed Tehran to "constantly strive to bring about the political, economic and cultural unity of the Islamic world."

Tehran's focus on pan-Islamism (as against Syria's pan-Arabism), was accompanied by a universal commitment to struggles against oppression worldwide. The country's constitution declared support for "the just struggles of the *mustad'afun*" (the downtrodden, lower classes, the meek) "against the *mustakbirun*" (the proud and mighty) "in every corner of the globe." While cynics might argue that the commitment to side with the oppressed was simply empty rhetoric, two points challenge this view. First, it was not so clear to political analysts in the West that the words were vacuous. At least one Iran expert "said that Iran faces constant decisions about whether it is a 'nation or a cause',"[2] which points to the leadership in Tehran taking the commitment seriously, even if the exigencies of managing a state in a world not of their own making may sometimes or even have often meant that support to the oppressed was not always possible. Grand Ayatollah Ali Khamenei, Iran's Supreme Leader, called himself "a revolution-ary," and his foreign policy decisions, concluded the U.S. Congress's official research service, were "ideology-based."[3] For these reasons, we should not read demagogy into the repub-lic's declaring in its constitution support for the oppressed. Second, Iran's support for the Ba'athist government in Damascus gave weight to the notion that the Iranian leadership took seriously both its opposition to imperialism and its sup-port for just struggles against the high and mighty.

Tehran was an energetic supporter of the Palestinian struggle for self-determination, a stance which could be attributed to its Islamist aspirations to unite the Islamic world. Ejecting the apparatus of the Zionist state from the historical realm of Islam and reversing the encroaching Judaization of Jerusalem, site of the Haram al-Sharif, from which Muhammad is believed to have ascended to heaven, would be a signal achievement in re-inte-grating the Muslim world. But were the facts that most Palestinians were Muslim and that Palestine was for centuries a Muslim-majority territory, the sole reasons Iran supported the Palestinian cause? Almost certainly. It seems unlikely that Tehran would have provided anywhere near the same level of support for non-Muslims who had been displaced by settlers colonizing territory outside the Islamic world. Tehran gener-ously funded the Muslim Brotherhood-affiliated Hamas, but not the secular Marxist PFLP, until Hamas sided with Sunni muja-hedeen against Tehran's allies in Damascus. Syria's Ba'athist had been one of Hamas's most ardent supporters, allowing Hamas's political wing to establish offices in Damascus—and for this decision Damascus had to bear the hostility of the United States and its military proxy, Israel, two countries whose combined power was many orders of magnitude greater than Syria's. For Hamas, the chances to contribute to the building of a Sunni Islamist state in Syria seemed to have proved more tempting than standing behind a long-time supporter. The Hamas leadership may have reasoned that an Islamist state in Syria would resume the backing to Hamas that the secular Arab nationalists had provided. In any event, once Hamas defected from what had been termed the Axis of Resistance, linking Iran, Syria and Hezbollah against U.S. efforts to completely dominate the Middle East, Tehran began to provide "financial and logistical support for the PFLP's political and military wings."[4] Hardly Islamist, the PFLP advocated a single secular democratic state in historic Palestine, in which Jews, Muslims and Christians would have equal rights; in other words, a democratic state for everyone, rather than a democratic state for Jews, and a Jewish state for the Arabs. Quite possibly, Tehran regarded the PFLP in much the same way Washington regarded Syria's Islamist fighters—as ideologically objectionable but useful as weapons to be wielded against a common enemy.

The Islamic Revolution's commitment to freedom from foreign domination very much echoed similar commitments made by the Arab nationalist states. In the first instance, Iran banned any "form of agreement resulting in foreign control over the natural resources, economy, army or culture of the country" as unconstitutional. Hence, foreign military bases on Iranian soil were forbidden,[5] a clear departure from the practice of Iran's Persian Gulf neighbors, Qatar, Bahrain, Kuwait, Oman, and the United Arab Emirates, which welcomed the U.S. military. Arab nationalist Libya ejected the United States from an air base near Tripoli, while neither Ba'athist Iraq nor Ba'athist Syria allowed the militaries of the United States to set up bases on their soil. Significantly, Syria, Libya, Iraq, and Iran, had histories of either direct or indirect foreign control. Under Arab nationalist rule, the three Arab republics, and under Islamic rule, the Persian republic, rejected foreign intrusions into their internal affairs. The Gulf Arab states, in contrast, had always been appendages of the world's dominant imperialist power, first Britain, and then, the United States. Domenico Losurdo argues that the string of U.S. aggressions since the first Gulf War of 1990-1991 were but individual campaigns in a single U.S.-led war for re-colonization of the world.[6] Washington's insistence that its global leadership was "essential" and "indispensable," that it could and would "lead the global economy," and that it would "mobilize the world to work" with it, was certainly consistent with Losurdo's argument.

Perhaps the signal event in Washington's efforts to bring Iran under U.S. domination was the CIA-orchestrated overthrow in 1953 of the Iranian prime minister Muhammad Mossadegh, who had provoked the enmity of the United States and Britain by nationalizing his country's oil industry. It will be recalled from an earlier chapter that the coup was engineered by Kermit Roosevelt, who only a few years later drafted a plan to overthrow a triumvirate of Communist and Ba'athist government leaders in Damascus. "In declassified documents, the CIA...acknowledged that the overthrow of Mossadegh was 'carried out under CIA direction as an act of U.S. foreign policy, conceived and approved at the highest levels of government,' with the aid of the British Secret Intelligence Service," reported *The Washington Post*. The "United States and Britain have never apologized for their role in the coup."[7] The overthrow of Mossadegh for seeking to use his country's oil resources to uplift the local population rather than allowing Western investors to reap the lion's share of the resource's benefit—the same anti-imperialist "crime" Gaddafi paid for with his life—was a clear instance in which U.S. foreign policy demonstrated that U.S. interests (specifically, those tied to corporate America) were in contradiction with Iran's. The contradiction of interests placed Iran's political and military leadership on Washington's regime change hit list.

U.S. officials were determined to turn the major benefits of Iran's economy over to U.S. banks, corporations and investors. Recognizing this, Iran's revolutionaries saw "the U.S. maintenance of a large military presence in the Persian Gulf region and in other countries around Iran" as reflecting U.S hostility and intent to overthrow the Islamic Revolution.[8]

Khamenei repudiated calls "for Iran's integration with the global economy,"[9] hewing closely to the Islamic Republic's constitution which called for "the complete elimination of imperialism and the prevention of foreign influence" and "the attainment of self-sufficiency in scientific, technological, industrial, agricultural and military domains." The constitution specified that the "economy of the Islamic Republic of Iran" would be based *inter alia* on the "prevention of foreign economic domination over the country's economy" and economic planning to "make the country self-sufficient and free from dependence." According to Khamenei, Tehran would seek "an Iran that is scientifically and technologically advanced enough to be self-sufficient, self-sufficient enough to be economically independent, and economically independent enough to be politically independent."[10] Tehran's determination to be free from foreign control resonated with the Arab nationalist project of achieving economic independence from foreign powers in order to achieve political self-determination.

While Iranian leaders were unlikely to use the word "socialist" to describe their country's politico-economic system, according to the CIA, Iran's economy was "marked by statist policies." The Iranian government directly owned and operated hundreds of state-owned enterprises and indirectly controlled many companies. "Private sector activity" in Iran, the U.S. intelligence service declared, was limited to "small-scale workshops, farming, some manufacturing, and services, in addition to medium-scale construction, cement production, mining, and metalworking."[11] Lucrative opportunities for U.S. banks, corporations and wealthy investors to reap attractive profits hardly existed.

The constitution of the Islamic Republic committed Tehran to "the planning of a correct and just economic order" with the aim of promoting welfare, eliminating poverty, and abolishing "all forms of deprivation with respect to food, housing, work, health care, and the provision of social insurance for all." The economy was to be organized into three sectors: state, cooperative and private. The state sector was "to include all large-scale and mother industries, foreign trade, major minerals, banking, insurance, power generation, dams and large-scale irrigation networks, radio and television, post, telegraph and telephone services, aviation, shipping, roads, railroads and the like." These industries were to be publicly owned and administered by the state. Meanwhile, the private sector was to be subordinate to the state and cooperative sectors, merely supplementing them. This was hardly the kind of business-friendly, pro-foreign investment climate the United States insisted all countries create to open up opportunities for U.S. investors, banks and corporations.

Iran's constitution also enshrined a host of economic rights—again, at variance with U.S. economic doctrine. Washington historically limited its definition of human rights to civil and political liberties, and only after it was forced, as a result of ideological competition with the anti-racist Soviet Union, to dismantle its white supremacist apartheid regime *avant la lettre* in the meridional states, a rectification that wasn't fully complete, in a *de jure* sense, until the mid-1960s. The United States government refused to countenance the inclusion of economic liberties and entitlements as officially recognized rights. In contradistinction to U.S. doctrine, Iran defined "social security with respect to retirement, unemployment, old age, disability, absence of a guardian, and benefits relating to being stranded, accidents, health services, and medical care and treatment" as universal rights to be paid for through "the national revenues and funds obtained through public contributions." This, U.S. officials may have harrumphed, was a "Soviet model."

CHAPTER SIX

WASHINGTON'S STATE
ISLAMIC ALLIES

Most people in the West remember the Arab Spring protests as touching the Arab republics—Tunisia, Egypt, Yemen, and of course, Libya and Syria. They seldom remember, or know at all, that upheavals occurred in most of the Arab monarchies, as well. There were protests in Saudi Arabia (the world's largest buyer of U.S. weapons), Bahrain (a British naval base from the early 1800s until the 1970s, when it became the home of the U.S. Fifth Fleet), as well as in Kuwait and Oman (also sites for a number of U.S. military installations). The protesters called for an end to monarchy and transition to representative democracy, along with a more equitable distribution of resources.[1]

Protests against royal dictators—the emirs, sultans and kings of the Gulf Arab states, who ruled their subjects with an iron fist, and were doted on by Washington as allies—received comparatively less media attention than did unrest in Libya and Syria. The attention they did receive lacked the moralizing quality of press reports that addressed insurrections in the two secular Arab nationalist states. We heard endlessly about the use of lethal force to quell internal disturbances in Libya and Syria, and less about the use of the armed power of the state to suppress uprisings in the Arab Gulf kingdoms. When the Saudi monarchy dispatched tanks to Bahrain to crush protests there,

Western journalists and commentators failed to mount the high moral horse from which they had excoriated Gaddafi and Assad for having the audacity to use the coercive powers of the state to contain armed rebellions. Rather than demonizing the Saudi authorities as vicious brutes who butchered a nascent movement for democracy, as they did authorities in Syria and Libya, Western media justified the monarchs' crackdowns in *realpolitik* terms.

The New York Times' Ethan Bronner, for example, weighed in with an article from the perspective of Bahrain's monarchy: "Crackdown Was Only Option, Bahrain Sunnis Say."[2] Neither *The New York Times*, nor any other major Western newspaper, ran articles from the perspective of the Libyan or Syrian governments. Indeed, comparable headlines, reading, "Crackdown Was Only Option, Libyan Government Says" or "Containing Islamist Insurrection Was Only Option, Syrian Government Says" were simply unimaginable.

Acting as a *de facto* public relations representative for Bahrain's monarchy, Bonner explained:

> "To many around the world, the events of the past week—the arrival of 2,000 troops from Saudi Arabia and other neighbors, the declaration of martial law, the forceful clearing out of Pearl Square, the military takeover of the main hospital and then the spiteful tearing down of the Pearl monument itself—seem like the brutal work of a desperate autocracy. But for Sunnis, who make up about a third of the country's citizenry but hold the main levers of power, it was the only choice of a country facing a rising tide of chaos that imperiled its livelihood and future."[3]

New York Times reporters Helene Cooper and Robert F. Worth put a *realpolitik* spin on the story, avoiding the moral lapidation favored in dealing with the Arab nationalists. They wrote:

> "On March 14, White House officials awoke to a nasty surprise: the Saudis had led a military incursion into Bahrain, followed by a crackdown in which the security forces cleared Pearl Square in the capital, Manama, by force...Mr. Obama...offered only veiled

criticisms. The reasons for Mr. Obama's reticence were clear: Bahrain sits just off the Saudi coast, and the Saudis were never going to allow a sudden flowering of democracy next door...In addition, the United States maintains a naval base in Bahrain...crucial for maintaining the flow of oil from the region."[4]

The U.S. government wasn't the only Western state lambasting Damascus for using its security apparatus to contain Islamist unrest, while looking the other way as Bahrain's monarchy bloodily cracked down on protesters calling for democracy. Britain also exercised a double standard, calling for Assad's departure while overlooking the crackdown in Bahrain. But the British went further than the Americans. While Washington at least offered veiled criticism of Manama, Britain did the opposite. Soon after Saudi tanks rolled into the Bahraini capital to smother the kingdom's version of the Arab Spring, Queen Elizabeth II invited King Hamid to the April 2011 royal wedding of Prince William and Kate Middleton. The next month, British prime minister David Cameron hosted Bahrain's Crown Prince, greeting him on the doorsteps of No.10 Downing Street with a firm handshake, thereby bringing a whole new meaning to the phrase "blood on your hands." A succession of British royals and politicians trekked off to Bahrain to ingratiate the United Kingdom with the Bahraini Kingdom: Prince Charles and Camilla, International Trade Minister Liam Fox, and Foreign Office Minister of State for Europe, Sir Alan Duncan. Patrick Cockburn wondered why the British government devoted "so much time and effort to cultivating the rulers of Bahrain," a state he described as "notorious for imprisoning and torturing its critics," to say nothing of deserving to be notorious for violently quelling street protests demanding democracy. Answering his own question, Cockburn pointed out that Britain cultivated Bahrain's royal tyranny in order to use the kingdom as a virtual aircraft carrier permanently stationed in the Gulf. It turned out that not only was Bahrain's bloody tyrant hosting the Royal Navy, he was footing the bill for an expansion of its naval base.[5]

Equally significant was the fact that Bahrain was open for business on terms favorable to Western investors. Foreign investment was welcomed, and the kingdom shunned the nonsense so many other countries insisted on of foreigners taking on local partners. There were no restrictions on repatriating profits and few restrictions on trade. The kingdom was committed to labor market "flexibility," had no minimum wage, and its social welfare programs were anemic, which allowed the kingdom to keep taxes low and local labor eager to work. Other than oil companies, corporations paid no income tax, and the personal income tax rate was no more than three percent. The banking sector was wide open, home to more than 400 privately owned banks and financial institutions. Economically, Bahrain was the very antithesis of the Arab world's secular nationalist governments, with their state-owned enterprises, foreign ownership restrictions, strictures on trade, robust social welfare programs and progressive tax systems.

The Arab Spring had two components: its reality, and its rhetoric. The Arab Gulf monarchies embraced the discourse of the Arab Spring in Libya and Syria, but crushed its reality at home.[6] The monarchs' patrons, officials of the United States, and the broader Western world, did the same: They welcomed, developed, shaped—indeed, championed—the rhetoric of the Arab Spring, selling it across the world as they did Apple smart phones and Hollywood movies. But they sold it with the greatest enthusiasm in connection with the two Arab countries that weren't in the U.S. orbit and didn't want to be. As for the countries that were already myrmidon parts of the empire, in those countries, the Arab Spring was banished, in both its rhetorical form, and in its actual expression. There, calls for the toppling of marionette kings, and subservient emirs and sultans, were greeted with little sympathy in Washington and among Western media commentators.

The gist of the real U.S. foreign policy, as opposed to the rhetorical one, was summed up in the words of a senior U.S. official who told *Washington Post* reporter Craig Whitlock that "countries that don't cooperate, we ream them as best we can" while the "countries that cooperate with us get a least a free pass."[7]

The kingdoms of Saudi Arabia and Bahrain were definitely countries which cooperated with the United States, specifically, with the U.S. corporate class. Accordingly, they got a free pass. In contrast, Libya, under Arab nationalist rule, didn't always cooperate with the United States. Its "resource nationalism" irked Western oil companies and therefore agitated the U.S. State Department, which wasn't going to tolerate foreign governments that nettled Big Oil by insisting on oil company bottom lines taking a back seat to the interests of local populations. Arab nationalist Syria hardly cooperated at all, either, committed, as it was, to the Ba'athist values of unity of the Arab world, freedom from outside domination, and Arab socialism. Accordingly, Washington reamed Libya and Syria as best it could.

When Saudi Arabia cracked down "on dissent and free speech," and allowed "its elite to fund Islamist extremists," the "United States...usually looked the other way," observed veteran *New York Times* reporter David Sanger.[8] By contrast, when the Syrian government used force to contain an armed Islamist uprising in 2011, Washington organized the funneling of weapons to mujahedeen to overthrow the secular government. *New York Times* reporters Mark Mazzetti and Matt Apuzzo enumerated the myriad ways in which Saudi Arabia cooperated with Washington to "explain why the United States [was] reluctant to openly criticize Saudi Arabia" for a number of outrages, among them: beheading the Saudi cleric Nimr al-Nimr, who led Arab Spring demonstrations challenging the Saudi royal family's anti-democratic tyranny; the kingdom's official misogyny (hardly something the United States, as self-appointed world champion of human rights, ought to have tolerated); and its "support for the extreme strain of Islam, Wahhabism, that...inspired many of the very terrorist groups the United States (was) fighting." There were three reasons Washington tolerated these abuses, Mazzetti and Apuzzo wrote: Saudi Arabia's vast oil reserves; its role as the spiritual anchor of the Sunni Muslim world; and its long intelligence relationship with the United States.[9]

What was significant about Saudi Arabia's vast oil reserves was that they were the source of immense profits for Western, and especially, U.S. oil companies. On top of this, the Saudi dynasty plowed much of Saudi Arabia's oil revenue into investments which benefited U.S. banks and corporations, including the U.S. arms industries, of which the Saudis were the world's number one customer. They also used their vast earnings from the sale of oil to fund various U.S. foreign policy projects, such as propping up military dictatorships in Egypt and monarchies in Bahrain, buying arms for the mujahedeen who fought the Soviets in Afghanistan in the 1980s, and more. What's more, because they sat atop vast reserves of oil, the Saudis could adjust production to control the price of oil on world markets in ways that benefited Uncle Sam and his corporate owning class.

The significance to Washington of Saudi Arabia's self-proclaimed role as the spiritual anchor of the Sunni Muslim world was two-fold. Historian David Motadel has written about how non-Muslim powers which become involved in the Islamic world have always actively sought to mobilize Islam against their enemies.[10] In WWI, the Kaiser "commissioned a proclamation of pan-Islamic jihad" against the Entente powers from the highest religious authority of the Ottoman Empire, to which Germany was allied. "Over the course of the war, Berlin and Constantinople made extensive efforts to incite, as Wilhelm II put it, 'the whole Mohammedan world to wild revolt' against the British, Russian and French empires."[11]

In WWII, Germany courted various spiritual anchors of the Muslim world "to stir up unrest behind enemy lines, most notably on the unstable Muslim fringes of the Soviet Union, as well as in British (and later Free French) colonial domains in Africa, the Middle East, and Asia."[12]

Mobilizing Islam to "provoke unrest, division and insurrection in territories ruled by rival or enemy powers, and also to conquer and pacify occupied territories in military conflicts"[13] wasn't unique to Germany. "During the Crimean War, the British, French and Ottomans tried to incite the Muslims on the Crimean Peninsula and in the Caucasus."[14] In WWII, Japan made efforts to mobilize Islam "across Asia against Britain, the Netherlands, China, and the Soviets." And Italian attempts to recruit Islam to its cause culminated in Mussolini improbably presenting himself as a "protector of Islam."[15]

Neither was the United States a stranger to mobilizing Islam for political purposes. It did so famously when "American intelligence services began to aid the Mujahedeen in Afghanistan six months before the Soviet intervention...drawing the Russians into the Afghan trap," as Zbigniew Brzezinski, the U.S. National Security Adviser who set the trap, called it. Brzezinski told *Le Nouvel Observateur* in 1998 that the "day that the Soviets officially crossed the border, I wrote to President Carter, essentially: 'We now have the opportunity of giving to the USSR its Vietnam War.'"[16] The Saudis were instrumental in the U.S. war effort against the Soviets and their secular allies in Afghanistan. In 1980, Brzezinski "cut a deal with Saudi Arabia: America would match, dollar for dollar, Saudi money going to the Afghan resistance."[17]

Just as the Kaiser used Germany's World War I alliance with the Ottoman Empire, then the spiritual leader of the world's Muslims, to mobilize Islam to serve Germany's foreign policy interests, so too, in the long tradition of imperialist powers mobilizing religion for profane ends, did Washington use its alliance with the Saudis, the spiritual anchor of the world's Sunni Muslims, to mobilize Sunni Islam to serve U.S. foreign policy goals.

That the Saudi royals were in a position to mount a credible claim to lead Sunni Islam was important to Washington, in a second, and related, respect. It served as a way of countering a second claimant to the mantle of leader of the world's Muslims, namely, the Islamic Republic of Iran, which, unlike the Kingdom of Saudi Arabia, was not, as we've seen, simpatico with U.S. domination of the Muslim world.

Western discourse in connection with relations between Tehran and Riyadh, which were frosty at best, was imbued with references to ancient sectarian animosities between orthodox and heterodox strains of Islam—but this was mistaken. The origins of the hostility were not to be found in an ancient dispute over who was the rightful successor to Muhammad as caliph, but in contrary views of the relationship of the Muslim world to its domination by the United States and the West. Iran's revolution, which broke the country's subordination to the West by overthrowing Washington's proxy, the Shah, aspired to represent the aspirations of the Muslim world to reclaim its independence. The Saudi royals, in contrast, had no intention of leading a break from U.S. ascendancy over the domain of Islam. They were supported by the British in their quest to become rulers of Arabia. They later became protégés of the United States. They were protected by the Pentagon. And they were effectively part of the U.S. economic elite. Opposing U.S. domination of the Muslim world would be inimical to their interests, for who would protect them from their own subjects who resented their oppression and saw them as frauds?

The "Al Sa'ud," wrote former CIA officer Robert Baer, were "reviled for failing to protect fellow Muslims in Palestine and Iraq and for standing by helplessly as Islam [was] humiliated."[18] Saudi subjects believed "that all the oil money [had] corrupted the ruling family beyond redemption, [and] that the Saudi leaders [had] defiled the faith by allowing U.S. troops into the kingdom."[19] That many politically-conscious Sunni Muslims saw through the Saudi royal veil, accounted ultimately for the rise of al-Qaeda and for a third claimant to the role of spiritual anchor of the Muslim world, namely, ISIS, or the Islamic State.

Al-Qaeda, and its descendant, Islamic State, shared the anti-imperialist aims of Iran's Islamic Revolution. The two Sunni Islamist organizations worked toward weakening Western influence in the Islamic world, through attacks on Western targets abroad (the far enemy). The purpose of these attacks was two-fold. First, to pressure Western governments to withdraw their military forces from the Muslim world; and, second, to pressure Western governments to abandon their support for local regimes. The collaborator regimes were nominally Muslim governments which were satellites (the near enemy) of the West. Saudi Arabia was emblematic of the al-Qaeda definition of the near enemy.

Islamic State was heavily influenced by the anti-Shi'a Wahhabi ideology, and, as a consequence, found no inspiration in the Islamic anti-imperialism of Shi'a Iran. Islamic State's sectarianism was perhaps its greatest Achilles' heel—and most salient feature. Even al-Qaeda's leader Ayman Zawahiri found the al-Qaeda offshoot's murderous intolerance of "infidels" objectionable, or, more to the point, impolitic. Unbelievers, in the Islamic State view, included Muslims who didn't subscribe to the interpretation of Islam promulgated by the self-proclaimed caliph, Abu Bakr al-Baghdadi.

The Iranians, wisely, rejected sectarianism for the obvious reason that invoking it would sabotage any hope of building Muslim unity, an exigency of achieving the revolution's anti-imperialist aims. (This paralleled the reason why such Arab nationalists as the Assads and Saddam embraced secularism and were therefore adamantly non-sectarian: to do otherwise would undermine any hope of bringing Arabs together as a single, coherent, and politically-effective force—a nation for itself, rather than only of itself.) What's more, as members of a minority Muslim sect, the Iranian leaders could hardly hope to appeal to Sunnis, the majority of Muslims with sectarian rhetoric, any more than the Assads in Syria could hope to build a stable basis for the rule of Arab nationalism in Damascus by pursuing a sectarian Alawite agenda. But more importantly, the Islamic Revolution didn't make appeals to identity based on sect because sect was irrelevant to its goals. Its objective was to achieve economic and political independence for Iran first and the Muslim world second, not to promote a particular branch of Islam. "Iran," said the country's president Hassan Rouhani, at the 71st session of the United Nations General

Assembly in 2016, "opposes any kind of sectarianism and any attempt to promote religious" differences among "the Muslim people."[20] This contrasted sharply with the aims of Saudi Arabia and Islamic State, which very much entailed the promotion of a Salafist Sunni interpretation of Islam. Indeed, as Rouhani was disavowing sectarianism at the General Assembly, two hundred Sunni Muslim clerics, including Egypt's Grand Imam, Ahmed el-Tateb of al-Azhar, were meeting in Grozny to denounce the Saudi state religion, Wahhabism, for promoting sectarianism.[21]

Nor did Islamic State share with Iran the objective of ending Western ascendancy in the Muslim domain as its primary aim. It did set this as a goal, to be sure, but as a secondary one, and not the principal one. Islamic State's paramount concern, instead, was to convert the Muslim world to a puritanical version of Sunni Islam, using force as the means, in a twenty-first century version of Ibn al Saud and Abd-al-Wahhab riding through eighteenth century Arabia slaughtering the unbelievers. Were al-Baghdadi's aims to have been realized, the Arab world would be ruled by a medieval Sunni interpretation of Islam, as Saudi Arabia was. However, al-Baghdadi's political Islam departed from that of the Saudis in rejecting monarchy as a form of government, and in repudiating subordination to non-Muslim powers. But, importantly, it was converting the Muslim world to a pristine Islam, as al-Baghdadi understood it, and not anti-imperialism, that was Islamic State's paramount aim. For this reason, the organization exerted considerable effort in suicide bombing Shi'ites, rather than devoting all its energies to waging war on the near and far enemies of Islam, as, say, the Muslim Brotherhood or al-Qaeda understood these categories. As John Mueller and Mark G. Stewart explained in their study of the policing of terrorism, *Chasing Ghosts*, "instead of focusing on doing damage against the far enemy, the United States in particular, [Islamic State] was mainly devoted to killing and terrorizing fellow Muslims and neighboring Christians that it [didn't] like."[22] But therein was the key to the Islamic

WASHINGTON'S STATE ISLAMIC ALLIES   179

State's ideology. Shi'ites, in the organization's view, were part of the near enemy. This made the Islamist organization preferable to al-Qaeda from Washington's and Tel Aviv's points of view, since the former's anti-Shi'a obsession kept it largely distracted from its war against the far enemy. It also made a mortal enemy of Iran.

Mazzetti and Apuzzo also cited Saudi Arabia's long intelligence relationship with the United States as one of the reasons Washington doted on the Saudi royal family, despite the royals' official misogyny, disdain for democracy, and entanglement with anti-U.S. terrorists. What the reporters were really referring to was the dynasty's helpfulness in regularly picking up all or part of the tab for various U.S. covert operations. Hence, when U.S. "President Obama secretly authorized the Central Intelligence Agency to begin arming Syria's...rebels in 2013, the spy agency knew it would have a willing partner to help pay for the covert operation. It was the same partner the C.I.A. [had] relied on for decades for money and discretion in far-off conflicts: the Kingdom of Saudi Arabia," the reporters wrote.[23] Mazzetti and Apuzzo added: "The support for the Syrian rebels [was] only the latest chapter in the decades-long relationship between the spy services of Saudi Arabia and the United States, an alliance that...endured through the Iran-contra scandal, support for the mujahedeen against the Soviets in Afghanistan and proxy fights in Africa. Sometimes, as in Syria, the two countries...worked in concert. In others, Saudi Arabia...simply [wrote] checks underwriting American covert activities."[24]

Washington didn't lead the campaigns to oust the secular Arab nationalist governments in Iraq, Libya and Syria because it was motivated to promote representative democracy. As we have seen, that this idea is a charming fiction is evidenced by the fact that the principal regional U.S. ally in the war on Syria, Saudi Arabia, was an absolute monarchy which used tanks, beheadings, and crucifixions to crush its own pro-democracy uprising, with nary a peep of protest from Washington. As Adam Coogle, a Middle East researcher at Human Rights

Watch put it, Washington had "always seemingly privileged economic interests over human rights concerns in its relationship" with Saudi Arabia.[25] Washington had also privileged economic interests over human rights in its dealings with secular Arab nationalist Iraq, Libya and Syria—except, unlike in Saudi Arabia, it sought to secure economic interests that the Arab nationalist governments—motivated by an ideology which stressed self-determination and Arab socialism—had been unwilling to grant.

Apart from Saudi Arabia, Turkey was perhaps Washington's most important regional ally in the war against Damascus's secular Arab nationalists. Turkey was a representative democracy, but had taken an increasingly authoritarian turn toward a destination which appeared to be an Islamized society where democracy was subordinate to the Quran as a source of legislation.

One of the principal leaders of Turkey's gradual Islamization was the country's president Recep Tayyip Erdogan. In 1996, as mayor of Istanbul, Erdogan stirred controversy by reading an Islamist poem that declared that "the minarets are our bayonets, the domes our helmets, and the mosques our barracks."[26] His Justice and Development Party (AKP) had "firm Islamist roots" in the Muslim Brotherhood,[27] from which sprang the principal internal opposition to Syria's secular Arab nationalists.

The AKP's program from the point it won its "first general election in 2002 [was] to reverse the secularization of Turkish society introduced by Kemal Ataturk, the founder of the republic in 1923. As the AKP tightened its grip on power, it chipped away at the secular institutions of the state and encouraged the Islamization of education and social behavior as well as seeking to cull non-Islamist officials and officers," according to Patrick Cockburn.[28]

The Wall Street Journal's Middle East specialist, Yaroslav Trofimov, saw modern Islamists like Erdogan as viewing "democracy not as a value in itself but merely as a tactic to bring about a 'true' Islamic order. To them, the voting booth was simply the most feasible way to dismantle the postcolonial, secular systems that, in the eyes of their followers, had failed to bring justice or development to ordinary Muslims." Trofimov pointed out that in 2005, Erdogan let slip "that he viewed democracy just as 'a vehicle'" to bringing about an Islamic state.[29] In Washington's view, too, Erdogan's Turkey was shifting "away from democracy," but it maintained close ties with the Muslim Brotherhood-connected leader because it saw him as "a key strategic ally."[30]

As Syria moved even closer to secular multi-party Western democracy, Turkey moved closer to Washington's other regional allies in the war on Syria, the Islamist anti-democracies, Saudi Arabia and Qatar, and toward Washington's allies on the ground, the jihadist fighters who sought to overthrow secular Arab nationalism in order to install a regime of rule by the Quran. Robert Fisk asked: "Turkey? Isn't this the place where the cops take over newspapers and lock up journalists, and where the army has been slaughtering large numbers of Kurds for decades, and where the president is turning into a miniature Sultan?"[31]

Washington's claim that it championed a fight for democracy in Syria, then, was as weak as the Entente's claim that its battle with the Central Powers in World War I was a crusade for rule by the people. One of the Entente's principal members, Russia, was led by an autocrat, Tsar Nicholas II, a class cohort of Saudi King Salman, Qatar's Emir Tamin, and Jordan's King Abdullah. In Washington's war on Syria, its principal regional allies, then, had as much commitment to democracy as did the Tsar...and the United States had as much commitment to fostering the spread of political rule by the masses as did Britain and France in WWI—which was none at all.

CHAPTER SEVEN

DIVIDE ET IMPERA

Mass movements can be organized around different aspects of personal identity such as race, class, religion, sect, ethnicity, language, sex, and position within the international division of labor.

The great imperialist powers often justified their domination of other countries and people on the basis of race. They presented themselves as superior races destined to rule over the "inferior" peoples of the world. One such "inferior" people, in the view of Europe's imperialists, was the Arabs, who occupied a territory stretching from the Atlantic to the Persian Gulf. The Arabs had made signal contributions to mathematics, astronomy, medicine, architecture, navigation, horticulture and philosophy, and had established great civilizations. But from 1516 to 1918 they were subjected to the rule of the tri-continental Turkish Empire. During WWI, the British fanned the flames of Arab aspirations to nationhood, promising to support Arab independence in return for aid in toppling the Turks.

Britain maintained hegemony over its vast, globe-girding empire by deepening existing religious and ethnic differences among subject populations, and even creating new ones. London then stepped in as arbiter to manage the conflicts it had deliberately intensified or created, presenting itself as indispensable to containing the feral passions of the savage and brutal locals.[1] The

British viewed the societies they colonized in ethno-religious terms, always emphasizing the differences within them, and presenting colonized people as combustible agglomerations of competing and hostile collectivities which were forever at odds with each other. And if subject populations weren't locked in struggle, the British machinated to ensure they became so.

Whereas Arab nationalists emphasized the commonalities among Arab speakers, the Great Powers emphasized the differences among them, as they did in connection with all the peoples they subjugated. The British denied that nations were coterminous with the territories they ruled, contending that countries were simply geographical expressions marking the territory of many antagonistic nations. The oversight of a rational, dispassionate, and civilized power was therefore essential and indispensable to keeping communities portrayed as riven by "ancient animosities" from tearing each other apart.

The weakness of the Great Powers' argument that ethno-religious divisions within colonized societies made the colonies ungovernable by the people within them was exposed in the following ironical survey of the United States offered by the British-Indian communist R. Palme Dutt:

"The subcontinent of the United States is characterized by the greatest diversity of climate and geographical features, while its inhabitants exhibit a similar diversity of race and religion. The customary talk of the United States as a single entity tends to obscure, to the casual...observer, the variegated assemblage of races and creeds which make up the whole. In the City of New York alone there are to be found nearly a hundred different national-ities, some of which are in such great numbers that New York is at once the largest Italian city, the largest Jewish city and the largest [African] city in the world. The contiguity of such diverse elements has been a fruitful cause of the most bitter communal conflicts. In the Southern States especially, this has led to inter-racial riots and murders...[P]ressing problems [are] presented by the separate existence of the Mormons in Utah, the Finns in Minnesota, the Mexican immigration...and the Japanese on the West Coast; not to speak of the survival...of the aboriginal inhabitants."[2]

Dutt observed that on the eve of the American Revolution, the British nobility described the American colonies as so thoroughly divided along ethno-religious lines that the unity of the American people was absurd to contemplate: "Great bodies of Dutch, Germans, French, Swedes, Scotch and Irish, scattered among the descendants of the English, contributed to the heterogeneous character of the colonies, and they comprised so many varieties of government, religious belief, commercial interests and social types, that their union appeared to many incredible on the eve of the Revolution."[3]

Indeed, one representative of the British nobility, having visited the North American colonies in 1759 and 1760, advanced an argument every imperialist power, including the United States, would make to justify their continued domination of a subjugated people: their presence was necessary to keep the colonized from a state of war against each other, a *bellum omnium contra omnes.*

"Fire and water are not more heterogeneous than the different colonies in North America...Such is the differences of character, of manner, of religion, of interest, of the different colonies, that I think, if I am not wholly ignorant of the human mind, were they left to themselves, there would be a civil war from one end of the continent to the other."[4]

The same style of thinking, with its stress on heterogeneity, and its conclusion that civil war is a necessary outcome of multiple ethno-sectarian communities existing in the same space, continued to inform imperialist discourse into the twenty-first century. U.S. politicians, including a vice-president, Joe Biden, proposed to divide Iraq into three separate communities, a Kurd state, a Shi'a state, and a Sunni state. In the wake of the U.S.-British invasion of Iraq in 2003, U.S. proconsul Paul Bremer, as we've seen, formalized Iraq's ethno-sectarian divisions by selecting representatives to a governing council on the basis of their ethnic and religious identities. In Syria, Western journalists placed considerable emphasis on the communal differences within Syria, and often cited these differences as the provenance of the conflict in the country. They presented it as if Syrians were fighting over ancient animosities related to religion, rather than over the question of whether the state should be secular, and oriented toward Arab nationalist goals, or Islamic, with its jurisprudence based on the Quran and Sunna. Painting the conflict as a sectarian one also obfuscated the role played by Washington in using mujahedeen as a proxy force to wage war on the Arab nationalists.

Robert Fisk observed that, "We always like divisive charts in the Middle East. Remember how Iraq was always the Shias at the bottom, Sunnis in the middle, Kurds at the top? We used to do this with Lebanon: Shias at the bottom (as usual), Shias in the east, Sunnis in Sidon and Tripoli, Christians east and north of Beirut. Never once has a Western newspaper shown a map of Bradford with Muslim and non-Muslim areas marked off, or a map of Washington divided into black and white people. No, that would suggest that our Western civilization is divvied up between tribes or races. Only the Arab world merits our ethnic distinctions."[5]

Even as late as June 2016, *The Wall Street Journal* was referring to the Syrian government as "Alawite-run."[6] This was akin to referring to the early Bolshevik government in Russia as "Jewish-run" because a number of the principal Bolsheviks were Jewish.

For its part, officials in the U.S. State Department insisted on understanding the conflict as a sectarian one, in which the United States had allied itself with the "Sunni" majority. U.S. officials could have understood the war differently, and still maintained the fiction that they were on the side of the majority. They could have said that the United States supported all Syrians, whether Sunni, Christian, Alawite, or otherwise, who opposed the Assad government. Instead, they insisted on framing the conflict in sectarian terms, likely because it fit with the discourse favored by the Sunni militants who Washington and its allies supported, and who had targeted the Assad government because it was secular. In support of the sectarian narrative,

U.S. officials added a further sectarian coloration: it was Assad and his "Alawite inner circle" who were bombing and starving the majority Sunni population out of a deep Alawite anti-Sunni malice. This led, through supreme sophistry, to the conclusion that the only way to defeat the Islamic State was to eliminate its alleged root cause: Assad and his Alawite inner circle,[7] whose supposed sectarian oppressions had created the conditions that led to the rise of Islamic State as a movement to defend Sunnis against the Syrian government's aggressions.

Root cause analysis is not tolerated in the United States when used to understand terrorist attacks against U.S. targets, but it turns out to be perfectly acceptable when used against governments, movements and groups Washington is hostile to. In any event, the understanding of State Department officials reversed the causal sequence. The Syrian government—unlike the Saudi monarchy which Washington doted upon and protected—was explicitly secular and non-sectarian, and implacably hostile to efforts to stir up sectarian tensions. To believe the Syrian government was pursuing an anti-Sunni campaign, when it was ideologically committed to anti-sectarianism, was tantamount to asserting that the promotion of free public health care and a significant reduction in the Pentagon budget were possible political outcomes of the George W. Bush administration. To the contrary, it wasn't Alawite oppression of the Sunni majority which sparked the conflict in Syria, for no such oppression existed; instead, the cause of the conflict lay in a Sunni political Islamist ideology which mobilized Sunni militants, many from abroad, against the Syrian government on dual grounds: (1) because the government was secular, and therefore seen to be idolatrous, since it put man above God; and (2) because it was led by a man whose faith the Sunni jihadists denounced as a heresy punishable by death. It would be more accurate to say that the jihadist allies of the United States were engaged in a war against seculars, as well as Christians, Jews, heterodox Muslims, and anyone else who didn't subscribe to their Salafist Sunni interpretation of Islam.

The Western establishment promoted sectarian conflict between Sunnis and Alawites by propagating the myth that Alawites ran Syria and oppressed the Sunni majority. At the same time, Saudi-propagated Wahhabism promoted hatred of Shi'ites and Alawites, inspiring fanatics to suicide-bomb Shi'ite and Alawite schools, mosques and neighborhoods, and to wage war against the "infidel" Assad, who U.S. propagandists were happy to falsely depict as the head of an Alawite-run government.

Slandering the Syrian government as an Alawite-led regime was tantamount to traducing the Kennedy administration as a Roman Catholic-led regime. It would be clear that anyone who tried to suggest that the principal goal of the Kennedy administration was to advance the interests of the president's co-religionists at the expense of the Protestant majority was deliberately attempting to foment anti-Kennedy animosity. It is no less true that unceasing references in the Western media to the Syrian government as an Alawite-dominated regime served the same purpose, namely, to incite animosity against Assad among the Sunni majority.

The claim that the Syrian government was Alawite-dominated was problematic on multiple levels. We wouldn't call the Kennedy administration a Roman Catholic regime or Roman Catholic-led or Roman Catholic-dominated, simply because the president was born into a Roman Catholic family and followed the Roman Catholic faith. Kennedy's faith bore no direct relationship to his decision to seek the presidency, nor to the policies he advanced in office. Nor did he seek the United States' top political office to champion the interests of the Roman Catholic community. Equally, we wouldn't say that Kennedy was surrounding himself with his co-religionist *qua* co-religionist when he appointed his brother, Bobby, also a Roman Catholic, to the cabinet post of attorney general. The key consideration in the president's decision to appoint his brother was loyalty based on kinship, not religion. Religion was incidental; a concomitant, but not the driving force, of Kennedy's decision.

While U.S. administrations have all been male-led and male-dominated, they have rarely, except in some circles, been branded as male-regimes. Male-regime implies something more than male-led or male-dominated. It says that the organizing principle of the regime is the pursuit of male interests against those of females. And since the pursuit of the interests of U.S. industrial and finance capital, and not of male interests, has been the paramount organizing principle of U.S. administrations, to say that U.S. administrations have been male regimes is false, even if they have been male dominated. Accordingly, to give U.S. administrations this designation would be to engage in a blatant attempt to arouse female antagonism. Calling U.S. administrations male regimes, then, would be inherently a political act with intended political consequences. Likewise, labeling the Syrian government as an Alawite regime was an inherently political act undertaken by Western state officials and the Western news media with the intended political consequences of diverting attention from the Assad government's Arab nationalist ideology, discrediting the government by presenting it as an instrument of sectarian oppression, and fomenting anti-government Sunni hostility.

The Assads appointed people of unquestioned loyalty to top positions in the state, and especially to leading posts in the military, the security establishment, and the president's Praetorian Guard. Being able to count on the loyalty of the army and police—the branches of the state in whose hands repose the state's coercive power and therefore on which political rule depends—is an imperative of political survival. A leader who fails to command the loyalty of the security services won't long be leader. In order for a vanguard political party to carry out its mission, it must retain power. And to retain power, it must, *inter alia*, defend itself from threats from within. Quite naturally, ties based on kinship and amity are the most trustworthy, and the Assads appointed friends and family to sensitive security posts within the state. "The political effectiveness of Assad's leadership depended heavily on firm control of the pervasive military and internal security and intelligence apparatus—the only countercoup forces available to an incumbent regime."[8]

Hafez al-Assad ushered in an unprecedented era of political stability in Syria by establishing a network of praetorian guards, countercoup military forces, and state security services, staffed by people close to him, on whom he could count for loyalty (though they sometimes proved not to be as loyal as he would have liked). A strong security apparatus to contend with a panoply of threats was a desideratum of political survival, and guarantor of stability in a country which, since independence, had only known instability. A strong security apparatus was necessary to eclipse threats emanating from Zionist forces. The Arab-Israeli War had ended in an armistice, not a peace treaty, and Syria and Israel were still officially at war. Israel, a colonial power with a history of going to war to expand its territory, was occupying Syrian territory in the Golan Heights, and posed a continuing threat of aggression. Internally, Sunni Islamist guerillas rejected the secularism of the Ba'ath revolution, while the traditional economic elite opposed the revolution's land reforms and socialist policies. What's more, political rivalries which had a tendency to engender *coups d'état* were a signal feature of Syria's post-independence political landscape, and Assad had to remain on the *qui vive* against another. For all these reasons, a strong state security apparatus was a *sine qua non*, and appointments to key military, security and intelligence positions of people Assad could implicitly trust were equally indispensable. As it happened, those close to him who were the most likely to be reliable allies tended to be family members, who, incidentally, shared his Alawite faith. Alawites may have accordingly been over-represented in the security apparatus of the state, but only concomitantly, and not as the outcome of a design to establish Alawite rule over a Sunni majority.

Ba'athist leaders bristled at the idea of anyone exploiting sectarian loyalties, which they considered injurious to building Arab unity. And they very much disliked being labeled as members of religious sects.[9] They were Arabs first, Syrians second, and their religious identity was politically irrelevant. John F. Kennedy would have bristled at political opponents insisting on understanding his policy decisions as "Roman Catholic," and would have abhorred quite rightly the insinuation that under his presidency the United States had come under Roman Catholic rule. He would be even more incensed, also with justification, had it been further asserted that because he led the country as a Roman Catholic that his administration was oppressing the Protestant majority. These would be the mischievous arguments of a political character seeking to discredit him.

The Middle East scholar Hanna Batutu pointed out that the same process of relying on kinship ties to build an inner circle of implicit loyalty—and this process incidentally producing a homogeneous group defined by familial, tribal and religious connections at the centre of political power—was at work in Arab nationalist Iraq, as well. Yielding to the exigencies of political survival, Saddam, as the Assads in Syria, surrounded himself with people of unquestioned loyalty. As a consequence, "the core of the ruling element of Iraq also [consisted] of a kinship group" which happened to comprise "members of a minority sect [Sunni Arabs]."[10] The Iraqi state under Saddam's leadership was a Ba'athist government, unreservedly secular and anti-sectarian. It was not a sectarian Sunni regime, as U.S. propaganda insisted, but a state in which many key positions were filled by Saddam loyalists, who happened to be kin of the Ba'ath Party leader, and therefore shared the same minority religion. They weren't appointed to leading roles in the state because they were Sunni, but because they were related to Saddam and therefore could be counted on to be loyal.

Nor did Saddam's government pursue a sectarian agenda. As a member of the Ba'ath Party, Saddam subscribed to the party's belief that sectarianism was inimical to the goal of building Arab unity. The party's founding document declared that all differences existing among Arabs, including religions ones, "are casual and fake." Saddam's vision, observed scholars Samuel Helfont and Michael Brill, was of "a nationalistic and socialist state. He promoted the view that [Arab] nationalism [would] alleviate divisiveness and sectarianism."[11] Saddam's view, shared by Arab nationalists in Syria, was the very antithesis of the U.S. and colonial view, which stressed emphasis on sect, and promoted divisiveness.

Before moving on, it should be acknowledged that not all the key figures in Arab nationalist Iraq were Sunni, or kin of Saddam. Tariq Aziz, Saddam's foreign minister, deputy prime minister, and close adviser, was Christian. And, as we've already seen, when the United States invaded Iraq in April 2003, it issued warrants for the arrest of the Iraqi government's top 55 figures, printing their photos and details on a deck of playing cards. Of the 55, the majority, 35, were Shi'a, an inconvenient truth which hardly comported with the U.S.-propagated myth of the Iraqi government as an instrument of Sunni oppression of the majority Shi'a. What's more, most of the early leaders of the Ba'ath Party in Iraq were Shi'a, including the founder of the Ba'ath Party's Iraqi branch.[12] Still, U.S. officials and Western media insisted on portraying Saddam's government as sectarian. For example, the U.S.-British invasion of Iraq in 2003 was portrayed in *The Wall Street Journal* as an operation that "reversed centuries of Sunni rule" in Iraq.[13] By the same logic, John F. Kennedy ended 185 years of Protestant rule in the United States when he became president in 1961. And Barack Obama ended 233 years of White rule to establish Black minority rule when he became president in 2009.

Along the same lines of challenging a popular misconception that the Arab nationalist Iraqi government was Sunni-led, British journalist Peter Oborne returned from a trip to Syria in 2014 to reveal a dissonant reality: only two of 30 members of Assad's cabinet belonged to the president's minority sect. "Only a handful of members of Assad's 30-strong cabinet (I was told two) are Alawite," reported Oborne. "The prime minister is Sunni, as are the interior minister, the justice minister, the foreign minister, even the defense minister." A government delegation which travelled to Geneva for peace talks was also almost entirely composed of Sunni Muslims, reported Oborne, who added that the delegates "would probably reject sectarian terms, and prefer to think of themselves just as Syrians"[14]—as indeed, Arab nationalists—with their stress on overcoming "casual and fake differences" among Arabs—would. Ba'athists, as well as many other Syrians, and Iraqis, too, prefer to think of themselves in non-sectarian terms. It's Westerners—following colonial tradition—who insist on affixing sectarian labels to Arabs.

Even the idea that Alawites were over-represented in key security positions in the Syrian state is a bit of an overstatement. During the years Hafez al-Assad was president many important posts in the Syrian state were occupied by individuals who were not linked to him by sect. Abdul Halim Khaddam, who held powerful posts as foreign minister and vice president for political and foreign affairs, was a Sunni, as were Armed Forces Chief of Staff Hikmat al-Shihabi and Minister of Defense Mustafa Tlas. Prime Minister Abd al-Karim Qasim, speaker of the legislature Mahmud az Zubi and Assad's Ba'ath Party deputy Abdallah al-Ahmar, were Sunni, as well. Their connection to Assad was through shared membership in a socio-economic class; they all came from the same modest rural background.[15] As Hafez al-Assad's biographer, the British journalist Patrick Seale pointed out, class alliances were always more important to Assad than sectarian identity.[16]

Sunnis were no less well represented in high positions of the state during the years Bashar al-Assad was president. A minister of defense, Fahd al-Freij, one of the most highly decorated officers in Syrian history, was Sunni, as were the intelligence chiefs Ali Mamlouk, Mohammad Dib Zaitoun and Rustom Ghazaleh. Mahmoud al-Khatutib, head of the investigation branch of the political directorate was a Sunni Muslim. Two Chiefs of General Staff, Hassan Turkmani and Hikmat Shihabi, were Sunni Muslims, while the Army Chief of Staff, Daoud Rajiha, was a

Greek Orthodox Christian. Prominent members of the General Staff, including Major General Ramadan Mahmoud Ramadan and Brigadier General Jihad Mohamed Sultan, were also Sunni Muslims.[17] Robert Fisk observed that "many of [Syria's] frontline generals, when I met them, turned out" also to come from the same Sunni sect to which the majority of Syrians belonged.[18] In the make-believe world of U.S. propaganda, there were no Arab nationalists in Damascus, only Alawite sectarians; the reality on the ground was quite otherwise.

Where, in all the public discussion of the conflict in Syria in the West, was there reference to Bashar al-Assad's ideology? We knew he was an Alawite, but references to him as a secular Arab nationalist were infrequent, if not altogether absent. Numberless references were made to Syria's government as "Alawite-led" and Alawite-run" and "Alawite-dominated"— misleading descriptions, as we've seen—but the number of references to Syria as the self-defined "den of Arabism," committed to bringing about the unity of the Arab world and freedom from foreign domination along an Arab socialist path were notable for their virtual absence. And yet these references would have helped promote an understanding of the origins and nature of the conflict. It was as if what we were supposed to understand was that the locals were brutes, inflamed by religious passions and lust for power, whose behavior conformed to no rational analysis or coherent set of political beliefs. Yet, surely, the political ideologies of the main parties to the conflict—the secular Arab nationalism of the Syrian government, the Sunni political Islam of the anti-government fighters, and even, indeed, the capitalist imperialism of the United States—were highly germane to putting the pieces of the Syrian conflict puzzle together. But apart from references to Wahhabism, discussions of the Syrian conflict steered clear of political ideology, as if all one needed to know about the war to understand it was that Assad was an Alawite and the rebels were mainly Sunni. In this, a path was prepared on which we were to travel to its final destination: the conclusion that the Syrian conflict was just another Third World eruption of ancient religious rivalries. And wasn't it fortunate that Washington could step in as the world's essential and indispensable power to put an end to the bloodbath?

CHAPTER EIGHT

ECHOES OF HITLER

There were echoes of Hitler in Syria's conflict, but they had nothing whatever to do with Bashar al-Assad, who, as we have seen, was falsely depicted as a dictator in order to manufacture consent for Western efforts to force a political transition in Syria. Instead, echoes of Hitler were to be found in the arguments the United States and its allies used to undermine Syrian pan-Arabist ideology by representing it as an instrument of Alawite rule. The practice of insinuating that a political ideology is a concealed instrument for the oppression of a majority by a religious minority parallels Hitler's propaganda campaign against Marxist internationalism, articulated in his *Mein Kampf.* In Hitler's hands, Marxist ideology, which commanded the allegiance of millions of German workers, was portrayed as a Trojan Horse of the Jews to establish political rule over the German majority. Hitler hated Marxists for promoting the solidarity of workers across national lines. In the Marxist view that "the working men have no country"[1] and in the Marxist call for "working men of all countries [to] unite!"[2] Hitler saw an abomination against an idea he cherished: that Germans constituted a great and powerful race which nature had foreordained to rule over less powerful nations. Only with Germanic unity could the great dream of German leadership, primacy, and indispensability—to borrow terms Washington uses to describe its own aspirations to global hegemony—be accomplished. How could Germans come together to realize the destiny which nature had set for them if they believed, as the Marxists contended was true, that workingmen had no country? Hitler thundered against Marxism for disparaging the nation, held by Marxists to be an invention of the capitalist class, and for denigrating the Fatherland, which Marxists portrayed as an instrument in the hands of the bourgeoisie for the exploitation of the working masses.[3]

In *Mein Kampf*, Hitler wrote that Zionism changed his attitude toward the Jews of Germany. At first, he regarded Jews as Germans as much as were the country's Roman Catholics and Lutherans. Jews weren't a race or nation, he felt, but followers of a faith. "In the Jew," wrote Hitler, "I saw only a man who was of a different religion, and therefore, on grounds of human tolerance, I was against the idea that he should be attacked because he had a different faith."[4] Only after encountering an Hasidic Jew, and seeing that he dressed differently from other Germans, did Hitler began to wonder whether Jews were "an entirely different people."[5] His indecision was finally removed, he recalled, "by the activities of a certain section of the Jews themselves. A great movement, called Zionism, arose among them. Its aim was to assert the national character of Judaism."[6] Thereafter, Hitler maintained that the Jews did not constitute a religious community but a race.[7] And so, Hitler came to believe, or at least to assert, that Germans Jews were members of a nation separate from the German nation. What's more, Hitler declared that the alien Jewish nation had set out to undermine the German race from within by spreading the "bacillus" of Marxist internationalism. Under Hitler's guidance, Jews and Judaism would be conflated with Marxism, social democracy, and internationalism.

Hitler also placed an equal sign between Jews and international finance, the stock market, democracy, both the Marxist and bourgeois press, and anything else he didn't like. The hated Bolshevik Revolution and German Revolution, for example, were both engineered, in his view, by the "race" he now despised. This was far from heterodox thinking at the time. Some members of the European elite attributed every social revolution to Jews, including the French Revolution of 1789.

Emblematic of the bearers of this creed was the philo-fascist Winston Churchill. An ardent defender of ruling class privilege and the British Empire's subjection of the colonies to dictatorship, he sang the praises of Mussolini, and made clear that his sympathies leaned more strongly toward fascism's defense of the class, racial and gender discrimination from which he and his class, race and sex benefitted, than toward the Bolshevik project of overcoming discrimination along the same lines.

In 1927, after a visit to Rome, Churchill rhapsodized about Mussolini's fascist movement. "What a man!" he enthused. "I have lost my heart...fascism has rendered a service to the entire world." Churchill added that if he were Italian, "I am sure I would have been with [the fascists] entirely from the beginning of [their] victorious struggle against the bestial appetites and passions of Leninism."[8] To lay to rest any doubts about his loyalties, Churchill told the British House of Commons, four years after Hitler came to power, that "I will not pretend that, if I had to choose between communism and Nazism, I would choose communism."[9]

Like Hitler, Churchill was a racist who believed in the supremacy of the white race, and hated the members of "races" and nations the European elite viewed as inferior. Indians, he described as "beastly people with a beastly religion." Palestinians were "beastly hordes who ate little but camel dung."[10] He said that he "did not really think that black people were as capable or efficient as white people" and that he hated "people with slit-eyes and pig-tails."[11] "By his mid-twenties," wrote Lawrence James, "Churchill had absorbed the current racial dogma that identified the Anglo-Saxon race as uniquely qualified to rule,"[12] different in only the details from Hitler's beliefs. The colonial despoliation of non-Europeans was acceptable, if not desirable, in Churchill's view, an argument Hitler, and much of Europe, including even some giants of the social democracy movement, among them the "evolutionary socialist" Eduard Bernstein, would applaud. Great wrongs had not been done to "the Red Indians of America or the black people of Australia," Churchill harrumphed. It was just that "a stronger race, a higher grade race, a more worldly wise race" had "come in and taken their place."[13] This was Hitler's ideology, but, no more Hitler's than that of European colonialism and its many champions, most of whom are revered and defended even to this day, where Hitler is not. For example, at the conclusion to the introduction of his study of Churchill, Lawrence James writes, "As for Churchill, I hope that readers who feel the need to judge him will do so according to the standards he set for himself and the empire." It is inconceivable that similar cautions would be issued to anyone who felt the need to judge Hitler.

Hitler, unlike the still widely admired Churchill, is reviled because he gave European colonial ideology an unforgivable twist. He turned it against Europe itself, seeking to build in Europe a great German Empire on the scale of the empires the Americans built through continental expansion and Britain built in the Far East. Except for the geography in which they were applied, the ideas were the same as those which had animated the European division of the world into colonies and spheres of influence. Karl Korsch, a German émigré Marxist wrote in 1942 that "the Nazis have simply extended to civilized European peoples the methods hitherto reserved for the natives or savages living outside civilization."[14]

Echoing Korsch, the Martinique Marxist Aimé Césaire pointed out the Nazism was simply an expression of European colonialism turned inward.

"People are surprised, they become indignant. They say: 'How strange! But never mind—it's Nazism, it will pass!' And they wait, and they hope; and they hide the truth from themselves, that it is barbarism, the supreme barbarism, the crowning barbarism that sums up all the daily barbarisms; that is Nazism, yes, but that before they were its victims, they were its accomplices; that they tolerated Nazism before it was inflicted on them, that they absolved it, shut their eyes to it, legitimized it, because, until then, it had been applied only to non-European peoples; that they have cultivated that Nazism, that they are responsible for it, and that before engulfing the whole edifice of Western Christian civilization in its redden waters, it oozes, seeps and trickles from every crack."[15]

Césaire added that what the West "cannot forgive Hitler for is not the crime itself, the crime against man, it is not the humiliation of man as such, it is the crime against the white man, the humiliation of the white man, and the fact that he applied to Europe colonialist procedures which until then had been reserved exclusively for the Arabs of Algeria, the 'coolies' of India, and the 'niggers' of Africa."[16]

To Churchill, the Indians of the Far East were a beastly people; to Hitler, the Slavs of Europe's East were equally beastly. Churchill justified the extermination of aboriginal Americans and Australians on the grounds that they were displaced by a superior race. Hitler justified his plan to enslave the Slavs and exterminate the Jews on grounds that they were sub-humans who had to give way to a superior race. Svend Lindqvist explained the continuity of the Nazi aims and methods with European colonialism with a literary allusion: "What was done in the heart of darkness," he wrote, "was repeated in the heart of Europe."[17]

In order to attack a doctrine of Marxist internationalism which had found favor among a large body of German proletarians, the future Fuhrer conflated working class ideology with Judaism, a faith with which most German workers could not identify since they were mostly Roman Catholics, Lutherans or atheists. The idea was to discredit Marxism by depicting it as an ideology created by a religious minority to dupe the majority and gain ascendancy over it. This was, *grosso modo*, how the Western establishment defined the Syrian government. Secular Arab nationalism was conflated with the Alawite faith, a faith with which most Syrians could not identify since they did not adhere to it. The idea was to discredit Ba'athism by depicting it as an ideology created by a religious minority to dupe the majority and gain ascendancy over it. This was precisely the argument made by the Syrian Muslim Brotherhood, whose leaders contended that the Alawite community used secular Arab nationalist ideology as a cover to surreptitiously advance a pro-Alawite sectarian agenda, with the aim of oppressing the Sunni Muslim majority and destroying Syria from within.[18]

This was the myth of a minority trying to dominate a majority by propagating an ideology of equality which denied the importance of the cleavage which set the minority apart. Hence, in Hitler's view, Jews sought to dominate non-Jews by creating and championing a Marxist internationalism which treated linguistic, ethnic, religious and national differences among workers as a distraction from their common economic interests. Hitler portrayed Marxist internationalism as a cunning Jewish plot to dominate non-Jews. Similarly, in the view of the Ba'athists' opponents, secular Arab nationalism was a cunning Alawite plot to dominate Sunni Muslims.

The view was problematic for a number of reasons.

First, the Alawites were not in power; the Ba'ath Party was, and the Ba'ath Party comprised, even at its highest levels, members of other faiths and Muslim sects, including many Sunnis. The over-representation of Jews in the Bolshevik leadership relative to their numbers in the Russian population did not mean that the first communist government was in reality a Jewish regime which exercised a Jewish tyranny over a Russian Orthodox Christian majority.

If Alawites were over-represented in the Ba'ath Party and Syrian state, it was not because these bodies had been captured by Alawites pursuing an agenda of Sunni oppression and Alawite supremacy; it was because religious minorities had been drawn to the party owing to its emphasis on secularism and freedom from sectarian discrimination—values which, implemented in the state, allowed the minorities to get out from under the heel of Sunni majority discrimination which had prevailed prior to the Ba'athists' rise to power. Hence, minorities in Syria were attracted to the Ba'athist ideology of non-sectarianism, for the obvious reason that a non-sectarian state was their best defense against the tyranny of a religious majority.

Additionally, the over-representation of Alawites in the security apparatus of the state had no immanent connection to religion, but was an imperative of political survival. The Assads recognized the necessity of appointing to key posts people whose loyalty could be implicitly relied upon. These were people with whom they had ties of kinship and amity, who happened, concomitantly, to share the same religion.

Finally, and decisively, the Assads were ideological, and their ideology was unequivocally anti-sectarian. It was not Alawite interests that Hafez al-Assad and his son, Bashar, sought to promote, but the interests of the Arab nation *en masse*. To do this, according to Ba'ath ideology, it was necessary for Arabs to overcome their divisions, including differences of sect. This could hardly be accomplished by establishing a sectarian regime in Damascus guided by an Alawite agenda.

U.S. imperialists opposed Ba'athist pan-Arabism for the same reason Hitler opposed Marxist internationalism: because its aim was to build a united front of oppressed people against their common enemy.

"In the years 1913 and 1914," Hitler wrote, "I expressed the opinion...that the problem of how the future of the German nation can be secured is the problem of how Marxism can be exterminated."[19] He referred to Marxism "as the most important problem in Germany"[20] and said that the *raison d'être* of the Nazi Party under his leadership was "to impede the triumphal advance of Marxists."[21] Exterminating Marxism was Hitler's primary concern. There was a parallel with U.S. imperialism. For the U.S. state, the problem of how the future of U.S. primacy in the oil-rich Middle East could be secured was the problem of how nationalist ideologies, which promoted goals of unity, freedom and socialism, could be exterminated. For Washington,

Arab and Islamic nationalism were important problems in the Middle East. And the key goal of the U.S. foreign policy in the region was to impede the triumphal advance of Arab and Islamic nationalists—the Nassers, the Assads, the Saddams, the Gaddafis, the Nasrallahs, the Ayatollahs.

The task before Hitler was to persuade the mass of Germans, many of whom subscribed to Marxist internationalist principles, to embrace the view that Germans made up a superior nation which nature compelled to expand its living space at the expense of lesser nations—or face extinction. To accomplish this task of persuasion, he accepted the Zionist view that Jews were a nation rather than merely a religious community. Next, he portrayed what was in reality a political division between two class ideologies, that of Marxism and that of the German nobility and bourgeoisie, as a racial division, with the Jewish "race" standing in for working class ideology and the German "race" standing in for the ideology of the Junkers and German industrialists and financiers. Marxism was branded as a "Jewish doctrine."[22] The leaders of Social Democracy "were the Jews."[23] The Jews were said to control the Social Democratic press.[24] Marxist internationalism sprang from the mind of Karl Marx, "the Jew." The Marxism practiced in Russia was labeled "Judeo-Bolshevism." Marxism was to equal Judaism and Judaism to equal Marxism. The two, in Hitler's view, would be presented as opposite faces of the same coin.

Hitler's goal in equating Marxism with Judaism was to make Marxism appear to the German worker as something alien, the creation of a tiny minority, not suitable to members of another—and altogether superior—nation. But there was also something sinister about this creation of Jewish minds, according to Hitler. It was not only the product of an alien race; Marxism was a way of duping German workers into servitude to the Jewish "race." "Marxism," wrote Hitler, "systematically aims at delivering the world into the hands of the Jews."[25] To the Syrian Muslim Brotherhood, secular Arab nationalism systematically aimed at delivering Syria into the hands of the Alawites.

Parallel ideas lurked beneath the surface of Western discourse on the conflict in Syria and the war on secular Arab nationalist Iraq. In the Western media, the Assads and Saddam were hardly ever called Arab nationalists. Instead, they were defined as members of minority sects and leaders of sectarian regimes, even though they didn't self-identify as members of a sect or lead governments with sectarian agendas. To the contrary, they led governments with explicitly anti-sectarian goals. Similar to Marxist internationalists, who sought to build unity among workers across national lines to pursue their common interests, the Assads and Saddam embraced Arab "internationalism," which sought to build unity among Arabs across sectarian and all other lines, including across the arbitrary frontiers drawn up in imperial map rooms which divided the Arab nation into dozens of states. But just as in Germany where Marxist internationalists, under Hitler's ministrations, were labeled Jews pursuing an agenda of ascendancy over the German majority, so too in the Middle East, pan-Arab nationalists, under the ministrations of U.S.-led propaganda, were labeled as members of minority sects pursuing a sectarian agenda of ascendancy over religious majorities. Hitler wanted Germans to understand Marxists as Jews, not as leaders of a working class movement against exploitation by Germany's elite. Similarly, Washington wanted secular Arab nationalists to be understood by Syria's Sunni majority as Alawites and by Iraq's Shi'ite majority as Sunnis, and not as leaders of a pan-Arabic movement against domination by the West. And so both Nazi propaganda and Western propaganda portrayed ideologies of emancipation as ideologies of racial and sectarian domination.

CHAPTER NINE

WALL STREET'S EMPIRE

"The two greatest obstacles to democracy in the United States are, first, the widespread delusion among the poor that we have a democracy, and second, the chronic terror among the rich, lest we get it."[1]

Edward Dowling

The United States has an empire, even if it's not often called one. More often, the U.S. Empire is widely referred to by various euphemisms, anodyne terms which make the unacceptable appear acceptable, if not desirable. For example, Steve A. Cook, a senior fellow at the high profile, Wall Street-led foreign policy think tank, the Council on Foreign Relations, called the U.S. Empire the "Washington-led global order," in one *Wall Street Journal* opinion piece.[2] The 2015 U.S. National Security Strategy spoke not of a U.S. empire but of "American global leadership." The U.S. Empire, so defined, opined the security strategy's authors, is "essential" and "indispensable," and is "a global force for good." Empires have invariably described themselves in this way. The critical question, however—to put it somewhat awkwardly—is, for whose good is the U.S. Empire a global force?

The U.S. Empire is a global force for the good of a parasitic elite at the apex of U.S. society which derives the bulk of its

income from rent, profits, and interest. It is intimately connected to the profit-making imperatives of U.S. businesses. In
2015, references in the National Security Strategy document
to U.S. global leadership were accompanied by the proclamation that "America can and must lead the global economy." U.S.
"global leadership" hardly seemed indistinguishable from
U.S. global *economic* leadership, or to put it more precisely, U.S.
leadership of the global economy on behalf of U.S. business
interests. Washington's security strategy document announced
that the U.S. "agenda is focused on lowering tariffs on American
products, breaking down barriers to [U.S.] goods and services,
and setting higher standards to level the playing field for
American...firms." At the same time, the United States
announced that it would open markets and level the playing
field for "American...businesses abroad... [and]...eliminate barriers to the full deployment of U.S. innovation," while ensuring
that "tomorrow's global trading system is consistent with
[U.S.] interests."

One way the United States would do this, was made clear in
the 2006 National Security Strategy: "The United States will
use military force, unilaterally if necessary...when our liveli-
hoods are at stake" the document warned. The readiness of
Wall Street's empire to use the United States' vast military
apparatus to enforce its economic agenda was made clear when
U.S. Defense Secretary, Robert Gates, let the world know that
the United States had "a national interest in...unimpeded economic development and commerce."[3] Foreign states, then,
which intended to "impede" the profit-making activities of U.S.
businesses, were warned that an important role for the U.S.
military was to ensure that markets remained open and playing fields level. If we define war as one state's attempt to impose
its will on another, by the creation of harm or its threat, then
Gates' statement, namely, that Washington would use the U.S.
military to impose its will on foreign states to open markets
and investment opportunities to U.S. corporations, banks and
investors, was an act of war-making.

Wall Street's tentacles reach in myriad ways into the U.S. foreign policy making process. Accordingly, U.S. foreign policy reflects the profit-making interests of the United States' largest corporations, biggest banks, and wealthiest investors. These entities and individuals have the money power to dominate foreign policy formation, and do so. Wall Street seeks a world without barriers to U.S. goods, services and investments—that is, a world in which U.S. banks, corporations and investors are free to accumulate capital, untrammeled by impediments that may be imposed by states which seek to manage their economies in ways that are not always conducive to U.S. exports and investment. For example, foreign states may use publicly-owned enterprises, protective tariff barriers, subsidies to local enterprises, barriers to market entry, and so on, to pursue public interest goals, such as reducing inequality, providing universal material security, and overcoming under development. Yet, no matter how favorable these policies are to local populations, they almost invariably limit corporate America's pursuit of profit. They are, therefore, anathema to Wall Street, a truth which can be quickly affirmed by reading through the Wall Street Journal/Heritage Foundation Index of Economic Freedom and noticing the rich denunciations these practices reliably elicit. Corporate America has the wherewithal to dominate policy formation in Washington, and uses its vast resources to do so. Consequently, U.S. foreign policy reflects a Wall Street agenda.

The U.S. Empire is a Wall Street-friendly global economic order enforced by a network of globe-girding U.S. military bases plus 10 force-projecting aircraft carriers, a number of proxy militaries and military alliances, along with a public persuasion apparatus, both state- and private business-owned, which shapes public opinion, defines the ideological environment, and sets the public policy agenda. The empire enforces its hegemony through means of coercion (its military and covert intelligence apparatus), means of persuasion (the media, universities, think tanks, and public relations industry), and its control over the World Bank and IMF. Wall Street is at the center of the empire in two ways: it provides the personnel who form the empire's power elite. The power elite comprises the politically active representatives of Wall Street interests who rotate between top-level positions in the state and high-level jobs in the corporate and banking worlds. Wall Street is also at the center of the U.S. Empire in defining the empire's goals. The empire is run by and for Wall Street.

Who Rules America?

Several authors have made the case that advanced capitalist societies—the United States being emblematic—are dominated politically by a wealthy class of billionaire bankers, wealthy investors, and corporate titans. These writers include Ralph Miliband (*The State and in Capitalist Society*), G. William Domhoff (*Who Rules America?*), Thomas Ferguson (*Golden Rule*) and Martin Gilens and Benjamin Page ("Testing Theories of American Politics: Elites, Internet Groups, and Average Citizens"), to name just a few. I've already cited Gilens and Page a number of times, but their research is so important that it's worthwhile to summarize again: "[E]conomic elites and organized groups representing business interests have substantial independent impacts on U.S. government policy, while average citizens and mass-based interest groups have little or no independent influence."[4] The Gilens and Page analysis comes from academe, but a careful reading of major newspapers furnishes scores of instances which resonate with the duo's conclusion. For example, *The New York Times* reported that a mere 158 families and the companies they own and control, mostly in finance and energy, contributed half the funds to Democratic and Republican presidential candidates in the 2016 presidential race,[5] from which the not unreasonable conclusion can be drawn that just 158 families and the companies they own and control had an impact on U.S. politics far in excess of their numbers (but not their wealth)—another way of saying that the United States is more a plutocracy than a democracy.

The enormous wealth commanded by members of the U.S. capitalist class allows them to use their money to shape electoral contests, spending just a small fraction of their income. For example, Chicago hedge fund billionaire Kenneth C. Giffen contributed $300,000 to Republican presidential candidates in the 2016 race, well beyond the capabilities of an average citizen. But Giffen's contribution represented less than one percent of his monthly income of $68.5 million.[6]

The titles of the following articles in major U.S. media further point to the role that wealth plays in shaping U.S. politics: "Trump picks billionaire Betsy DeVos, school voucher advocate, as education secretary;"[7] "Trump expected to tap billionaire investor Wilbur Ross for commerce secretary;"[8] "Hillary, Jeb and $$$$$$;"[9] "Bloomberg starts 'Super PAC', seeking national influence;"[10] "The businessman behind the Obama budget;"[11] "Which millionaires are you voting for?"[12] "Close ties to Goldman enrich Romney's public and private lives;"[13] "Conservative nonprofit acts as stealth business lobbyist;"[14] "Number of millionaires in Congress: 261;"[15] "White House opens door to big donors, and lobbyists slip in;"[16] "Obama sends pro-business signal with adviser choice;"[17] "Wall Street ties linger as image issue for Hillary Clinton;"[18] "Obama's not-so-hot date with Wall Street."[19]

The title of the last article appeared to indicate that limits exist on Wall Street's influence in Washington (the not-so-hot date) but in point of fact the article described U.S. politics as a contest between various factions of the capitalist class to persuade average voters to back their favored candidate. This calls to mind the wry observation that the art of politics resides in the wealthy persuading the rest of us to use our votes to keep their representatives in power.

However, the influence of the dominant economic class on politics extends well beyond the electoral arena. The late Marxist sociologist Albert Szymanski offered a concise summary of the mechanisms the wealthy use to dominate U.S. politics.

Szymanski on the Theory of the State[20]

There is a wealthy class that dominates the U.S. state and the U.S. government and runs the state in its interest and against the interests of the vast majority of people. There are various ways that the wealthy class is able to dominate the U.S. government even though there are elections in which everyone is eligible to vote. There are at least seven different ways by which the wealthy are able to control the U.S. government. The first four are instrumental mechanisms. The last three are structural mechanisms. Instrumental mechanisms refer to ways in which the rich directly intervene in the U.S. government. Structural mechanisms refer to those conditions that constrain the decision-making process. They operate independently of instrumental mechanisms. Hence, even if wealthy people don't influence the government, the government is compelled by the ideological environment, the imperative of maintaining business confidence to avert economic crises and military intervention to make decisions in the interests of big business.

The direct mechanisms are:

- The placement of wealthy individuals or elite corporate executives in the top policy-making positions in the state.
- The pressure exerted on elected representatives and regulatory commissioners by lobbyists to legislate and rule in favor of business interests.
- Campaign funding. Politicians have to do the bidding of business if they want to receive the campaign funds they need to seriously contest elections.
- The role of key policy-formation groups, including the Trilateral Commission, the Council on Foreign Relations, the Business Council—very powerful, exclusive, private organizations that formulate public policies and are able to transmit them to the government by putting their people in top positions, holding regular conferences, and sending reports to the government.

There are seven or eight full-time lobbyists in Washington D.C. for every elected member of Congress. Virtually all work for big business.

Congress people, heads of regulatory commissions, and top generals are recruited by large corporations at the end of their public service careers to work as lobbyists, usually earning more money than they make in public service. Aware of the lucrative possibilities for their post public service careers, they ingratiate themselves with their prospective employers by acting in their interests while in politics, to ensure that they're later offered remunerative positions.

There are no teeth in laws aimed at limiting the role of money in election campaigns. Consequently, the wealthy are able to spend as much as they want to get politicians who are sympathetic to their interests elected.

Policy-formation organizations are generally composed of two-thirds elite business people and one-third academics, major intellectuals and other influential people. They hold seminars and meetings with government officials, as well as transmit many policy recommendations to the government.

The structural mechanisms:

- Ideological hegemony: The ability of business to put ideas in our heads, so that we think like them, and thereby act the way they want us to act.
- Business strikes: Businesses' ability to move outside a jurisdiction if the state's policies are not conducive to profit-making. Businesses' freedom to invest their capital as they see fit limits what governments can do.
- Military hegemony: If a government gets out of line and encroaches on business interests the military can take over.

Most people get their news and political values from the major media and educational system. Major media are major private corporations interlocked with major banks. But not only are they major private businesses themselves, they depend on advertising from major businesses. They are, then, doubly dependent on big business. If the media's content becomes anti-business, sponsors cancel. So how we get our ideas is doubly controlled by big business.

The boards of trustees of universities are generally dominated by business people. Business people also make the major contributions to universities and therefore are in a position to influence what academics study.

Hence, schools and mass media are dominated by big businesses. We get our political values and ideas from the mass media and schools—hence, from big business.

We think our decisions about who we vote for are freely made, but our political ideas and values have been instilled by big business through the institutions of the mass media and education system which it dominates. All mass media and all universities are pro-business.

Suppose a state tripled the minimum wage and gave corporations six months to stop polluting. Businesses would move to another jurisdiction where wages were lower and there were no laws against pollution. Massive unemployment would ensue. In the next election, the government would be blamed for the economic crisis. It would lose the election to a right-wing party that would promise to bring jobs back by passing business-friendly legislation. It might propose to abolish the minimum wage altogether and to rescind all laws against pollution.

As long as business is free to invest or not invest—as long as it makes the economic decisions—the government has to structure the environment to serve businesses' profit-making imperative; otherwise it will face a serious economic crisis. The only way to circumvent this structural constraint is to deny private business the freedom to make economic decisions, which is to say to nationalize them, so that capital cannot be relocated or made idle and is mobilized in the interests of a majority of people, rather than a wealthy minority of owners.

There are only eight countries in the world of say 160 capitalist countries that unremittingly had elections and parliamentary forms from about 1940: Britain, Ireland, the United States, Canada, Australia, New Zealand, Switzerland and Sweden. All others had a dictatorship or military government at some point. Hence, the normal state for capitalist economies is to have military rule. Only the wealthiest capitalist states haven't had military rule. But when a capitalist country encounters a severe crisis that challenges capitalist rule, it resorts to military rule.

Often the military takes over, and then relinquishes power. When this happens, civilian governments know that if they implement anti-business policies, the military will intervene once again. Hence, they are careful to remain within the bounds of acceptable big business policy. If ever there were a deep crisis in the United States that threatened capitalist rule, U.S. generals would act as their counterparts in other capitalist countries have.

The Council on Foreign Relations

Szymanski cites the elite policy-formation organization, the Council on Foreign Relations, as one of the principal organizations through which corporate America's policy preferences are transmitted to the U.S. government. Laurence H. Shoup wrote a major treatise on the Council, titled *Wall Street's Think Tank*, an update of an earlier analysis he co-authored with William Minter, titled *Imperial Brain Trust*. Shoup argues that the Council is the major organization through which the U.S. capitalist class establishes its agency and direction, becoming a class for itself. As such, it is worth a closer look.

The Council is a private organization with a chairman (for years David Rockefeller, who, as of this writing, remains the honorary chairman) and board members (typically billionaires or near billionaires) and approximately 5,000 members, who are selected by the board. The *raison d'être* of the organization is to bring together intellectuals, prominent business people, leading members of the media, state officials, and top military leaders, into an exclusive club which formulates foreign policy recommendations and promotes them to the public and government. The Council's interlocks with the U.S. state are extensive. Beginning with the Carter Administration and moving forward to the Obama Administration, Shoup found that 80 percent of the key cabinet positions, which he defined as State, Defense, Treasury, National Security Adviser, and U.S. Ambassador to the UN, were filled by Council members. Presidents (George H.W. Bush and Bill Clinton) and vice-presidents (George H.W. Bush and Richard Cheney) were members at the time they were elected to these posts. One president, Carter, became a member after leaving the presidency.

Here are the numbers of Council members as of 2016 who filled key positions in the U.S. state (they were usually members of the Council *before* they were appointed to these posts): Secretary of Treasury, 10; National Security Adviser, 10; U.S. Ambassador to the United Nations, nine; Secretary of State, eight; Secretary of Defense, eight; CIA Director, eight; Chairman of the Joint Chiefs, four; Head of the Federal Reserve, four; World Bank President, three; President, two; Vice-President, two; Director of National Intelligence, two; Director of the National Security Agency, one.

Seventeen members of Barack Obama's administration were members of the billionaire-directed private club: James Jones Jr. (national security adviser); Thomas Donilon (national security adviser); Susan Rice (national security adviser, U.S. ambassador to the UN); Timothy Geithner (treasury); Jack Lew (treasury); Robert Gates (defense); Chuck Hagel (defense); Ashton Carter (defense); David Petraeus (CIA); Robert Zoellick (World Bank); Janet Napolitano (homeland security); John Bryson (commerce); Penny Pritzker (commerce); Ernest Moniz (energy); Sylvia Burwell (health and human services); Mary Jo White (securities and exchange); and Michael Froman (U.S. trade representative). John Kerry, while not a Council member, was married to near billionaire Teresa Heinz Kerry, who was.

On top of placing its members in key state positions, the Council also directly influences policy by dominating external advisory boards established to advise the secretaries of state and defense and the director of the CIA. The Foreign Affairs Policy Board acts "to provide the Secretary of State, the Deputy Secretaries of State, and the Director of Policy Planning with independent, informed advice and opinion concerning matters of U.S. foreign policy." It consists of 20 advisers, 18 of whom belonged to the Council as members in 2016. The Defense Policy Board provides "the Secretary of Defense, Deputy Secretary of Defense and the Under Secretary of Defense for Policy with independent, informed advice and opinion concerning major matters of defense policy." In 2016, 14 of its 22 members belonged to the Council. On September 10, 2009 then CIA Director Leon Panetta announced the establishment of an external advisory board of "distinguished men and women" who would visit CIA headquarters "periodically and offer their views on managing [the CIA] and its relationships with key customers, partners, and the public." 10 of the 14 advisers Panetta named to the board—the majority—were Council on Foreign Relations members.

The Council is interlocked with other influential foreign policy-related organizations, including the Trilateral Commission (an international version of the Council, reaching beyond the United States to include counterparts in Canada, Western Europe, and Japan), Human Rights Watch and the International Crisis Group.

Human Rights Watch has a number of connections to the Council. Its 2016 co-chair Joel Motley; vice-chair John Studzinski (global head of the investment firm Blackstone); board member Michael Gellert; executive director Kenneth Roth; and deputy executive director Caroll Bogert, were all members of the Council on Foreign Relations. A major source of funding for the rights group was Council member George Soros' Open Society Institute.

The International Crisis Group has extensive overlaps with the Council. In 2016, the group's Chairman Emeritus, George J. Mitchell, was a Council member, as were the following trustees:

Mort Abramowitz; Samuel Berger; Wesley Clark; Thomas R. Pickering; Olympia Snowe; George Soros; and Lawrence Summers. Council members who served as the group's advisers included Zbigniew Brzezinski; Stanley Fischer; Carla Hills; Swanee Hunt; James V. Kimsey and Jessica T. Mathews. Soros and Rockefeller were major sources of funding.

In 2016, the Council membership included an assortment of billionaires and prominent business people, including Peter Ackerman (supporter of non-violent overthrow movements and head of the CIA-interlocked Freedom House); Bruce Kovner; Henry R. Kravis; Penny Pritzker; David M. Rubenstein; Frederick W. Smith; George Soros; Leonard A. Lauder; Mortimer B. Zuckerman; Eric E. Schmidt; Stephen Schwarzman; John Paulson; Lloyd Blankfein; Edgar Bronfman Jr.; Jamie Dimon; Louis V. Gerstner, Jr.; and a number of Rockefellers, a Roosevelt, and members of other wealthy families. It also included a media mogul, Rupert Murdoch, and prominent journalists: Tom Brokaw; Leslie H. Gelb; Robert W. Kagan; Charles Krauthammer; Nicholas D. Kristof; Lewis H. Lapham; Judith Miller; Peggy Noonan; Walter Pincus; John Podhoretz; Dan Rather; David E. Sanger; Diane Sawyer; George Stephanopoulos; and Barbara Walters. Not only does the Council place its members in key positions in the state and in influential civil society organizations, it also co-opts leading media figures to promote the Council's views to the public.

Targeting Countries with Publicly-Owned Economies

Significantly, every country in which the United States has intervened militarily either directly or through proxies, or threatened militarily, since WWII, has had a largely publicly owned economy in which the state has played a decisive role. Or it has had a democratized economy where productive assets have been redistributed from private (usually foreign) investors to workers and farmers, and in which room for U.S. banks, U.S. corporations and U.S. investors to exploit the countries' land, labor, markets and resources has been limited, if not altogether prohibited. These include the Soviet Union and its allied socialist countries; China; North Korea; Nicaragua; Yugoslavia; Iraq; Libya; Iran; and Syria. We might expect that a foreign policy dominated by a wealthy investor class would react to the restrictions of communists, socialists and economic nationalists on U.S. profit-making as obstacles to overcome, even at great cost to the lives of others. For example, as we've already seen, when asked in 1996 about a UN estimate that U.S.-led sanctions had killed 500,000 Iraqi children under the age of five, then U.S. secretary of state Madeleine Albright (a Council member) told 60 Minutes that "It's a hard choice, but I think, we think, it's worth it."[21] Losurdo has pointed out that the Clinton administration's murder through sanctions-related hunger and disease of hundreds of thousands of Iraqis is a crime far in excess of any of which Soviet leader Joseph Stalin can been accused, since the deaths attributed to Stalin were the consequences of decisions he took as defensive responses to a permanent state of emergency the USSR faced during his years in power, including the aggressions of Nazi Germany and Imperial Japan and the Cold War—aggressions which threatened the very existence of the Soviet Union. By contrast, the United States faced no security threat from Iraq. Even so, then U.S. president Bill Clinton (a Council member) chose to sacrifice the lives of numberless Iraqis in pursuit of the foreign policy goal of establishing U.S. hegemony in the Middle East to facilitate the accumulation of capital by his country's economic elite.[21] If Stalin is portrayed as a monster, then by what greater category of monster must we describe George H. W. Bush, Bill Clinton, and George W. Bush, who led wars of aggression (either military, economic, or both) on Arab nationalist Iraq? It is one thing to take decisions which lead to innumerable deaths in response to significant threats against one's country (as Stalin did), and quite another to kill numberless people in the absence of a threat in pursuit of foreign policy goals related to the profit-making interests of bankers, investors and oil companies (as the Bushes and Clinton did).

220 WASHINGTON'S LONG WAR ON SYRIA

We need not tarry too long on the idea that the intervention of the United States and its allies in the struggle in Arab nationalist Syria was motivated in any way by considerations of human rights and democracy, since, as we've seen in earlier chapters (a) the United States counted as its principal allies in the Middle East, despotic regimes whose disdain for human rights as elemental as suffrage and the right of women to drive automobiles (in the case of Saudi Arabia) knows no parallel, and yet Washington was perfectly willing to dote on these anti-democratic monarchies, emirates and dictatorships, selling them arms, establishing military bases on their territory and protecting them against condemnation in international forums and from the opposition of democratic forces at home; and (b) these same tyrannies were the major supporters, along with the United States, of sectarian Sunni jihadists who sought to establish an Islamic state in Syria, in place of a secular, pluralist, and democratic state. When jihadists' attacks were directed at Syrians, the brutality of these sectarian fanatics was mechanically noted then passed over quickly by the Western news media, in contrast to the copious coverage afforded to equivalent butchery aimed at Western targets. Hence, an Islamic State attack in Paris in November, 2015 was given wide-ranging media coverage and elevated to an event of earth-shattering proportions, while similar attacks carried out almost daily in Syria and Iraq, and in Syria by "rebels," including the Islamists dubbed "moderates," were largely ignored. For example, in August 2013, Islamic State, the Nusra Front, Ahrar al-Sham and other Islamist fanatics slaughtered more than 200 Alawite villagers, and at the same time kidnapped more than 100 women and children.[23] There was no Western media-orchestrated outpouring of grief for these victims of Washington's Sunni Islamist allies of convenience.

There was a confluence of factors that conduced to making the Syrian government a target for U.S.-sponsored regime change through militant Sunni Islamist proxies, but two appear to be primary.

The first was the status of the Syrian government as the last bastion of Arab nationalism. Arab nationalism threatened the ability of the U.S. corporate class to draw a Himalaya of profits from North Africa to the Persian Gulf, the traditional range of the Arab nation. Instead of a free flow of profits to the United States, facilitated by Arab kings, sultans and emirs who had no legitimacy with their own people and relied on Washington's support to continue their despotic rule, the proceeds of the sale of the region's petroleum resources would be used for the region's own internal development, if Arab nationalist aspirations were brought to fruition. It was necessary, from the point of view of U.S. foreign policy planners, to eradicate the carriers of the Arab nationalist contagion.

The second was the existence in Syria of a major role for the state in the ownership and control of the economy. The idea of state control of industry and enterprise is an anathema to the U.S. foreign policy establishment, as well we would expect it to be, given the enormous influence of bankers, investors and major corporations in Washington, in no small measure exercised through the Council on Foreign Relations. U.S. capital is always looking for places to export to and invest in. It is no accident that one of the first tasks undertaken by the dictator Washington initially installed in Iraq in 2003, L. Paul Bremer (not surprisingly, a member of the Council), was to remove most of the restrictions which the toppled Arab nationalist government in Baghdad had imposed on imports and foreign investment. Tariffs and duties were abolished; scores of Iraqi enterprises were put on the auction block; much of the economy was opened to foreign investment; foreign investors were allowed to repatriate 100 percent of their profits; and a regressive 15 percent flat tax was established.[24]

Likewise, much of the growing U.S. hostility to China, signaled in the Obama administration's military pivot to the Asia-Pacific region and the Council's call for Washington to "balance the rise of China" (which is to say, block its rise), was based on opposition to the significant role the Chinese Communist Party played in

China's economy. Saying that Washington was opposed to state economic control was another way of saying that the U.S. foreign policy establishment bristled at restrictions which prevented U.S. investors and businesses from fully realizing the profit potential of Chinese land, labor, resources, and markets. U.S. investors, U.S. business people and U.S. bankers wanted China as a wonderful source of profits, an aspiration that failed to comport fully with China's own development strategy.

Similarly, the significant management of Syria's economy by Arab nationalists in Damascus at the expense of U.S. investors and U.S. corporations was a major consideration behind the decision taken by the big business-dominated U.S. foreign policy establishment to attempt to engineer the de-Ba'athification of Syria.

It is said that countries have interests, not friends, but is there any democratic or geographically legitimate sense in which they have economic interests in someone else's territory? Only imperialists have economic interests beyond their own borders, enforced through threat and coercion. The fact that U.S. state officials regularly invoked the phrase "our vital interests" in other countries in order to justify interventions was a measure of how unabashedly imperialist U.S. foreign policy is. The vital interests the United States claimed to have in the Middle East, Asia and Europe were no more valid than were the vital interests Nazi Germany claimed to have in Eastern Europe, fascist Italy claimed to have in the Mediterranean, Imperial Japan claimed to have in East Asia, and imperialist Britain and France claimed to have in Asia and Africa.

An analysis of who exercises sway over public policy making in Washington leads to an inescapable conclusion: U.S. foreign policy has a class content. It is that of bankers, investors and major shareholders of the United States' key corporations who, through instrumental and functional mechanisms, dominate U.S. public affairs. This class has an interest in unimpeded access to the land, labor, resources and markets of the entire world for purposes of making itself ever wealthier.

It even has an interest beyond the planet earth. In 2015, "President Obama...signed the U.S. Commercial Space Launch Competitiveness Act (H.R. 2262) into law...recogniz[ing] the right of U.S. citizens to own asteroid resources."[25] The bill, which can be found on the U.S. Congress website, reads: "(Sec. 202) This bill directs the President, acting through appropriate federal agencies, to:...promote the right of U.S. commercial entities to explore outer space and utilize space resources, in accordance with such obligations, free from harmful interference, and to transfer or sell such resources." A U.S. law promoting the commercial exploitation of outer space calls to mind the words of the arch-British imperialist, Sir Cecil Rhodes, who was instrumental in founding one of the Council on Foreign Relation's predecessor organizations. Rhodes said: "The world is nearly all parceled out, and what there is left of it, is being divided up, conquered and colonized. To think of these stars that you see overhead at night, these vast worlds, which we can never reach. I would annex the planets if I could. I often think of that."[26] While the bill didn't authorize the annexation of the stars, it did direct the president to promote a right for U.S. investors to own asteroid resources. In doing so it sought to accomplish what, in previous centuries, annexation was used to bring about, namely, opportunities for proprietary classes to expand their wealth by giving them access to new territory.

Because the U.S. owning class—which is to say, corporate America—has an interest in unimpeded access to the land, labor, resources and markets of the entire world for the purposes of making itself ever wealthier, U.S. foreign policy is, and has always been, hostile to foreign populations which aspire to control their own wealth-producing assets for their own purposes. This was no less true in connection with Syria, where Bashar al-Assad's government represented the last bastion of Arab nationalism, an ideology hostile to U.S. corporate control of the Arab world, and which played a significant role in Syria's economic affairs at the expense of U.S. investors. By contrast with the imperialist character of U.S. foreign policy, the thinking of

Syria's Arab nationalists was democratic and geographically valid: "Syria," in Assad's view was "an independent state working for the interests of its people, rather than making the Syrian people work for the interests of the West."[27] U.S. foreign policy sought to turn this on its head. In the view of U.S. planners, Syria was to become a U.S. client state which would collude in making the Syrian people work for the economic interests of a parasitic elite of billionaires, wealthy investors, and major shareholders who sat atop U.S. society and aspired to rule the world.

CONCLUSION

At the center of the U.S. war on Syria were four major forces.

The first was U.S. imperialism, known by its anodyne appellation, "U.S. global leadership." U.S. imperialism seeks to offer U.S. corporations, banks and investors untrammeled access to export and investment opportunities anywhere in the world, regardless of the wishes of the people who live in whichever part of the world U.S. capitalists are driven to nestle in, settle in, and establish connections in. The centrality of U.S. business agendas in U.S. foreign policy is easily confirmed by observing the frequency with which the following concepts appear in U.S. government foreign policy strategy documents: economic freedom, free enterprise, open economies, level playing fields, elimination of barriers, overcoming trade tariffs, and unimpeded commerce.

There are two reasons why U.S. imperialism is driven by the economic agenda of North America's wealthiest investors, largest banks, and richest corporations.

The first reason is that corporate America is compelled by the very nature of capitalism to unremittingly seek opportunities for the unceasing accumulation of capital. The appetites of profit-making enterprises are illimitable, incapable of being satisfied by domestic markets and opportunities at home. Indeed, capitalist expansionary appetites reach even beyond the planet. Where Cecil Rhodes dreamed of annexing the stars, corporate America demands the right to exploit the commercial opportunities inhered in the stars—or at least the asteroids.

The second reason that the profit-making agenda of the highest economic stratum of U.S. society lies at the centre of U.S. global leadership is because economic power is largely coterminous with political power. The U.S. economic elite doesn't always get its way in competition with other sections of U.S. society, but its money power greatly increases the chances it will. As the political scientists Gilens and Page showed in their 2014 study of over 1,700 policy issues, "economic elites and organized groups representing business interests have substantial impacts on government policy, while average citizens and mass-based interest groups have little or no independent influence."[1]

There are a multitude of ways in which the U.S. economic elite—the country's capitalist class—uses its money power to obtrude its preferences and imperatives on U.S. foreign policy.

The U.S. corporate elite is over-represented in key positions in the U.S. state relative to its numbers in the population and dominates important public policy decision-making processes. For example, most members of the U.S. Congress are millionaires, whose millions have come from their connections to business enterprises. (The median net worth of U.S. senators in 2012 was over \$2.7 million.[2]) Most of the people appointed to U.S. cabinet positions come from high-level positions in the corporate world.

Various mechanisms allow the U.S. corporate community to impose its policy preferences on the state. First, it has a vast network of lobbyists representing its point of view to government. Large corporations, for example, have entire departments dedicated to pressuring government officials to accommodate the interests of individual enterprises. Industries have lobbyists to represent the common interests of firms that comprise the industry. And there are lobby groups, spanning multiple industries, which advocate on behalf of the corporate community as a whole. And what are the corporate community's common interests when operating abroad? Open markets, a level playing field, low wages and low taxes, and unimpeded access to investment opportunities. Is it any wonder that these concepts show up frequently as goals in U.S. foreign policy strategy documents?

The corporate community owns the mass media and has a vast public relations network to get its point of view across to the public. It finances political campaigns. And it shapes the behavior of politicians by holding out the promise of very lucrative post-political careers in the executive suite and positions on corporate boards to politicians who champion the interests of the corporate community while in power.

High-level executives frequently rotate between senior jobs in the corporate world and important posts in public service. For example, the connections between the New York investment bank Goldman Sachs and the U.S. Treasury Department are so multifarious that the firm is known by its competitors as Government Sachs. Former Goldman executives who moved on to government positions include Robert Rubin and Henry Paulson, who served as U.S. Secretaries of the Treasury. The list also includes numerous other Goldman Sachs alumni who have held less visible, though still very important positions in the U.S. state and elsewhere. For example, Goldman alumnus Mark Carney headed the Bank of Canada and Bank of England and former Goldman executive Mario Draghi headed the European Central Bank. *The New York Times* wrote that the investment bank "has a history and culture of encouraging its partners to take leadership roles in public service" and that "it is a widely held view within the bank that no matter how much money you pile up, you are not a true Goldman star until you make your mark in the political sphere."[3]

Goldman Sachs had strong ties to the Clintons. As president, Bill Clinton appointed Goldman co-chair Robert Rubin to the post of Treasury Secretary. Goldman chair and CEO Lloyd Blankfein (a member of the Council on Foreign Relations) raised funds for Hillary Clinton's first presidential bid, and also paid Clinton $675,000 to deliver three speeches at Goldman events after she left the State Department. Blankfein was one of the guests at Clinton's 64th birthday celebration. (Blankfein's predecessor as Goldman's top executive was Henry Paulson, who served as Treasury Secretary in the George W. Bush administration.) "Over 20-plus years," observed *The New York Times*, "Goldman provided the Clintons with some of their most influential advisors, millions of dollars in campaign contributions and speaking fees, and financial support to the family foundation's charitable programs."[4]

But it's not only Goldman Sachs that has had a significant footprint in the state: former high-level executives from scores of major enterprises hold senior positions in the bureaucracy.

The view that capitalist democracies are dominated by the super-rich is not as heterodox as might be imagined. Consider the following passages from the Nobel Prize-winning economist Paul Krugman's *New York Times'* columns:

> "You see, the rich are different from you and me: they have more influence. It's partly a matter of campaign contributions, but it's also a matter of social pressure, since politicians spend a lot of time hanging out with the wealthy."[5]

Krugman again:

> "...assured paychecks for the ideologically loyal are an important part of the system. Scientists willing to deny the existence of man-made climate change, economists willing to declare that tax cuts for the rich are essential to growth, strategic thinkers willing to provide rationales for wars of choice, lawyers willing to provide defenses of torture, all can count on support from a network of organizations that may seem independent on the surface but are largely financed by a handful of ultra wealthy families."[6]

In another of his *New York Times'* columns, Krugman observed that "policy makers [cater] almost exclusively to the interests of...those who derive lots of income from assets." The "only real beneficiaries" of government economic policy, concluded Krugman, are "bankers and wealthy individuals with lots of bonds in their portfolios." "And that," concluded the economist turned columnist, "explains why creditor interests bulk so large in policy; not only is this the class that makes big campaign contributions, it's the class that has personal access to policy makers—many of whom go to work for these people when they exit government through the revolving door."[7]

The sway over public policy that the U.S. corporate community exercises is exerted just as strongly, if not more powerfully, in foreign policy as it is in domestic affairs. People have a stronger interest in domestic policy because it has more immediate and direct effects on them. They're more likely to understand domestic policy because the matters with which it deals are closer to home and directly affect them. In contrast, for most U.S. citizens, the effects of, say, U.S. military missions abroad are remote and indirect and, when undertaken by secretive Special Forces or drones operating under covert programs, hidden from view altogether. Therefore, citizens are more likely to mount opposition to domestic policy that is hostile to their interests (because they're more likely to see and feel and understand it) than to foreign policy (whose effects are often distant and indirect and difficult to discern). As a consequence, the corporate community has virtually a clear field to dominate foreign policy with very little, if any, opposition from other sectors of U.S. society.

There are a number of high-prestige, corporate-funded think tanks which deal with foreign policy. Most foreign policy think tanks receive corporate funding, are directed by members of the corporate community, and make foreign policy recommendations to the government reflecting the interests of the corporate community.

Corporate community-controlled think tanks and advocacy organizations also provide "experts" to the media to comment on matters of public policy. Journalists consult them for background on public policy stories. Because opinion is swayed most by voices perceived as authoritative and utterly independent, think tank experts pose as disinterested savants with special knowledge and thus serve a role of leading public opinion in directions that are favorable to the corporate community.

To illustrate, consider the Institute for the Study of War, or ISW, a foreign policy think tank. The ISW is funded by the U.S. arms industry. Its sponsors include a who's who of weapons manufacturers from Raytheon to General Dynamics, Northrop Grumman to DynCorp. In 2016, the think tank was headed by Jack Keane, a retired U.S. general. Keane sat on the boards of MetLife, Allied Bartan Security Services, and weapons industry giant General Dynamics.[8] Anyone of an unbiased mind would recognize that the ISW and its corporate sponsors had an interest in promoting the use of the U.S. military as an apparatus of U.S. foreign policy. War was good for the profits of the think tank's sponsors.

The ISW played two roles: a policy formation role and a public opinion shaping role. As part of its policy formation role, it created policy recommendations for the government that favored a robust military and its frequent use. As part of its public opinion shaping role, it ran advocacy campaigns to support a muscular military. Keane played a lead role in public advocacy through the cooperation of the mass media, which enlisted his services as an "impartial" military analyst. Keane appeared frequently on CNN to promote U.S. military intervention in Iraq and Syria—two countries whose secular Arab nationalist orientations, with their rejection of the United States' self-proclaimed role as leader of the global economy, were clearly against the interests of corporate America, an important part of which was the weapons industry which bankrolled Keane's think tank.

There were dozens of other representatives of the weapons industry who appeared regularly in the mass media as "impartial" experts. The list included retired Marine Corp general James Mattis, who was on the board of General Dynamics; retired U.S. general Anthony Zinni, who was on the board of the British arms company, BAE Systems; John Garret, a retired Marine colonel who worked as a military analyst for Fox News, and who was a lobbyist for the Pentagon provider Patton Boggs; and James Marks, a retired U.S. Army general who was CNN's military analyst for three years while working as a senior-level executive at the weapons manufacturer McNeil Technologies.[9]

Another organization that illustrated the connection between the corporate community and the U.S. state was the Committee for the Liberation of Iraq, which lobbied the U.S. government to wage war on Arab nationalist Iraq. Two of NBC's most prominent military analysts, Barry McCaffrey and Wayne Downing, were both members of the committee and board members of several major arms suppliers. Their connections to the weapons industry were never acknowledged by NBC.

Military analysts like McCaffrey and Downing often had direct connections to the U.S. state. This was revealed in a 2008 *New York Times* expose by reporter David Barstow. Barstow found that mass media military analysts were receiving talking notes directly from the Pentagon.

Barstow wrote:

> "To the public, these men are members of a familiar fraternity, presented tens of thousands of times on television and radio as 'military analysts' whose long service has equipped them to give authoritative and unfettered judgments about the most pressing issues of the post-Sept. 11 world. [But most] of the analysts have ties to military contractors vested in the very war policies they are asked to assess on air. [They represent] a vast assemblage of contractors scrambling for hundreds of billions in military business generated by [the Pentagon and often get] more airtime than network reporters...framing how viewers ought to interpret events."[10]

An important part of the corporate community's public opinion shaping network, then, is the provision to the mass media of misleadingly labeled "independent analysts" who frame how viewers and readers ought to interpret events in order to persuade the public to back policies that favor corporate community interests. The parallel in domestic policy is the mass media's reliance on bank economists and CEOs as experts on economic policy. To be sure, there are some left voices given access to the mass media, but the viewpoint of labor and the left is overwhelmed by an avalanche of pro-corporate views, and the inclusion of a few voices from the other side allows the mass media to claim that they offer a variety of views across the political spectrum.

The most important element of the corporate community's public opinion-shaping network is the mass media. The mass media are large corporations themselves, and are an integral part of the corporate community. They promote positions that are compatible with and conducive to their own interests and to the interests of the larger corporate community to which they belong. This view is almost axiomatic. There would be no controversy in the claim that a newspaper owned by labor unions would promote positions that are compatible with the interests of organized labor. Nor would there be much disagreement with the view that a news network owned by environmentalists would have a certain point of view on fracking and pipelines. Clearly, then, we should expect media owned by wealthy business owners to reflect the viewpoint of wealthy business owners. And that means that since most people get most of what they know about foreign policy from the mass media, most of what they know about foreign policy reflects the viewpoint of the U.S. corporate elite.

The corporate community's public opinion shaping network also includes polling firms to monitor the opinions of the public, and public relations firms to develop programs to shape public opinion. Additionally, the corporate community draws on its expertise in commercial marketing to do political marketing, to shape the opinions of voters, legislators, and political decision-makers to favor policies that promote the corporate community's interests, in the same way they shape the brand choices of consumers. A community that has developed marketing into a science uses the same science to mobilize public opinion in support of policies of interest to it in the state.

A rival theory of the state to the instrumental view presented above holds that capitalism as a system structures the environment in which governments operate, compelling them to formulate policy in the interests of the corporate community. One implication of this view is that the political orientations of the people who hold high-level positions in the capitalist state are largely irrelevant. According to the theory, the logic of capitalism structures the policy boundaries within which policy- and decision-makers operate, forcing conservatives, liberals, social democrats, and even communists who elect to work within the capitalist system, to operate within the same narrow policy space. Critical to this view is the idea that the prosperity and stability of a capitalist society depends on the private owners of capital earning sufficient profits. If they cannot generate enough profit, they cease to invest, and economic activity grinds to a halt. To maintain stability, governments must pursue policies to support the profit-making activities of their business communities. To do otherwise would precipitate an economic crisis, and the government would lose the support of the public. Hence, governments either support the profit-making activities of the private owners of capital, and avoid crises that would challenge their continued rule, or pursue policies which interfere with capital accumulation, in which case they fall into crisis, are defeated at the next election, and are replaced by a successor government which reinstates policies to support profitability and restore capitalist economic stability.

The structural and instrumental theories represent complementary processes by which the U.S. state operates in the interests of a social upper class based in the business community. Not only does the need for governments to maintain stability and prosperity within a capitalist society limit the realistic range of policy alternatives to those that are supportive of profit-making, but the immense wealth of the corporate community allows the U.S. business elite, at the same time, to dominate the political process to shape policies of interest to it in the state through think tanks, advocacy organizations, lobbyists, and the placement of its representatives in important public policy decision-making posts.

We can be certain, then, that U.S. foreign policy will always be inimical to foreign states which seek to place the interests of local populations above the foreign investment and export interests of U.S. investors, banks and corporations, since the U.S. state is dominated by these capitalist forces.

The second force at the center of the U.S. war on Syria was secular Arab nationalism, a program to overcome the legacy of underdevelopment and disunity which European colonialism had brought to the Arab world and which left it vulnerable to domination by the U.S. state and its economic agenda. Secular Arab nationalism was wholly antithetical to U.S. global leadership, regarding it as neither essential nor indispensable, but undesirable, exploitative, and to be resisted and defended against. The fact that secular Arab nationalism was so thoroughly at odds with the values of the U.S. capitalist class, and its aspirations to lead an integrated global economy shaped to serve its profit-making interests, led Washington to work toward the overthrow of three secular Arab nationalist states: Iraq, Libya and Syria. Attempts to overthrow Arab nationalists intensified beginning in 1990.

The year 1990 is significant. By this point, the leadership of the Soviet Union—which had backed the secular Arab nationalist states—had capitulated in its struggle with the capitalist world, and the USSR was on the cusp of dissolution. The Soviet Union's contribution to de-colonization had been incalculable. But now, with the USSR's demise imminent, the United States was about to become the world's lone superpower. It immediately embarked on the project of capitalizing on the opportunity afforded by the suicide in progress of the first, and most powerful, communist state. It would integrate the world into a U.S.-led global order, free from the opposition to this project that the Soviet Union would have otherwise exerted.

Through a U.S.-led war lasting over a decade, and comprising military intervention, economic blockade and finally invasion, Iraq was purged of its Arab nationalist leadership, its Arab socialist economy was dismantled, and a constitution was drafted under U.S. supervision to bar secular Arab nationalists from ever again holding positions of influence in Baghdad. The United States also maneuvered to base Iraq's politics on ethno-sectarian divisions, undermining the efforts of Arab national-ists to build Arab unity and foster harmony within Iraq across ethnic, religious and tribal lines. That the country's Arab nationalist leader, Saddam, was known by a single name was an outcome of the Ba'ath Party's efforts to overcome tribal div-isions by banning the use of tribal names.

Washington had colluded with Saddam for years to eradicate what the U.S. foreign policy establishment regarded as greater threats to U.S. profit-making interests in the Middle East than secular Arab nationalism, namely, communism and Iran's Islamic Revolution. The Ba'athists were not communists, how-ever much hardliners in Washington regarded them as such, and the Syrian Ba'athists, who cooperated with both commun-ists at home and in Moscow, nevertheless maintained some distance from them, regarding communism with suspicion. Saddam went further by working with the CIA to wage a war on communists in Iraq. He also proved useful to the United States in engaging Iran's Islamic Republic in war. As we've seen, after 1979, the Iranians vigorously rejected U.S. leadership, and committed themselves to the project of uniting the Islamic world against U.S. domination. Washington provided Iraq with weapons and intelligence to help prosecute its war against Iran.

But in 1990, Saddam significantly raised the level of threat posed by Arab nationalism to U.S. profit-making in the Middle East by invading Kuwait, creating the threat, from Washington's standpoint, that Arab nationalists were poised to invade Arabia, a demarche that would likely bring the peninsula's cornucopia of oil profits under the control of an Arab nationalist agenda. This would have been a major setback to U.S. corporate activ-ity in the Arab world on two counts.

First, the peninsula's oil wealth would be used for the uplift of Arabs *en masse*, rather than for the narrow enrichment of the Saudi monarchy and U.S. oil firms. Iraq's Ba'athists had already used Iraq's publicly-owned oil industry to remake Iraqi society, building vast new infrastructure, and creating what a former U.S. State Department official had called a "golden age." "Schools, universities, hospitals, factories, theaters and museums proliferated; employment became so universal that a labor shortage developed."[11] Imagine what the Arab nationalists might have accomplished with the addition of Arabia's oil wealth.

Second, if Iraq's Arab nationalists were successful in using revenue from the sale of Iraq's and Arabia's oil to create an Arab golden age across Iraq and the Arabian Peninsula, they would inspire Arabs elsewhere. The entire Arab world might organize against U.S. corporate influence. This was the great Arab nightmare in embryo for the U.S. capitalist class: Secular Arab nationalism might create "a vastly important Arab center of gravity with worldwide influence"[12] which would deny to U.S. banks, corporations and investors the open markets, level playing fields, and pro-foreign investment policies they demanded.

To address this threat, the Pentagon mobilized, driving Iraqi forces out of Kuwait, and establishing a prophylactic troop presence on the peninsula. The latter development, perceived by Osama bin Laden as a U.S. invasion of the Islamic homeland, did much to spur the growth of al-Qaeda as a force mobilizing mujahedeen against the United States, rather than in alliance with it, as the Islamist guerillas had acted in Afghanistan. (Later, in Syria, al-Qaeda would revert to its role as U.S. ally of convenience to counter Damascus's secular Arab nationalists.) A decade-long regime of sanctions followed, undermining the golden age the Arab nationalists had created in Iraq, and weakening the state so severely that it was left virtually defenseless. In 2003, Washington and London invaded the country and quickly de-Ba'athified the Iraqi state, dismantled its socialist economy, and created a business climate which welcomed U.S. imports and investment.

In 2011, Washington and two of its major European allies, Britain and France—formerly the world's greatest colonial powers—teamed up with Islamist guerillas to overthrow Libya's secular Arab nationalist leader, Muammar Gaddafi. Gaddafi had come to power in 1969, overthrowing Britain's protégée King Idris I. Oil had been discovered in Libya in 1959, but the oil revenues which began to flow to the state were not used to uplift the majority of Libyans. The king, his retinue, and Western oil companies, monopolized the benefits of Libya's oil, while the king's subjects lived lives that were nasty, brutish and short. In the mid 1960s, the capital, Tripoli, was a huge network of slums, without running water or electricity. Inspired by the "Lion of the Desert" Umar al-Mukhtar, who led a rebellion against Italian colonization of Libya, and the great Arab nationalist leader, Gamal Abdel Nasser, Gaddafi set about to liberate Libya from Western domination and to use his country's oil wealth to overcome the colonial legacy of its underdevelopment. He ejected the U.S. Air Force from a military base it had inherited from the British, located near Tripoli. The Pentagon valued the air base for its proximity to the Soviet Union. Gaddafi also pursued an Arab socialist program of state control, planning and guidance of the economy. Using revenues from the sale of the country's oil, Libya's Arab nationalists overcame their country's backwardness to a large degree, enormously improving "the lives of the settled, coastal people," enabling them to live "beyond the dreams of their fathers and grandfathers."[13]

Gaddafi posed the same challenges to U.S. foreign policy that other Arab nationalists had, and these challenges were the most acute where the nationalists sat atop oceans of oil. They exercised control over resources that U.S. oil majors coveted, and the nationalists weren't willing to give the oil companies access to this lucrative natural resource on terms which didn't establish local interests as prior and senior. Access to oil revenue allowed the nationalists, through *dirigiste* economic policies, to uplift their populations, creating inspiring examples of what Arab nationalism, harnessing oil wealth, could accomplish. There was, then, a huge danger that the Arab nationalist principles of unity, independence, and socialism would be replicated elsewhere in the Arab world, to the detriment of corporate America.

Gaddafi's robust Arab nationalism was a major irritant to Western oil companies and to the U.S. State Department. The oil companies complained that Gaddafi's government was driving hard bargains, and restricting access to Libya's most productive oil fields to the state-owned oil company. The U.S. State Department complained that Libya was practicing "resource nationalism" and reprobated the Gaddafi government's "increasingly nationalistic policies in the energy sector." *The New York Times* summed up the West's troubles with Libya: The Arab nationalist, the U.S. newspaper observed, "proved to be a problematic partner for international oil companies."[14] Gone were the days when the Libyan monarch made generous deals with the privately-owned oil majors, and got a cut of the action for his "helpfulness." This, in effect, was the same model beloved by the aristocrats of the Arabian Peninsula, many of them, princes, emirs and sultans, trained at the British elite military academy, Sandhurst. The model was: scratch the oil companies' backs, and Washington will scratch yours. Because he was a nationalist, galvanized by the dream of Libyan self-determination, Gaddafi never accepted the paradigm of pandering to Western economic interests. He was, for that reason, long a U.S. government target for elimination. When he was finally brought down, a deed accomplished by the U.S. corporate elite's military muscle, NATO, in alliance with Islamists who objected to the Arab nationalist's secularism, there remained only one Arab nationalist state: Syria, the "den of Arabism."

Washington's objections to Arab nationalist Syria were the same as its objections to Iraq and Libya under Arab nationalist rule—that it would become "a focus of Arab nationalistic struggle against an American regional presence and interests."[15] The Assad government opposed the U.S. take-over of Iraq, and refused to cooperate with Washington in integrating the freshly conquered Iraq into the U.S. Empire. The government in Damascus was implacably hostile to Israel, as a democracy for Jews, and Jewish state for Arabs, implanted by Europeans at the center of the Arab world. Washington objected to the aid Damascus provided to groups fighting for Palestinian self-determination as well as to its alliance with Hezbollah, whose *raison d'être* was to safeguard Lebanese sovereignty against Israeli expansionism. U.S. officials objected even more strenuously to the alliance the Arab nationalists maintained with Iran, a state which championed the independence of the Islamic world from U.S. global leadership. Neither did Syria's alliance with Russia, a so-called "peer competitor" of the United States, endear the Assad government to U.S. strategists. Finally, the economy the Ba'athists shaped in Syria—"largely state-controlled...dominated by...(the) public sector" and "based largely on Soviet models," as U.S. government researchers described it in 2005,[16] left little room for the pursuit of profit by U.S. banks, corporations and investors. The global economy which the United States said it could and would lead, with the open markets, level playing fields, and free enterprise Washington envisioned for it, was completely repudiated by Syria's Arab nationalists. Assad refused to fall into step behind U.S. global leadership, regarding it as neither essential nor indispensable, and recognizing that it was committed to prioritizing private U.S. economic interests over the aspirations and development requirements of the formerly colonized world, including Syrians. "Syria," Assad boldly declared, "is an independent state working for the interests of its people, rather than making the Syrian people work for the interests of the West."[17] This must have seemed like a slap in the face to the country that insisted it would lead the world. Owing to his defiance, Assad, and his Arab nationalist colleagues, would have to go. The Syrian state would be de-Ba'athified, as the Iraqi state had been earlier.

The third force at the center of the U.S. war on Syria was the political Islam of the Muslim Brotherhood, an Islamist reaction to the Arab world's encounter with European imperialism.

The Muslim Brotherhood, under the leadership of Hasan al-Banna, objected to the gradual de-Islamization of Egypt that was being effected by Britain's control of the country. Egypt's jurisprudence, formerly based on the Quran, as well as on the Sunna, the record of the Prophet Muhammad's deeds and words, was increasingly being replaced by laws formulated by men, without reference to Islam. The jurisdiction of Islamic religious courts was being attenuated, and usury and the consumption of alcohol, anathematized by Islam, had begun to flourish. The Muslim Brotherhood pledged to restore Islamic traditions in regions under the influence of the West. The Brothers' were opposed to all Western ideologies which offered an alternative to Islam as the basis for organizing politics, law, and conduct. These included imperialism, as well as secularism, Marxism, and nationalism. The Brotherhood's mission was reflected in its promise to make "the Quran our constitution."

Syria's Muslim Brotherhood clashed early with the Ba'athists for obvious reasons. The Arab nationalists proposed to create a secular state, and sought to mobilize Arabs against their domination by the West by building a mass movement on the basis of shared ethnicity. By contrast, the Brothers proposed to restore Islam to the state and sought to mobilize Arabs on the basis of a fundamentalist Sunni interpretation of it. The secular nationalists—as the secularizing reformer Ataturk had done in Turkey—emulated Western modernity in order to overcome the backwardness that had allowed the Western world to dominate their countries. They would create secular societies and build modern economies in the Western fashion. The Brothers saw matters differently. Islam had once been a great military and economic power, greater than Europe. The solution to the decline of the Muslim world relative to the West was to return to the early days of Islam, when the Islamic world was a force to be reckoned with—militarily, economically, and scientifically. Like Marxists who saw the solution to the demise of communism in a return to the original works of Marx, before the "encrustations" of Leninism, Stalinism and Maoism would lead the world proletariat from what the "Salafist" Marxists saw as the one true path, the Brothers saw the solution to the decline of the Muslim world relative to the West in a return to Islam as it was practiced by the faith's original adherents.

Through the late 1940s and 1950s, Syria's Muslim Brothers and secular Arab nationalists were implacable foes, often engaging in bloody street battles. During one skirmish, a young Ba'athist activist named Hafez al-Assad was knifed by a Muslim Brother. The enmity between the vying forces continued after the Ba'athists came to power—becoming fiercer and more determined.

From the 1970s and into the second decade of the twenty-first century, the Muslim Brotherhood remained the most formidable internal opposition to secular Arab nationalist rule in Syria. The Brothers organized demonstrations, riots, and guerilla attacks against the Syrian state. The Ba'athists made efforts to accommodate the Islamists, with little success, and more often strenuously repressed the Brothers, sometimes bloodily. The struggle between the two would become a death feud.

Imperialist powers are accustomed to practicing a strategy of divide and rule, which often involves finding groups which have grievances against the local rulers and recruiting them as allies. For example, the Spanish built a great empire in the Americas by "finding local allies among the subordinated Indian peoples who helped topple the dominant native power in each region."[18] In Syria, the Muslim Brothers were the equivalent, as potential imperialist allies, of subordinated Indian peoples. They were happy to take whatever assistance Washington was willing to offer to try to force their shared enemy, the secular Arab nationalists, from power. There was evidence that the West was arming Muslim Brother guerillas as early as the 1980s, and secret U.S. diplomatic cables obtained by WikiLeaks revealed that the Bush administration began working with the Muslim Brothers to topple the Assad government in 2005, if not earlier. By 2012, a leaked U.S. Defense

Intelligence document showed that the Brothers were at the forefront of the insurrection against the Ba'athists, along with other Salafists and the al-Qaeda aligned AQI, forerunner of Islamic State. Al-Qaeda had been greatly influenced by the thinking of the Muslim Brotherhood's chief ideologue in the 1960s and 1970s, Sayyid Qutb. The two Islamist organizations that would come to dominate the fight on the ground against Syria's secular Arab nationalists, Islamic State and Jabhat al-Nusra, were Muslim Brotherhood-inspired al-Qaeda progeny.

The Saudi tyranny promoted an alternative political Islamist creed, the fourth force in Wall Street's war on Syria. Based on the thinking of the itinerant Islamic preacher Abd-al-Wahhab, who formed a political alliance with the Saud family in the eighteenth century, Wahhabism encouraged Sunni Muslims to self-identify as Sunnis in opposition to Shi'a "heretics." This divisive ideology undermined Arab unity and promoted intra-Arab strife, to the delight of the Arab world's oppressors—the United States, Israel and the Arab monarchs and military dictators who served as imperial minions. Wahhabism—which the Saudi tyranny spent enormous sums promoting throughout the Arab and Islamic worlds—was significant in the struggle for the control of the Syrian state for its role in fostering divisions among Arabs, encouraging them to fight among themselves over the question of who was the legitimate successor to Muhammad as caliph, rather than against U.S. domination and the local rulers who facilitated it.

The United States also endeavored to deepen sectarian cleavages in Syria by framing the conflict between secular Arab nationalists and Sunni political Islam as a battle between an Alawite minority, which had control of the state, and a Sunni Muslim majority, which had risen up against oppression by Alawite rulers. The basis of this myth lay in the fact that Syria's religious minorities were attracted to the Ba'ath Party to a greater extent than were Sunni Muslims, and when the Ba'athists came to power, the imbalance was reflected in the personnel of the state.

Ba'athism appealed strongly to religious minorities for three reasons. The first reason was because the Ba'athists' espoused secularism. Religious minorities perceived correctly that they would lead more secure lives in a secular state than they would under Muslim Brotherhood rule, where heterodox interpretations of Islam would be regarded with suspicion, and non-Muslim creeds would be frowned upon, and where politics, conduct and jurisprudence would be based on an alien faith.

The second reason Ba'athism had a strong appeal to religious minorities was because the Arab nationalists anathematized sectarianism, regarding attempts to elevate one sect above others as detrimental to the goal of building Arab unity. Ba'athist rule was regarded as a bulwark against the possibility of the Sunni majority exercising a majoritarian religious oppression.

Thirdly, class and religion intersected in Syria. Religious minority communities were disproportionately represented among poor, rural, laborers. Landowners and merchants, in contrast, tended to be Sunni. As a consequence, the Ba'ath Party's commitment to socialism attracted the poorest Syrians, who, at the same time, typically adhered to minority faiths. Sunni Muslims who were drawn to the Ba'athist program also tended to be of humble origin.

The tendency of a particular religious faith to be disproportionately represented in a political party has been replicated in other places and in other times. For example, there was a popular association of Jews with communism dating from the Bolshevik Revolution.[19] Jews were over-represented in the Bolshevik Party leadership, and many towering names in the communist movement were Jews. A "great many – perhaps most – American communists" were Jews. One FBI estimate held that in the late 1940s, "50 to 60 percent of Communist Party members were Jews."[20] Of course, it didn't follow that because most, or many, communists were Jews, that most, or many Jews, were communists. To draw this inference is to commit, what in formal logic, is known as the error of transposing the conditional. But some people, Hitler perhaps the most notable, believed they could discredit the communist movement by fostering a popular association of Judaism with communism through this very same transpositional error. The goal was to insinuate that because many Marxists were Jews that Marxism was the disguised political program of a religious minority. (Marxist internationalism had been developed, Hitler sneered, by the Jew Karl Marx.)

The same technique was used by the Muslim Brotherhood, and later U.S. state officials, along with the U.S. mass media, to foster a popular association between the Alawite faith and Syria's secular Arab nationalist government. Ba'athism, thus, was presented as the disguised political program of Syria's Alawite minority (advanced—the Muslim Brothers would sneer—by the Alawite heretics Hafez al-Assad and his son, Bashar). The U.S. contribution to wrapping an ideological struggle between secular Arab nationalism and Sunni political Islam in sectarian garb omitted the obvious Sunni Islamist language of the Muslim Brothers; Assad, for example, wasn't denounced by U.S. officials as a heretic. But his government was frequently referred to as Alawite-led, Alawite-dominated, and Alawite-controlled, while the insurrectionists were just as frequently described as overwhelmingly Sunni. A parallel practice would have been for Western journalists to have referred to the first Bolshevik government as Jewish-led, Jewish-dominated, and Jewish-controlled, and the insurrectionists who opposed it as overwhelmingly Russian Orthodox Christians. The West—its politicians and mass media—thus sought to shape an understanding of the conflict as one in which a religious minority was fighting to maintain an oppressive sectarian rule over the Sunni majority. Hitler had done the same by presenting Marxist internationalism as the tool of a religious minority, Jews, to stealthily bring about the oppression of the majority of Germans.

It was hoped, it seemed, that in describing the insurrectionists as overwhelmingly Sunni, that people would be lured into committing the error of transposing the conditional to erroneously conclude that Sunnis—who made up the large majority of Syria's population—were overwhelmingly opposed to the Syrian government. There was no evidence that this was true; on the contrary, there existed evidence that it wasn't. On the eve of the insurrection's outbreak, *Time* magazine reported that even "critics concede that Assad is popular" and that he had endeared himself, "personally, to the public." A week after the outbreak of violence in Daraa, *Time's* Rania Abouzeid would report that "there do not appear to be widespread calls for the fall of the regime or the removal of the relatively popular President." Moreover, the demands issued by the protesters and clerics did not include calls for Assad to step down. And the protests never reached a critical mass. On the contrary, the government continued to enjoy "the loyalty" of "a large part of the population," reported *Time*.[21] Over a month after the outbreak of violence in Daraa, the *New York Times'* Anthony Shadid would report that "the protests, so far, seemed to fall short of the popular upheaval of revolutions in Egypt and Tunisia."[22]

That the government commanded popular support was affirmed when the British survey firm YouGov conducted a poll in late 2011 showing that 55 percent of Syrians wanted Assad to stay. The poll received almost no mention in the Western media, prompting the British journalist Jonathan Steele to ask: "Suppose a respectable opinion poll found that most Syrians are in favor of Bashar al-Assad remaining as president, would that not be major news?" Steele described the poll findings as "inconvenient facts" which were suppressed because Western media coverage of the events in Syria had ceased "to be fair" and had turned into "a propaganda weapon."[23]

Descriptions of the Syrian government as Alawite-led were more than a little over-stated. Most members of Assad's cabinet belonged to Syria's Sunni majority—as most key members of the Saddam government in Iraq had belonged to Iraq's Shi'a majority. Despite this, both secular Arab nationalist governments were portrayed by U.S. officials as instruments of rule by a sectarian minority. Many key posts in Syria's security apparatus were occupied by Sunnis, and many of Syria's front-line generals were Sunni Muslims. What's more, the majority of the Syrian Arab Army's personnel were Sunni, making the Syrian army the largest Sunni fighting force in the country. Hafez al-Assad's right hand man, Mustafa Tlass, who served as defense minister for 30 years, was Sunni. And Bashar al-Assad's wife, Asma al-Assad (formerly Akhras), belonged to a prominent family of Sunni Muslims from Homs.

When Assad wasn't being falsely presented by Western sources as the leader of an oppressive sectarian minority, he was being misleadingly portrayed as a dictator with blood on his hands who was suppressing a movement for democratic change. This discourse was problematic for all sorts of reasons.

First, there was no evidence that the spring 2011 protests had any democratic content. On the contrary, the protesters' demands related to the release of political prisoners (mostly Muslim Brothers), the abolition of the wartime emergency law, and an end to corruption. *Time* magazine reported that Islam played a prominent role in the protests.[24] The government almost immediately announced a series of reforms in response to the unrest, including "greater freedom for the news media and political parties, and a reconsideration of the emergency rule."[25] Before the end of April 2011, Damascus had rescinded "the country's 48-year-old emergency law" and abolished "the Supreme State Security Court."[26] These concessions, however, did not stop the insurrection.

Second, Assad ruled with the consent of the governed. His name had been put forward in a presidential referendum and a majority of voters had approved. While this fell short of the multi-candidate presidential elections favored in the West, it was far more democratic than the hereditary succession that brought the king of Saudi Arabia and emir of Qatar, key U.S. allies in the war against Syria, to power in their countries. U.S. officials steered clear of describing the Saudi monarch as a dictator, even though he ruled by decree. Nor did they describe him as a despot with blood on his hands, despite his using tanks, mass arrests and executions to put down an uprising demanding a transition from tyranny to representative democracy in his own country. The Saudi autocrat also sent his tanks into Bahrain to bloodily suppress a pro-democracy uprising there.

Syria had an elected legislative body, and candidates from a number of parties stood for election in multi-candidate contests. The Saudis and Qataris had neither popular parliaments nor political parties. What's more, the Assad government took significant steps to move Syria even closer to Western-style representative democracy, amending the country's constitution in 2012 to transform presidential elections into multi-candidate contests. Assad stood for election against other candidates and won. Hence, in 2011 Syria was closer to the Western model of democracy than virtually all other Arab countries, and was certainly closer to Western-style democracy than were Washington's principal Arab allies, which were all monarchical or military dictatorships. By 2012, Syria had moved even closer to the Western model. If the uprising was driven by thirst for Western-style democracy, why did it continue after democratic reforms were enacted?

Third, the insurrectionists weren't democrats; they were Islamists whose goal was to establish an Islamic state in which the Quran, not democratic decision-making, would be the basis of the country's jurisprudence. Even the Free Syrian Army, falsely portrayed as an army of secular democrats, was largely Islamist; it was the military wing of the Muslim Brotherhood-dominated Syrian National Council. This explained why there was not a single reference to democracy in the army's stated goals. Its only objective, it said, was to overthrow Assad. That goal continued to guide the insurrectionists' mission, even after Assad made reforms to make Syria more like a Western-style representative democracy.

Hence, the conflict was misrepresented as a struggle between Alawite minority rulers and an oppressed Sunni majority and also as a dictatorship trying to crush popular aspirations for democracy. The clash between Sunni political Islam and secular

Arab nationalism—the post-independence leitmotif of Syria's political life—was nowhere in evidence in the way in which the conflict was limned in the West. The role played by U.S. imperialism was occasionally admitted for discussion, but even here the specific reasons for U.S. imperialist antagonism to the Syrian government were hardly ever spelled out, or even hinted at. If U.S. state officials or U.S. mass media outlets acknowledged the secular Arab ideology of the Syrian government, I'm not aware of it. References to Syria's socialist economy and Assad's refusal to fall in behind the United States' self-proclaimed role as leader of the global order—in order to assert Syrian interests and sovereignty—were notable for their absence.

The work of the scholar Lisa Stampnitzky on terrorism discourse is useful in illuminating the discourse on the Syrian conflict.[27] Stampnitzky argues that terrorism discourse is shaped by taboos which prevent serious analysis of the phenomenon. The taboos prevent one from seeing a terrorist as a rational actor with coherent, intelligible, goals. Instead, "terrorist" becomes a term of moral lapidation, and a demand to close off all inquiry into the "terrorist's" motivations, grievances and goals. Terrorists are to be understood as evil and irrational. It is unthinkable to contemplate that they may have legitimate complaints and rational objectives.

In the discourse on the Syrian conflict, "brutal dictator" and "Alawite sectarian" were used as terms comparable to "terrorist" to assert a moral judgment and to close all inquiry into the ideology of the Assad government. We were not to understand Damascus's secular Arab nationalists in political terms—as actors guided by the goals of fostering Arab unity, achieving self-determination, and using state ownership, guidance and economic planning to overcome underdevelopment. Instead, we were led to view the Assad government in moral terms. This was done by replacing analysis with moral stone throwing. Hence, Syria's Ba'athists were labeled as "dictatorial," "sectarian" and "brutal," while efforts to explore the Arab nationalists' aims, motivations and ideology were virtually absent from public discourse. Inquiry into the ideological basis of the government's actions was taboo. The entire purpose of the discourse on the Syrian conflict was to discredit the secular Arab nationalist government by hiding its ideology and goals beneath a patina of rhetoric about its alleged brutality and evil. The Assad government, itself, did the same to discredit the insurgents. Assad and key state officials employed the discourse of terrorism to discredit Syria's mujahedeen as energetically as did politicians in the West to discredit Islamists who carried out attacks on Western targets. Insurgents were regularly demonized as "terrorists" and even "mercenaries," the latter obloquy a reference to the fact that many insurgents received remuneration from the outside powers which financed the rebellion. This was a questionable rendering since a mercenary is motivated solely by lucre, and it was clear that most insurgents were ideologically driven. It was true that the insurgents used terrorist methods, and that Western politicians used the same discourse of terrorism to discredit al-Qaeda, but it was also clear that when Syrian government officials fulminated against terrorists, their objective, apart from expressing their indignation, was to tendentiously influence the way in which the conflict was understood. The Assad government wanted us to see the insurgents in moral terms, as evil, irrational actors, rather than in political terms, as rational actors with a competing view of how the state and society ought to be organized. This paralleled U.S. efforts to shape public opinion to view the Assad government in the same moral terms, as monstrous, autocratic, and sectarian—evil, in other words—rather than in political terms, as rational actors with a view of how Syrian society, and the broader Arab world, should be organized, that differed from the views of Sunni political Islamists and U.S. imperialists.

The ideology of the insurgents was just as important to understanding the conflict as was that of the secular Arab nationalists who controlled the state. But political Islam was only occasionally addressed in public discourse as a driving force of the conflict. Instead, the preferred discourse in the West was one of moral approbation where the insurgents were concerned. Discourse about "moderate rebels" was unceasing. The words "moderate" and "rebels" intimated that Islamist guerillas were not Islamists at all, but secular pro-democrats, though the head of U.S. National Intelligence, James Clapper, scotched that fiction when he pointed out that "moderates" meant "not belonging to Islamic State," a category which included such Islamist groups as Jabhat al-Nusra, Ahrar al-Sham and the Muslim Brotherhood. But like the YouGov poll which showed Assad had the support of a majority of Syrians, this inconvenient truth was suppressed.

Wall Street's war on Syria was also an ideological war on U.S. citizens. By reducing the Syrian government to a single person, Assad, and by repeatedly denouncing him as an Alawite dictator with blood on his hands, a number of ideological tasks were accomplished. First, a justification was provided for Washington's leading a campaign to force the Syrian president to step down. After all, if Assad was a monster, it was necessary and just that the United Sates lead the "international community" to undertake this exigent moral task. Second, Washington's implacable opposition to the Syrian government—rooted in the Arab nationalists' refusal to pander to the profit-making imperatives of Wall Street—was hidden behind a moral veil. We were to believe that Washington was impelled to force Assad from power by the United States' (self-proclaimed) pro-democratic sentiments, rather than because Syria's secular Arab nationalists embraced a Wall Street-unfriendly program of fostering Arab unity, promoting independence and pursuing Arab socialism. Third, by portraying Assad as a bloody tyrant, Washington framed its role in working to overthrow him as an indication that the United States was, indeed, a force for good in the world.

To be sure, the United States government is a force for good in the world, though hardly for the good of all, and only for the good of an infinitesimally small fraction of the world's population, namely, the class of billionaire investors, mega-rich bankers, and wealthy CEOs based in the United States. Owing to the immense money power of this small-in-numbers class, it exercises outsized influence over U.S. public policy, ensuring that the powerful apparatus of the U.S. state is used on its behalf to get its way in the world. The values which secular Arab nationalists promoted were antithetical to U.S. capitalist class interests, which were embodied in U.S. imperialist ideology. That ideology encouraged states to fall in behind U.S. leadership, described as "essential" and "indispensable," and demanded that economies be open to U.S. goods, services and investments—and on terms favorable to U.S. corporate profit-making. In defiance, Arab nationalist states in Syria and Iraq instilled in schoolchildren the values of self-determination, Arab socialism, and Arab unity—entirely at odds with what Wall Street-dominated Washington called "American values and interests." Of course, these values and interests related to U.S. global economic "leadership," whose purpose was to protect and promote the pursuit of profit by U.S. capitalists. Corporate America was to receive unimpeded access to markets and investment opportunities anywhere in the world, regardless of the wishes of the people who lived in whatever part of the world the quest for profits drove it. The U.S.-superintended global economy, into which all countries would be integrated—by force if necessary—was to be regulated by markets, not economic plans drawn up by the state to serve the public interest. Moreover, it was to operate on the basis of enterprises owned by wealthy investors and great banks—preferably American—and not states. And its goal would be profit-making, not the satisfaction of human needs.

In the U.S. war on Syria, the power-elite representatives of the U.S. capitalist class—the Wall Street-connected cabinet level officials, the top bureaucrats, and members of the United States' most prestigious think tanks—struck an alliance of convenience with the Syrian government's Islamist foes, to bring down a Ba'ath Arab Socialist Party government which was "a focus of Arab nationalistic struggle against an American regional presence and interests."[28] Washington had already done the same to two other foci of Arab nationalistic struggle: Saddam's government in Iraq, and Gaddafi's government in Libya. All three campaigns represented but individual battles in a greater overall war to effectively re-colonize the planet by integrating the last Arab champions of colonial emancipation into a U.S.-led global order in which Wall Street's interests would have primacy.

BIBLIOGRAPHY

Ayoob, Mohammed. *The Many Faces of Political Islam: Religions and Politics in the Muslim Word*. The University of Michigan Press, 2008.

Baer, Robert. *Sleeping with the Devil: How Washington Sold Our Soul for Saudi Crude*. Three Rivers Press, 2003.

Césaire, Aimé. *Discourse on Colonialism*. Monthly Review Press, 2000.

Collelo, Thomas, ed. *A Country Study: Syria*. Washington, D.C.: Federal Research Division, Library of Congress, 1988.

Cumings, Bruce, Ervand Abrahamian and Moshe Ma'oz. *Inventing the Axis of Evil: The Truth about North Korea, Iran, and Syria*. The New Press, 2004.

Dawisha, Adeed. *Arab Nationalism in the Twentieth Century*. Princeton University Press, 2005.

Domhoff, William G. *Who Rules America? Power and Politics*. McGraw Hill, 2002.

Dutt, R. Palme. *The Problem of India*. New York: International Publishers, 1943.

Dreyfuss, Robert. *Devil's Game: How the United States Helped Unleash Fundamentalist Islam*. Holt, 2005.

Ferguson, Thomas. *Golden Rule: The Investment Theory of Party Competition and the Logic of Money-Driven Political Systems*. The University of Chicago Press, 1995.

Haldane, J.B.S. *Callinicus: A Defence of Chemical Warfare*. Kegan Paul, Trench, Trubner & Co., 1925.

Hitler, Adolph. *Mein Kampf: The Official 1939 Edition*. CODA Books, 2011.

James, Lawrence. *Churchill and Empire: A Portrait of an Imperialist*. Pegasus Books, 2015.

Khaled, Leila (ed. George Hajjar). *My People Shall Live: The Autobiography of a Revolutionary*. Hodder and Stoughton, 1973.

Khalidi, Rashid. *The Iron Cage: The Story of the Palestinian Struggle for Statehood.* Beacon Press, 2007.

Lindqvist, Svend. *The Dead Do Not Die: Exterminate All The Brutes and Terra Nullius.* The New Press, 2014.

Losurdo, Domenic. *War and Revolution: Rethinking the 20th Century.* Verso, 2015.

Macpherson, C.B. *The Real World of Democracy.* CBC Enterprises, 1965.

Matthiesen, Toby. *Sectarian Gulf: Bahrain, Saudi Arabia, and the Arab Spring That Wasn't.* Stanford Briefs. Stanford University Press, 2013.

Miliband, Ralph. *The State in Capitalist Society.* Merlin Press, 2009.

Motadel, David. *Islam and Nazi Germany's War.* The Belknap Press of Harvard University Press, 2014.

Mueller, John. *Overblown: How Politicians and the Terrorism Industry Inflate National Security Threats, and Why We Believe Them.* Free Press, 2006.

Mueller, John and Mark G. Stewart. *Chasing Ghosts: The Policing of Terrorism.* Oxford University Press, 2016.

Muttitt, Greg. *Fuel on the Fire: Oil and Politics in Occupied Iraq.* The New Press, 2012.

Novick, Peter. *The Holocaust in American Life.* Houghton Mifflin, 2000.

Olusoga, David and Casper W Erichsen. *The Kaiser's Holocaust: Germany's Forgotten Genocide and the Colonial Roots of Nazism.* Faber and Faber, 2010.

Pape, Robert A. *Dying to Win: The Strategic Logic of Suicide Terrorism.* Random House, 2005.

Polk, William R. *Understanding Iraq.* Harper Perennial, 2005.

Polk, William R. *Understanding Iran: Everything You Need to Know, From Persia to the Islamic Republic, From Cyrus to Ahmadinejad.* Palgrave MacMillan, 2009.

Polk, William R. *Humpty Dumpty: The Fate of Regime Change.* Panda Press, 2013.

Barry Rubin, ed. *Revolutionaries and Reformers: Contemporary Islamist Movements in the Middle East.* State University of New York Press, 2003.

Seale, Patrick. *Asad of Syria: The Struggle for the Middle East.* University of California Press, 1995.

Shoup, Laurence H. *Wall Street's Think Tank: The Council on Foreign Relations and the Empire of Neoliberal Geopolitics, 1976-2014.* Monthly Review Press, 2015.

Shoup, Laurence H. and William Minter. *Imperial Brain Trust: The Council on Foreign Relations & United States Foreign Policy.* Authors Choice Press, 2004.

Smith, S.A. *The Russian Revolution.* Sterling, 2002.

Stampnitzky, Lisa. *Disciplining Terror: How Experts Invented Terrorism.* Cambridge University Press, 2013.

Szymanski, Albert. *The Logic of Imperialism.* Praeger, 1983.

Szymanski, Albert. *Human Rights in the Soviet Union.* Zed Books, 1984.

Taylor, Alan. *Colonial America: A Very Short Introduction.* Oxford University Press, 2013.

Toye, Richard. *Churchill's Empire: The World that Made Him and the World he Made.* St. Martins Griffen, 2011.

Van Dam, Nikolaos. *The Struggle for Power in Syria: Politics and Society under Asad and the Ba'ath Party.* I.B. Tauris, 2011.

Vine, David. *Base Nation: How U.S. Military Bases Abroad Harm America and the World.* Metropolitan Books, 2015.

NOTES

Introduction

1. "Syrian rebels elect head of new military command," *Reuters,* December 8, 2012.
2. Bassem Mroue and Benn Hubbard, "Syria rebels create new unified military command," *Associated Press,* December 8, 2012.
3. Inti Landauro and Stacy Meichtry, "Rebels in Syria move to show moderation," *The Wall Street Journal,* June 27, 2013.
4. Belen Fernandez, review of *The Jihadis Return: ISIS and the New Sunni Uprising,* by Patrick Cockburn, *The Middle East Eye,* September 3, 2014.
5. Craig Whitlock, "Niger rapidly emerging as a key U.S. partner," *The Washington Post,* April 14, 2013.
6. Alfred B. Prados and Jeremy M. Sharp, "Syria: Political Conditions and Relations with the United States After the Iraq War," *Congressional Research Service,* February 28, 2005.
7. Report of the Defense Science Board Task Force on Strategic Communications, September 2004, Office of the Undersecretary of Defense for Acquisition, Technology and Logistics, quoted in Glenn Greenwald, "when the State Department tries to choose Muslim thought leaders to win 'hearts and minds'." *The Intercept,* December 15, 2015.
8. Martin Gilens and Benjamin I. Page, "Testing Theories of American Politics: Elites, Interest Groups, and Average Citizens," *Perspectives on Politics,* Fall, 2014.
9. Statement by Robert Mugabe at the 71st Session of the United Nations General Assembly, September 21, 2016.
10. Fisher, "Obama acknowledging."
11. Barack Obama, *State of the Union Address,* January 13, 2016, https://www.whitehouse.gov/sotu.
12. U.S. Department of State, *FY 2004-2009 Department of State and USAID Strategic Plan.* http://www.state.gov/s/d/rm/rls/dosstrat/2004/index.htm.

13. The White House, Washington. *National Security Strategy*, February 2015. https://www.whitehouse.gov/sites/default/files/docs/2015_national_security_strategy.pdf.

14. Robert Baer, *Sleeping with the Devil: How Washington Sold Our Soul for Saudi Crude*, (Three Rivers Press, 2003), 127.

15. Ibid.

16. Jay Solomon, "To check Syria, U.S. explores bond with Muslim Brothers," *The Wall Street Journal*, July 25, 2007.

17. Robert Dreyfuss, *Devil's Game: How the United States Helped Unleash Fundamentalist Islam* (Holt, 2005), 37.

18. *National Security Strategy*, February 2015.

19. "President al-Assad: Basis for any political solution for crisis in Syria is what the Syrian people want." (interview with Argentina's Clarin newspaper and Telam news agency), *Syria Online*, http://www.syriaonline.sy/?f=Details&catid=12&pageid=5835.

20. J.B.S. Haldane, *Callinicus: A Defence of Chemical Warfare* (Kegan Paul, Trench, Trubner & Co., 1925), 5-6.

21. Ibid, 49.

22. John Mueller and Karl Mueller, "Sanctions of Mass Destruction," *Foreign Affairs*, May/June 1999.

23. Ibid.

24. Stephen Gowans, "Rethinking chemical Weapons," *what's left*, June 27, 2015.

25. John Mueller and Karl Mueller, "Sanctions of Mass Destruction," *Foreign Affairs*, May/June 1999.

26. "A 1993 analysis by the Office of Technology Assessment of the U.S. Congress finds that a ton of sarin gas perfectly delivered under absolutely ideal conditions over a heavily populated area against unprotected people would cause between 3,000 and 8,000 deaths. Under slightly less ideal circumstances—if there is a moderate wind or if the sun is out, for example—the death rate would be one-tenth as great." (John Mueller, *Overblown: How Politicians and the Terrorism Industry Inflate National Security Threats, and Why We Believe Them* (Free Press, 2006), 18.) The UN estimated that rockets carrying a payload of between 11 and 16 gallons of chemical agent were used in the 2013 chemical weapons attack in Ghouta, Syria. ("Syria chemical attack: What we know," *BBC*, September 24, 2013.) Assuming an average payload of 13 gallons and 358 gallons per ton, then 13 gallons of sarin gas perfectly delivered under absolutely ideal conditions over a heavily populated area against unprotected people would cause between 108 and 290 deaths.

27. Mueller & Mueller, "Sanctions."

Chapter one • The Den of Arabism

1. William R. Polk, "Understanding Syria: From pre-civil war to post-Assad," *The Atlantic*, December 10, 2013.
2. Adeed Dawisha, *Arab Nationalism in the Twentieth Century* (Princeton University Press, 2005), 3.
3. Polk, "Understanding Syria."
4. Dawisha, *Arab Nationalism*, 3.
5. Rashid Khalidi, *The Iron Cage: The story of the Palestinian Struggle for Statehood* (Beacon Press, 2007).
6. Leila Khalid, *My People Shall Live: The Autobiography of a Revolutionary*, (Hodder and Stoughton, 1973).
7. Martin Kramer, "Arab Nationalism: Mistaken Identity," *Daedalus* 122.3 (1993): 171-206.
8. Polk, "Understanding Syria."
9. *The National Security Strategy of the United States of America*, February 2015.
10. The White House, Washington. *National Security Strategy*, March 2006. https://www.comw.org/qdr/fulltext/nss2006.pdf.
11. *National Security Strategy*, March 2006.
12. Greg Muttitt, *Fuel on the Fire: Oil and Politics in Occupied Iraq*, The New Press, 2012, p. 73.
13. Ibid.
14. Ibid.
15. Muttitt, *Fuel on the Fire*, 75.
16. Samuel Helfont and Michael Brill, "Saddam ISIS? The Terrorist Group's Real Origin Story," *Foreign Affairs*, January 12, 2016.
17. Muttitt, *Fuel on the Fire*, 78.
18. Baer, *Sleeping with the Devil*, 123.
19. Baer, *Sleeping with the Devil*, 193.
20. C.B. Macpherson, *The Real World of Democracy* (CBC Enterprises, 1965), 26-27.
21. Domenico Losurdo, *War and Revolution: Rethinking the 20th Century* (Verso, 2015).
22. S.A. Smith, *The Russian Revolution* (Sterling, 2002), 118.
23. Albert Szymanski, *Human Rights in the Soviet Union* (Zed Books, 1984), 210.
24. Domenico Losurdo, *War and Revolution: Rethinking the 20th Century* (Verso, 2015), 258.
25. Samuel Black, "The changing political utility of nuclear weapons: Nuclear threats from 1970 to 2010," *The Stimson Center*, August 2010.
26. C.B. Macpherson, *The Real World*, 27.

27. Martin Gilens and Benjamin I. Page, "Testing Theories of American Politics: Elites, Interest Groups, and Average Citizens," *Perspectives on Politics*, Fall 2014.
28. "A Letter to G. Myasnikov," *Lenin's Collected Works, 1st English Edition*, vol. 32, (Progress Publishers, 1965), 504-509.
29. David M. Herszenhorn, "For Syria, Reliant on Russia for weapons and food, old bonds run deep," *The New York Times*, February 18, 2012.
30. Zeina Karam, "In rare public appearance, Syrian president denies role in Houla massacre," *The Associated Press*, June 3, 2012.
31. Bashar al-Assad May 19, 2013 interview with Clarin newspaper and Telam news agency.
32. Ibid.
33. *National Security Strategy*, February 2015.
34. Ibid.
35. U.S. State Department website, Accessed February 8, 2012, http://www.state.gov/r/pa/ei/bgn/3580.htm#econ.
36. *The National Security Strategy of the United States of America*, September 2002.
37. *National Security Strategy*, February 2015.
38. *National Security Strategy*, March 2006.
39. William R. Polk, *Humpty Dumpty: The Fate of Regime Change* (Panda Press, 2013), 279.
40. Polk, *Humpty Dumpty*, 275.
41. Polk, *Humpty Dumpty*, 278.
42. Polk, *Humpty Dumpty*, 281-282.
43. Benoit Faucon, "For big oil, the Libya opening that wasn't," *The Wall Street Journal*, May 4, 2012.
44. Guy Chazan, "For West's oil firms, no love lost in Libya," *The Wall Street Journal*, April 15, 2011.
45. Steven Mufson, "Conflict in Libya: U.S. oil companies sit on sidelines as Gaddafi maintains hold," *The Washington Post*, June 10, 2011.
46. Ibid.
47. Ibid.
48. Clifford Kraus, "The Scramble for Access to Libya's Oil Wealth Begins," *The New York Times*, August 22, 2011.
49. Greg Muttitt, *Fuel on the Fire: Oil and Politics in Occupied Iraq* (The New Press, 2012), 315.
50. Ibid.
51. Bruce Cumings, Ervand Abrahamian and Moshe Ma'oz, *Inventing the Axis of Evil: The Truth about North Korea, Iran, and Syria*, (The New Press, 2004), 185.
52. Blair Shewchuck, "Saddam or Mr. Hussein?" *CBC News Online*, February 2003.

53. Muttitt, *Fuel*, 113.
54. William R. Polk, *Understanding Iraq* (Harper Perennial, 2005), 127-128.
55. Polk, *Understanding Iraq*, 127-128.
56. Polk, *Humpty Dumpty*, 248.
57. Ibid.
58. Ibid.
59. Dreyfuss, *Devil's Game*, 99.
60. Bernard Lewis, "Rethinking the Middle East," *Foreign Affairs*, September 1, 1992.
61. Laurence H. Shoup, *Wall Street's Think Tank: The Council on Foreign Relations and the Empire of Neoliberal Geopolitics, 1976-2014*, Monthly Review Press, 2015, p. 215.
62. Amy Harder and Colleen McCain Nelson, "Obama administration rejects Keystone XL pipeline, citing climate concerns," *The Wall Street Journal*, November 6, 2015.
63. Juan Forero, "Center of gravity in oil world shifts to America," *The Washington Post*, May 25, 2012.
64. Juliet Eilperin, "Canadian government overhauling environmental rules to aid oil extraction," *The Washington Post*, June 3, 2012.
65. Clifford Kraus and Eric Lipton, "U.S. inches toward goal of energy independence," *The New York Times*, March 22, 2012.
66. Albert Szymanski, *The Logic of Imperialism*, (Praeger, 1983), 167.
67. Szymanski, *Imperialism*, 166.
68. Muttitt, *Fuel*, 74.
69. Muttitt, *Fuel*, 87.
70. *Coalition Provisional Authority Order Number 1*, May 16, 2003, http://www.iraqcoalition.org/regulations/20030516_CPAORD_1_De-Ba_athification_of_Iraqi_Society_.pdf.
71. Muttitt, *Fuel*, 229.
72. Polk, *Understanding Iraq*, 205.
73. Polk, *Understanding Iraq*, 206.
74. Ibid.
75. Marjorie Cohn, "Want endless war? Love the U.S. empire? Well, Hillary Clinton's your choice," *Truthdig*, February 1, 2016, http://www.truthdig.com/report/item/want_endless_war_love_the_us_empire_hillary_clintons_your_choice_20160201.
76. Ian Cobain, "Britain's secret wars," *The Guardian*, September 8, 2016.
77. Ibid.
78. Ibid.
79. Ibid.
80. Ibid.
81. Ibid.

82. Jamie Merrrill, "Major British defense deal with Oman comes under fire," *Middle East Eye*, May 20, 2016.
83. Yohann Koshy, "The Middle East correspondents who predicted the rise of ISIS tells us about his 30-year career," *Vice*, March 25, 2016.
84. Polk, *Humpty Dumpty*, 248.
85. Shirley Ceresto, "Socialism, capitalism and inequality," *The Insurgent Sociologist*, Spring 1982.
86. David Vine, *Base Nation: How U.S. Military Bases Abroad Harm America and the World* (Metropolitan Books, 2015).
87. Craig Whitlock, "Niger rapidly emerging as a key U.S. partner," *The Washington Post*, April 14, 2013.

Chapter two • Regime Change

1. "Resources of hope," *Al-Ahram Weekly* (631), April 2, 2003.
2. Cumings, Abrahamian and Ma'oz, *Inventing the Axis of Evil*, 207.
3. Ben Fenton, "Macmillan backed Syria assassination plot," *The Guardian*, September 27, 2003.
4. Ibid.
5. Ibid.
6. Dreyfus, *Devil's Game*, 199-200.
7. Cumings, Abrahamian and Ma'oz, *Inventing the Axis of Evil*, 182.
8. Dreyfus, *Devil's Game*, 199-200.
9. Cumings, Abrahamian and Ma'oz, *Inventing the Axis of Evil*, 183.
10. Jay Solomon, "To check Syria, U.S. explores bond with Muslim Brothers," *The Wall Street Journal*, July 25, 2007.
11. Cumings, Abrahamian and Ma'oz, *Inventing the Axis of Evil*, 183; Dreyfus, *Devil's Game*, 200.
12. Gareth Porter, "The real U.S. Syria scandal: supporting sectarian war," August 30, 2016, http://www.middleeasteye.net/columns/real-us-syria-scandal-supporting-sectarian-war-1378989458.
13. Baer, *Sleeping with the Devil*, 207.
14. Nikolas Van Dam, *The Struggle for Power in Syria: Politics and Society under Asad and the Ba'ath Party*, (I.B. Taurus, 2011), 98.
15. Van Dam, *Struggle*, 107-108.
16. Dreyfus, *Devil's Game*, 200-201.
17. Robert Fisk, "Conspiracy of silence in the Arab world," *The Independent*, February 9, 2007.
18. Dreyfus, *Devil's Game*, 205.
19. Polk, "Understanding Syria."
20. Dreyfus, *Devil's Game*, 205.
21. Ibid.
22. Polk, "Understanding Syria."

23. Van Dam, *Struggle.*
24. Patrick Cockburn, "Confused about the U.S. response to Isis in Syria? Look to the CIA's relationship with Saudi Arabia," *The Independent,* June 17, 2016.
25. Jay Solomon, "To check Syria, U.S. explores bond with Muslim Brothers," *The Wall Street Journal,* July 25, 2007.
26. Liad Porat, "The Syrian Muslim Brotherhood and the Asad Regime," *Crown Center for Middle East Studies,* Brandeis University, December 2010, No. 47.
27. Solomon, "To check Syria."
28. Ibid.
29. Porat, "The Syrian Muslim Brotherhood."
30. Ibid.
31. DIA document leaked to Judicial Watch, Inc., a conservative, non-partisan educational foundation, which promotes transparency, accountability and integrity in government, politics and the law. http://www.judicialwatch.org/wp-content/uploads/2015/05/Pg.-291-Pgs.-287-293-JW-v-DOD-and-State-14-812-DOD-Release-2015-04-10-final-version11.pdf .
32. Alfred B. Prados and Jeremy M. Sharp, "Syria: Political Conditions and Relations with the United States After the Iraq War," Congressional Research Service, February 28, 2005.
33. Andrew Browne, "Rodrigo Duterte throws a grenade in Washington's China strategy," *The Wall Street Journal,* September 7, 2016.
34. Max Fisher, "Obama acknowledging U.S. misdeeds abroad, quietly reframes American power," *The New York Times,* September 7, 2016.
35. "Address by President Obama to the 71st Session of the United Nations General Assembly," September 20, 2016.
36. Fisher, "Obama acknowledging."
37. Fisher, "Obama acknowledging."
38. Alfred B. Prados and Jeremy M. Sharp, "Syria: Political Conditions and Relations with the United States After the Iraq War," *Congressional Research Service,* February 28, 2005.
39. Ibid.
40. Ibid.
41. Ibid.
42. Ibid.
43. Alfred B. Prados, "Syria: U.S. Relations and Bilateral Issues," *Congressional Research Service,* March 13, 2006.
44. Ibid.
45. Ibid.
46. Ibid.
47. Ibid.

48. Prados and Sharp, "Syria: Political Conditions and Relations."
49. Ibid.
50. Ibid.
51. *National Security Strategy*, March 2006.
52. National Security Strategy, September 2002.
53. Prados, "Syria: U.S. Relations and Bilateral Issues."
54. Ibid.
55. Ibid.
56. Nada Bakri, "Sanctions pose growing threat to Syria's Assad," *The New York Times*, October 10, 2011.
57. Joby Warrick and Alice Fordham, "Syria running out of cash as sanctions take toll, but Assad avoids economic pain," *The Washington Post*, April 24, 2012.
58. Patrick Cockburn, "U.S. and E.U. sanctions are ruining ordinary Syrians' lives, yet Bashar al-Assad hangs on to power," *The Independent*, October 7, 2016.
59. Ibid.
60. Prados, "Syria: U.S. Relations and Bilateral Issues."
61. Jay Solomon, "To check Syria, U.S. explores bond with Muslim Brothers," *The Wall Street Journal*, July 25, 2007.
62. "U.S. admits funding Syrian opposition," *CBC News*, April 18, 2011.
63. Craig Whitlock, "U.S. secretly backed Syrian opposition groups, cables released by WikiLeaks show," *The Washington Post*, April 17, 2011.
64. Patrick Cockburn, "Syria in 2016 will be like the Balkans in 1914 as explosive violence breaks out on an international scale," *The Independent*, December 12, 2015.
65. "Gen. Wesley Clark Weighs Presidential Bid: 'I Think About It Every Day,'" *Democracy Now!*, March 2, 2007.
66. Ibid.
67. *National Security Strategy*, September 2002.
68. National Security Strategy, March 2006.
69. "Address by President Obama to the 71st Session of the United Nations General Assembly," September 20, 2016.

Chapter three • The 2011 Distemper

1. Aryn Baker, "Syria is not Egypt, but might it one day be Tunisia?" *Time*, February 4, 2011.
2. Rania Abouzeid, "The Syrian style of repression: Thugs and lectures," *Time*, February 27, 2011.
3. Rania Abouzeid, "Sitting pretty in Syria: Why few go backing Bashar," *Time*, March 6, 2011.

4. Rania Abouzeid, "The youth of Syria: the rebels are on pause," *Time*, March 6, 2011.
5. Ibid.
6. "Officers fire on crowd as Syrian protests grow," *The New York Times*, March 20, 2011.
7. Nicholas Blanford, "Can the Syrian regime divide and conquer its opposition?" *Time*, April 9, 2011.
8. Robert Fisk, "Welcome to Dera'a, Syria's graveyard of terrorists," *The Independent*, July 6, 2016.
9. "President Assad to ARD TV: Terrorists breached cessation of hostilities agreement from the very first hour, Syrian Army refrained from retaliating," Interview, *SANA*, March 1, 2016.
10. Ibid.
11. "Officers fire on crowd."
12. Rania Abouzeid, "Arab Spring: Is a revolution starting up in Syria?" *Time*, March 20, 2011; Rania Abouzeid, "Syria's revolt: How graffiti stirred an uprising," *Time*, March 22, 2011.
13. "Officers fire on crowd."
14. Rania Abouzeid, "Arab Spring: Is a revolution starting up in Syria?" *Time*, March 20, 2011.
15. "Thousands march to protest Syria killings," *The New York Times*, March 24, 2011.
16 Rania Abouzeid, "Assad and reform: Damned if he does, doomed if he doesn't," *Time*, April 22, 2011.
17. "Officers fire on crowd."
18. Aryn Baker, "Syria is not Egypt, but might it one day be Tunisia?" *Time*, February 4, 2011.
19. Nicholas Blanford, "Can the Syrian regime divide and conquer its opposition?" *Time*, April 9, 2011.
20. Rania Abouzeid, "Syria's Friday of dignity becomes a day of death," *Time*, March 25, 2011.
21. Ibid.
22. "Syrie: un autre eclarage du conflict qui dure depuis 5 ans," *Be Curious TV* video, May 23, 2016. http://www.globalresearch.ca/syria-aleppo-doctor-demolishes-imperialist-propaganda-and-media-warmongering/5531157.
23. Nicholas Blanford, "Can the Syrian regime divide and conquer its opposition?" *Time*, April 9, 2011.
24. Anthony Shadid, "Security forces kill dozens in uprisings around Syria," *The New York Times*, April 22, 2011.
25. Rania Abouzeid, "Syria's Friday of dignity becomes a day of death," *Time*, March 25, 2011.
26. Peter Novick, *The Holocaust in American Life* (Houghton Mifflin, 1999) p. 33.

27. "Seymour Hersh's latest bombshell: U.S. military undermined Obama on Syria with tacit help to Assad," *Democracy Now*, December 22, 2015.

28. Fabrice Balanche, "The Alawi Community and the Syria Crisis," *Middle East Institute*, May 14, 2015.

29. Anthony Shadid, "Syria broadens deadly crackdown on protesters," *The New York Times*, May 8, 2011.

30. Rania Abouzeid, "Meet the Islamist militants fighting alongside Syria's rebels," *Time*, July 26, 2012.

31. Rania Abouzeid, "Interview with official of Jabhat al-Nusra, Syria's Islamist militia group," *Time*, December 25, 2015.

32. Robert Fisk, "Syrian civil war: West failed to factor in Bashar al-Assad's Iranian backers as the conflict developed," *The Independent*, March 13, 2016.

33. Anthony Shadid, "Syria broadens deadly crackdown on protesters," *The New York Times*, May 8, 2011.

34. Nada Bakri, "Syria allows Red Cross officials to visit prison," *The New York Times*, September 5, 2011.

35. Nada Bakri, "Syrian opposition calls for protection from crackdown," *The New York Times*, October 25, 2011.

36. "President al-Assad to Portuguese State TV: International system failed to accomplish its duty... Western officials have no desire to combat terrorism, Interview, *SANA*, March 5, 2015.

37. Yohann Koshy, "The Middle East correspondents who predicted the rise of ISIS tells us about his 30-year career," *Vice*, March 25, 2016.

38. James R. Clapper, "James Clapper on Global Intelligence Challenges," March 2, 2015. Jr.Council on Foreign Relations, http://www.cfr.org/ homeland-security/james-clapper-global-intelligence-challenges/ p36195.

39. Rania Abouzeid, "Sitting pretty in Syria: Why few go backing Bashar," *Time*, March 6, 2011.

40. Rania Abouzeid, "The youth of Syria: the rebels are on pause," *Time*, March 6, 2011.

41. "Can the Syrian regime divide and conquer its opposition?" *Time*, April 9, 2011.

42. Anthony Shadid, "Security forces kill dozens in uprisings around Syria," *The New York Times*, April 22, 2011.

43. William Blum, "The Anti-Empire Report," No. 146, November 6, 2016.

44. Samuel Black, "The changing political utility of nuclear weapons: Nuclear threats from 1970 to 2010," *The Stimson Center*, August 2010.

45. Craig Whitlock, "U.S. secretly backed Syrian opposition groups, cables released by Wikileaks show," *The Washington Post*, April 17, 2011.

46. Lenin, "A Letter to G. Myasnikov," 504-509.

47. Patrick Seale, "In Syria, this is no plan for peace," *The Guardian (UK)*, May 27, 2012.

48. "President Assad to ARD TV: Terrorists breached cessation of hostilities agreement from the very first hour, Syrian Army refrained from retaliating," Interview, *SANA*, March 1, 2016.

49. Nicholas D. Kristof, "Bahrain pulls a Qaddafi," *The New York Times*, March 16, 2011.

50. Nick Cumming-Bruce, "U.N. accuses Yemen of using deadly force in protests," *The New York Times*, September 14, 2011.

51. "Saudi response to increasing violence in Eastern Province," Stratfor, January 17, 2012.

52. Steve Chase, "Saudi Arabia's al-Qatif a growing hotbed of opposition," *The Globe and Mail*, May 13, 2016.

53. Steven Chase, "Saudis use armoured vehicles to suppress internal dissent, videos show," *The Globe and Mail*, May 11, 2016.

54. Kareem Fahim, "As hopes for reform fade in Bahrain, protesters turn anger on the United states," *The New York Times*, June 24, 2012.

55. Alex Delmar-Morgan, "Protests, investigator pressure Bahrain," *The Wall Street Journal*, March 9, 2012.

56. Greg Miller and Karen De Young, "Secret CIA effort in Syria faces large funding cut," *The Washington Post*, June 12, 2015; Greg Millar and Adam Entous, "Plans to send heavier weapons to CIA-backed rebels in Syria stall amid White House scepticism," *The Washington Post*, October 23, 2016.

57. Margherita Stancati and Nathan Hodge, "Karzai's Afghan legacy rests on fragile unity," *The Wall Street Journal*, September 28, 2014.

58. Henry Fountain, "Researchers link Syrian conflict to drought made worse by climate change," *The New York Times*, March 2, 2015.

59. Aryn Baker, "Syria is not Egypt, but might it one day be Tunisia?" *Time*, February 4, 2011.

60. DIA document leaked to Judicial Watch, Inc., a conservative, non-partisan educational foundation, which promotes transparency, accountability and integrity in government, politics and the law. Judicial Watch website. http://www.judicialwatch.org/wp-content/uploads/2015/05/Pg.-291-Pgs.-287-293-JW-v-DOD-and-State-14-812-DOD-Release-2015-04-10-final-version11.pdf.

61. Yaroslav Trofimov, "Jordan's election poses a test for Muslim Brotherhood's change," *The Wall Street Journal*, August 25, 2016.

62. David N. Gibbs, "Afghanistan: The Soviet Invasion in Retrospect," *International Politics* 37.2 (2000): 241-242.

Chapter four • The Myth of the Moderate Rebel

1. Country study, 256.

2. Porat, 2010.

3. Ibid.
4. Nicholas Blanford, "Can the Syrian regime divide and conquer its opposition?" *Time*, April 9, 2011.
5. Nour Malas, Joe Parkinson and Jay Solomon, "Nations pledge aid to rebels in Syria," *The Wall Street Journal*, April 1, 2012.
6. Nour Malas, "'Friends' of Syria expected to spar over arming rebels," *The Wall Street Journal*, February 21, 2012.
7. Karen DeYoung and Liz Sly, "Syrian rebels get influx of arms with gulf neighbors' money, U.S. coordination," *The Washington Post*, May 15, 2012.
8. Robert F. Worth, "Egypt is arena for influence of Arab rivals," *The New York Times*, July 9, 2013.
9. Nour Malas and Siobhan Gorman, "Syrian brass defect, buoying rebels," *The Wall Street Journal*, March 9, 2012.
10. Anne Barnard, "Syria opposition group is routed and divided," *The New York Times*, March 14, 2012.
11. Charles Levinson, "As Syria strikes kill scores, opposition seeks backing," *The Wall Street Journal*, February 10, 2012.
12. Greg Miller and Joby Warrick, "In Syria conflict, U.S. struggles to fill intelligence gaps," *The Washington Post*, July 23, 2012.
13. Malas, Parkinson and Solomon, "Nations pledge aid to rebels in Syria."
14. "As Assad Makes Gains, Will New U.S. Strategy for Syria Change the Dynamics?" *PBS Newshour*, June 14, 2013, http://www.pbs.org/newshour/bb/world/jan-june13/syria2_06-14.html.
15. Patrick Seale, "Syria's long war," *Middle East Online*, September 26, 2012.
16. Ibid.
17. Bassem Mroue and Benn Hubbard, "Syria rebels create new unified military command," *Associated Press*, December 8, 2012.
18. Michael R. Gordon and Anne Barnard, "U.S. places militant Syrian rebel group on list of terrorist organizations." *The New York Times*, December 10, 2012.
19. Rania Abouzeid, "Syria's secular and Islamist rebels: Who are the Saudis and the Qataris arming?" Time, September 18, 2012.
20. Bassem Mroue and Benn Hubbard, "Syria rebels create new unified military command," *Associated Press*, December 8, 2012; "Muslim Brotherhood undermining Syrian rebel unity," AFP, August 20, 2012.
21. Neil MacFarquhar and Hwaida Saad, "As Syrian war drags on, Jihadists take bigger role," *The New York Times*, July 29, 2012.
22. Inti Landauro and Stacy Meichtry, "Rebels in Syria move to show moderation," *The Wall Street Journal*, June 27, 2013.
23. Rania Abouzeid, "Syria's secular and Islamist rebels: Who are the Saudis and the Qataris arming?" Time, September 18, 2012.
24. Sam Dagher, "Militants seize oil field, expand Syrian domain," *The Wall Street Journal*, July 3, 2014.

25. Maria Abi-Habib, "Al-Qaeda emissary in Syria killed by rival Islamist rebels," *The Wall Street Journal* , Feb. 23, 2014.

26. Sam Dagher, "Syria's Bashar al-Assad Tries to Force the West to Choose between Regime, Islamic State," The Wall Street Journal, October 9, 2015.

27. Asa Fitch, "Syrian rebels issue demands for U.N. hostages," *The Wall Street Journal*, September 2, 2014.

28. Rania Abouzeid, "Meet the Islamist militants fighting alongside Syria's rebels," *Time*, July 26, 2012; Rania Abouzeid, "Interview with official of Jabhat al-Nusra, Syria's Islamist militia group," *Time*, Dec 25, 2015.

29. Bassem Mroue and Benn Hubbard, "Syria rebels create new unified military command," *Associated Press*, December 8, 2012.

30. Rania Abouzeid, "Interview with official of Jabhat al-Nusra, Syria's Islamist militia group," *Time*, Dec 25, 2015.

31. Ibid.

32. Alice Fordham, "As Syria prepares to vote on new constitution, some still support Assad," *The Washington Post*, February 25, 2012.

33. Patrick Cockburn, "Syria and Iraq: Why U.S. policy is fraught with danger," *The Independent,* September 9, 2014.

34. Anne Barnard, "Syria opposition group is routed and divided," *The New York Times*, March 14, 2012.

35. Greg Miller and Joby Warrick, "In Syria conflict, U.S. struggles to fill intelligence gaps," *The Washington Post*, July 23, 2012.

36. Jabhat al-Nusra, Australian National Security website, https://www.nationalsecurity.gov.au/Listedterroristorganisations/Pages/Jabhatal-Nusra.aspx.

37. Scott Shane, "Saudis and extremism: 'Both the arsonists and the firefighters,'" *The New York Times*, August 25, 2016.

38. Robert A. Pape, *Dying to Win: The Strategic Logic of Suicide Terrorism* (Random House, 2005), 54.

39. Baer, *Sleeping with the Devil,* 127.

40. Baer, *Sleeping with the Devil,* 105.

41. Solomon, "To check Syria, U.S. explores bond with Muslim Brothers."

42. Ayoob, *Political Islam*, 72.

43. Eric Schmitt, "Al-Qaeda turns to Syria, with a plan to challenge ISIS," *The New York Times*, May 15, 2016.

44. Sam Dagher, "Militants seize oil field, expand Syrian domain," *The Wall Street Journal*, July 3, 2014.

45. Siobhan Gorman and Maria Abi-Habib, "Syria airstrikes roil rebel alliances," *The Wall Street Journal*, September 26, 2014.

46. Jay Solomon, "U.S., Russia agree to implement Syria cease-fire," *The Wall Street Journal,* February 22, 2016.

47. Farnaz Fassihi, "U.N. Security Council unanimously votes to adopt France's counterterrorism resolution," *The Wall Street Journal*, November 20, 2015.

48. Sam Dagher, "Syria's Bashar al-Assad Tries to Force the West to Choose between Regime, Islamic State," *The Wall Street Journal*, October 9, 2015.

49. Michael R. Gordon and Anne Barnard, "U.S. places militant Syrian rebel group on list of terrorist organizations," *The New York Times*, December 10, 2012.

50. Neil Mac Farquhar, "Questions linger over Russia's endgame in Syria, Ukraine and Europe," *The New York Times*, February 23, 2016.

51. Anne Barnard and Michael R. Gordon, "Goals diverge and perils remain as U.S. and Turkey take on ISIS," *The New York Times*, July 27, 2015.

52. Karen Zraick and Anne Barnard, "Syrian war could turn on the battle for Aleppo," *The New York Times*, February 12, 2016.

53. Karen de Young, "U.S. Russia hold Syria cease-fire talks as deadline passes without action," *The Washington Post*, February 19, 2016.

54. Patrick Cockburn, "Britain is on the verge of entering into a long war in Syria based on wishful thinking and poor information," *The Independent*, December 1, 2015.

55. Ben Hubbard, "A look at the Army of Conquest, a prominent rebel alliance in Syria," *The New York Times*, October 1, 2015.

56. Andrew E. Kramer and Anne Barnard, "Russian soldiers join Syria fight," *The New York Times*, October 5, 2015.

57. Jay Solomon and Nour Malas, "U.S. tries to isolate Syria's militant Islamists," *The Wall Street Journal*, December 5, 2012.

58. Ibid.

59. Tim Arango, Anne Barnard and Hwaida Saad, "Syrian rebels tied to al-Qaeda play key role in war," *The New York Times*, December 8, 2012.

60. Patrick Cockburn, "Syrian ceasefire begins—and the U.S. and Russia have the power to make sure it sticks," *The Independent*, September 12, 2016.

61. "James Clapper on Global Intelligence Challenges," Council on Foreign Relations, March 2, 2015, http://www.cfr.org/homeland-security/james-clapper-global-intelligence-challenges/p36195.

62. Maria Abi-Habib, "Islamic State remains unchallenged from its sanctuary in Syria," *The Wall Street Journal*, August 10, 2014.

63. Matthew Dalton, "Reports on Islamic state plans in Europe fueled French move to prepare Syria strikes, *The Wall Street Journal*, September 15, 2015.

64. Patrick Cockburn, "Government has no strategy, no plan and only 'phantom' allies in Syria, scathing Commons report reveals," *The Independent*, September 22, 2016.

65. Anne Barnard and Hwaida Saad, "ISIS fighters seize control of Syrian city of Palmyra, and ancient ruins," *The New York Times*, May 20, 2015.

66. Patrick Cockburn, "Chilcot report: Tony Blair, the Iraq war, and the words of mass destruction that continue to deceive," *The Independent*, July 4, 2016.

67. Robert Fisk, "I read the Chilcot report as I travelled across Syria this week and saw for myself what Blair's actions caused," *The Independent*, July 7, 2016.

68. Patrick Cockburn, "A young price may cost Syria and Yemen dear," *The Independent*, April 5, 2015.

69. Jay Solomon and Nour Malas, "Qatar's ties to militants strain alliance," *The Wall Street Journal*, February 23, 2015.

70. "Vice President Biden Delivered Remarks on Foreign Policy," *Harvard University Institute of Politics*, video, (see quote at 53:20), https://www.youtube.com/watch?v=dcKVCtg5dxM.

71. David E. Sanger, "John Kerry adds voice to those urging bigger push against Islamic State in Syria," *The New York Times*, November 23, 2015.

72. Patrick Cockburn, "Syria conflict: Turkish threats of intervention after Ankara bombing taken seriously by Barack Obama," *The Independent*, February 20, 2016.

73. Patrick Cockburn, "Syrian civil war: Jabhat al-Nusra's massacre of Druze villagers shows they're just as nasty as Isis," *The Independent*, June 14, 2015.

74. Ewen MacAskill, "Who are these 70,000 Syrian fighters David Cameron is relying on?" *The Guardian*, November 30, 2015.

75. Ian Cobain, Alice Ross, Rob Evans and Mona Mahmood, "How Britain funds the 'propaganda war' against Isis in Syria," *The Guardian*, May 3, 2016.

76. Ben Hubbard, "Islamist rebels create dilemma on Syria policy," *The New York Times*, April 27, 2013.

77. Ibid.

78. Nour Malas, "Islamists gain momentum in Syria," *The Wall Street Journal*, February 27, 2013.

79. Thomas L. Friedman, "Obama on the world," *The New York Times*, August 8, 2014.

80. Patrick Cockburn, "The West has been in denial over how to tackle the threat of Islamic State," *Evening Standard*, November 19, 2015.

81. Robert Fisk, "David Cameron, there aren't 70,000 moderate fighters in Syria—and whoever heard of a moderate with a Kalashnikov anyway?" *The Independent*, November 29, 2015.

82. Ben Hubbard, "Warily, Jordan assists rebels in Syrian war," *The New York Times*, April 10, 2014.

83. Adam Entous, Siobhan Gorman and Nour Malas, "CIA expands role in Syria fight," *The Wall Street Journal*, March 22, 2013.

84. Mazzetti, Barnard and Schmitt, "Military success in Syria."

85. Greg Miller and Karen De Young, "Secret CIA effort in Syria faces large funding cut," *The Washington Post*, June 12, 2015.

86. Mark Mazzetti and Matt Apuzzo, "U.S. relies heavily on Saudi money to support Syrian rebels," *The New York Times*, January 23, 2016.

87. Greg Miller and Karen De Young, "Secret CIA effort in Syria faces large funding cut," *The Washington Post*, June 12, 2015.
88. Erin Banco, "Syrian rebel groups merge to take on Assad in Dera'a, but deep divisions remain," *International Business Times*, June 26, 2015.
89. Robert F. Worth, "Egypt is arena for influence of Arab rivals," *The New York Times*, July 9, 2013.
90. Mazzetti, Barnard and Schmitt, "Military success in Syria."
91. Liam Stack, "In slap at Syria, Turkey shelters anti-Assad fighters," *The New York Times*, October 27, 2011.
92. Yaroslav Trofimov, "Porous Syria-Turkey border poses challenge in fight against Islamic State," *The Wall Street Journal*, February 19, 2015.
93. Jay Solomon and Nour Malas, "Qatar's ties."
94. Seymour M. Hersh, "Military to Military," *London Review of Books*, 7 January 2016.
95. Erin Banco, "In Syria's north, opposition is making a comeback thanks to one rebel group, and to Turkey," *International Business Times*, June 19, 2015.
96. Mark Mazzetti and Matt Apuzzo, "U.S. relies heavily on Saudi money to support Syrian rebels," *The New York Times*, January 23, 2016.
97. Patrick Cockburn, "Egypt plane crash: This attack shows that Russia is hurting ISIS," *Independent*. November 7, 2015.
98. Ben Hubbard, "Warily."
99. Mark Mazzetti, Anne Barnard and Eric Schmitt, "Military success in Syria gives Putin upper hand in U.S. proxy war," *The New York Times*, August 6, 2016.
100. Karen DeYoung and Liz Sly, "Syrian rebels get influx of arms with gulf neighbors' money, U.S. coordination," *The Washington Post*, May 15, 2012.
101. Yaroslav Trofimov "To U.S. allies, Al-Qaeda affiliate in Syria becomes the Lesser Evil," *The Wall Street Journal*, June 11, 2015.
102. Mark Mazzetti and Matt Apuzzo, "U.S. relies heavily on Saudi money to support Syrian rebels," *The New York Times*, January 23, 2016.
103. Seale, "Syria's long war."
104. Ibid.

Chapter five • The Ba'athists' Islamic Ally

1. Kenneth Katzman, "Iran's Foreign Policy," *Congressional Research Service*, August 24, 2016.
2. Ibid.
3. Ibid.
4. Hazem Baloushal, "Iran increases aid to PFLP," *Palestine Pulse*, September 17, 2013.

5. Aresu Eqbali and Asa Fitch, "Russian raids on Syria from Iranian air base finished, Tehran says," *The Wall Street Journal*, August 22, 2016.

6. Domenico Losurdo, "Zielscheiben des Westens," *Junge Welt*, January 27, 2016; "Washington Views Russia, China as Its Main 'Targets'?" *CaribFlame*, January 30, 2016.

7. Adam Taylor, "It's not just Hiroshima: The many other things America hasn't apologized for," *The Washington Post*, May 26, 2016.

8. Kenneth Katzman, "Iran's Foreign Policy," *Congressional Research Service*, August 24, 2016.

9. "Iran's top leader says U.S. should not be trusted," Xinhua, June 3, 2016.

10. William R. Polk, *Understanding Iran: Everything You Need to Know, From Persia to the Islamic Republic, From Cyrus to Ahmadinejad* (Palgrave MacMillan, 2009), 212.

11. "CIA World Factbook, Iran," Central Intelligence Agency, accessed May 29, 2016, https://www.cia.gov/library/publications/the-world-factbook/geos/ir.html.

Chapter six • Washington's Islamic Allies

1. Toby Matthiesen, *Sectarian Gulf: Bahrain, Saudi Arabia, and the Arab Spring That Wasn't* (Stanford Briefs, 2013), ix.

2. Ethan Bronner, "Crackdown Was Only Option, Bahrain Sunnis Say," *The New York Times*, March 20, 2011.

3. Ibid.

4. Helene Cooper and Robert F. Worth, "In Arab Sprint, Obama Finds a Sharp Test," *The New York Times*, September 24, 2012.

5. Patrick Cockburn, "Saudi Arabia is the flagging horse of the Gulf—but Britain is still backing it as an answer to Brexit," *The Independent*, September 20, 2016.

6. Matthiesen, *Sectarian Gulf*, ix.

7. Craig Whitlock, "Niger rapidly emerging as a key U.S. partner," *The Washington Post*, April 14, 2013.

8. David E. Sanger, "U.S. struggles to explain alliance with Saudis," *The New York Times*, January 4, 2016.

9. Mark Mazzetti and Matt Apuzzo, "U.S. relies heavily on Saudi money to support Syrian rebels," *The New York Times*, January 23, 2016.

10. David Motadel, *Islam and Nazi Germany's War*, (The Belknap Press of Harvard University Press, 2014) 321.

11. Motadel, *Islam and Nazi Germany's War*, 8.

12. Ibid, 3.

13. Ibid, 9.

14. Ibid, 8.

15. Ibid, 6.

16. David N. Gibbs, "Afghanistan: The Soviet Invasion in Retrospect," *International Politics* 37.2, 2000, 241-242.
17. Baer, *Sleeping with the Devil,* 100.
18. Baer, *Sleeping with the Devil,* xxxii.
19. Ibid.
20. Statement by Dr. Hassan Rouhani at the General Debate of the General Assembly of the United Nations, 22 September 2016.
21. Robert Fisk, "For the first time, Saudi Arabia is being attacked by both Sunni and Shia leaders," *The Independent,* September 22, 2016.
22. John Mueller and Mark G. Stewart, *Chasing Ghosts: The Policing of Terrorism,* (Oxford University Press, 2016) 46.
23. Mark Mazzetti and Matt Apuzzo, "U.S. relies heavily on Saudi money to support Syrian rebels," *The New York Times,* January 23, 2016.
24. Ibid.
25. Jay Solomon, "Obama's Mideast plan faces a new hurdle," *The Wall Street Journal,* January 3, 2016.
26. Bulens Aras and Omer Caha, "Fethullah Gulen and His Liberal 'Turkish Islam,'" 149 in Barry Rubin (Ed.), *Revolutionaries and Reformers: Contemporary Islamist Movements in the Middle East* (State University of New York Press, 2003).
27. Ayoob, *Political Islam,* 96.
28. Patrick Cockburn, "Is Erdogan using the coup to make Turkey a fully Islamic country?" *The Uniz Review: An Alternative Media Selection,* July 18, 2016.
29. Yaroslav Trofimov, "The crisis of political Islam," *The Wall Street Journal,* July 22, 2016.
30. Carol E. Lee and Thomas Grove, "Joe Biden attempts to smooth relations with Turkey," *The Wall Street Journal,* August 24, 2016.
31. Robert Fisk, "The 'one for one' refugee policy means we're picking and choosing among desperate people," *The Independent,* April 8, 2016.

Chapter seven • Divide et Impera

1. Rashid Khalidi, *The Iron Cage: The story of the Palestinian Struggle for Statehood* (Beacon Press, 2007).
2. R. Palme Dutt, *The Problem of India,* 91.
3. Ibid.
4. R. Palme Dutt, *The Problem of India,* 91-92.
5. Robert Fisk, "Alawite history reveals the complexities of Syria that West not does not understand," *The Independent,* March 3, 2013.
6. Yaroslav Trofimov, "Can victories against Islamic state last without support of Sunnis?" *The Wall Street Journal,* June 9, 2016.
7. Maria Abi-Habib, "U.S. State Department officials call for strikes against Syria's Assad," *The Wall Street Journal,* June 16, 2016.

8. Thomas Collelo, ed., *A Country Study: Syria* (Washington, D.C.: Federal Research Division, Library of Congress), 186.

9. Van Dam, *Struggle.*

10. Hanna Batatu, "Some observations on the social roots of Syria's ruling, military group and the causes for its dominance," *Middle East Journal*, 35.3, 331 – 344.

11. Samuel Helfont and Michael Brill, "Saddam ISIS? The Terrorist Group's Real Origin Story," *Foreign Affairs*, June 12, 2016.

12. Muttitt, *Fuel*, 78.

13. Tamer El-Ghobashy and Nour Malas, "Iraq says military has retaken central Fallujah from Islamic State," *The Wall Street Journal*, June 17, 2016.

14. Peter Oborne, "Syria: As the bombs fall, the people of Damascus rally around Bashar al-Assad," *The Telegraph*, April 17, 2014.

15. Thomas Collelo, ed., *A Country Study.*

16. Patrick Seale, *Asad of Syria: The Struggle for the Middle East* (University of California Press, 1995).

17. Kamal Alam, "Why Assad's army has not defected," *The National Interest*, February 12, 2016.

18. Robert Fisk, "Syrian civil war: West failed to factor in Bashar al-Assad's backers as the conflict developed," *The Independent*, March 13, 2016.

Chapter eight • Echoes of Hitler

1. Adolph Hitler, *Mein Kampf: The Official 1939 Edition*, (CODA Books, 2011), 26.

2. Hitler, *Mein Kampf*, 41.

3. Hitler, *Mein Kampf*, 34.

4. Hitler, *Mein Kampf*, 42.

5. Hitler, *Mein Kampf*, 44.

6. Ibid.

7. Hitler, *Mein Kampf*, 148.

8. Michael Dickenson, "Winston Churchill: The Imperial Master," *Counterpunch*, January 28, 2015.

9. "The Churchill you didn't know," *The Guardian*, November 28, 2002.

10. Garikai Chengu, "Winston Churchill: Britain's 'Greatest Briton' left a legacy of global conflict and crimes against humanity," *Global Research*, January 23, 2016.

11. Richard Toye. *Churchill's Empire: The World that Made Him and the World he Made.* St. Martins Griffen, 2011.

12. Lawrence James, *Churchill and Empire: A Portrait of an Imperialist* (Pegasus Books, 2015).

13. Garikai Chengu, "Winston Churchill: Britain's 'Greatest Briton' left a legacy of global conflict and crimes against humanity," *Global Research*, January 23, 2016.

14. David Olusoga and Casper W. Erichsen, *The Kaiser's Holocaust: Germany's Forgotten Genocide and the Colonial Roots of Nazism*, Faber and Faber, 2010, 329.
15. Aimé Césaire, *Discourse on Colonialism* (Monthly Review Press, 2000), 36.
16. Césaire, *Discourse*, 36.
17. Svend Lindqvist, *The Dead Do Not Die: Exterminate All The Brutes and Terra Nullius, The New Press*, 2014, p. 178.
18. Liad Porat, "The Syrian Muslim Brotherhood and the Asad Regime." *Crown Center for Middle East Studies, Brandeis University*, December 2010, No. 47.
19. Hitler, *Mein Kampf*, 106.
20. Hitler, *Mein Kampf*, 106.
21. Hitler, *Mein Kampf*, 235.
22. Hitler, *Mein Kampf*, 49.
23. Hitler, *Mein Kampf*, 46.
24. Hitler, *Mein Kampf*, 47.
25. Hitler, *Mein Kampf*, 25.

Chapter nine • Wall Street's Empire

1. Edward Dowling, *Chicago Daily News*, July 28, 1941, cited in Heather King, "Father Edward Dowling, S.J.," *Catholic Education Resource Center*, http://www.catholiceducation.org/en/faith-and-character/faith-and-character/father-edward-dowling-s-j.html.
2. Steve A. Cook and Michael J. Koplow, "Turkey is no longer a reliable ally," *The Wall Street Journal*, August 10, 2016.
3. Thom Shanker, "U.S. and China soften tone over disputed seas," *The New York Times*, October 12, 2010.
4. Martin Gilens and Benjamin I. Page, "Testing Theories of American Politics: Elites, Internet Groups, and Average Citizens," *Perspectives in Politics*, Fall 2014.
5. Nicholas Confessore, Sarah Cohen and Karen Yourish, "The families funding the 2016 presidential election," *The New York Times*, October 10, 2015.
6. Nicholas Confessore, Sarah Cohen and Karen Yourish, "The families funding the 2016 presidential election," *The New York Times*, October 10, 2015.
7. *The Washington Post*, November 23, 2016.
8. *The Washington Post*, November 24, 2016.
9. *New York Times*, February 21, 2015.
10. *New York Times*, October 17, 2012.
11. *Wall Street Journal*, July 13, 2012.

12. *New York Times*, October 13, 2012.
13. *New York Times*, January 27, 2012.
14. *New York Times*, April 21, 2012.
15. *CBS News*, November 17, 2010.
16. *New York Times*, April 14, 2012.
17. *New York Times*, January 21, 2011.
18. *New York Times*, November 21, 2015.
19. *New York Times*, May 2, 2012.
20. Transcript of audio file containing lecture by Albert Szymanski. The audio file is no longer available on the internet.
21. *60 Minutes*, May 12, 1996.
22. Domenico Losurdo, "Flight from history? The communist movement between self-criticism and self-contempt," *Nature, Society and Thought*, 2000, 1393: 457-514.
23. Sam Dagher and Raja Abdulrahim, "Russian fighter jet downed in region with diverse mix of rebel groups," *The Wall Street Journal*, November 24, 2015.
24. Shoup, *Wall Street's Think Tank*, 220.
25. "President Obama Signs Bill Recognizing Asteroid Resource Property Rights Into Law," *Planetary Resources*, November 25, 2015, http://www.planetaryresources.com/2015/11/president-obama-signs-bill-recognizing-asteroid-resource-property-rights-into-law/.
26. Laurence H. Shoup & William Minter, *Imperial Brain Trust: The Council on Foreign Relations & United States Foreign Policy* (Authors Choice Press, 2004) 6.
27. "President al-Assad: Basis for any political solution for crisis in Syria is what the Syrian people want," http://www.syriaonline.sy/?f=Details&catid=12&pageid=5835.

Conclusion

1. Martin Gilens and Benjamin I. Page, "Testing Theories of American Politics: Elites, Interest Groups, and Average Citizens," *Perspectives on Politics*, 12.3 (2014): 564.
2. Russ Choma, "Millionaires' club: For first time, most lawmakers are worth $1 million-plus," opensecrets.org, *Centre for Responsive Politics*, January 9, 2014.
3. Julie Creswell and Ben White, "The Guys from 'Government Sachs,'" *The New York Times*, October 19, 2008.
4. Nicholas Confessore and Susanne Craig, "2008 crisis deepened the ties between Clintons and Goldman Sachs," *The New York Times*, September 24, 2016.
5. Paul Krugman, "The angry rich," *The New York Times*, September 19, 2010.

6. Paul Krugman, "Fear and favor," *The New York Times*, October 3, 2010.
7. Paul Krugman, "Rule by rentiers," *The New York Times*, June 9, 2011.
8. Lee Fang, "Who's Paying the Pro-War Pundits?" *The Nation*, September 16, 2014.
9. Ibid.
10. David Barstow, "Behind TV Analysts, Pentagon's Hidden Hand," *The New York Times*, April 20, 2008.
11. William R. Polk, *Understanding Iraq*, Harper Perennial, 2005, Pp. 127-128.
12. Dreyfuss, *Devil's Game*, 99.
13. Polk, *Humpty Dumpty*, 278.
14. Clifford Kraus, "The Scramble for Access to Libya's Oil Wealth Begins," *The New York Times*, August 22, 2011.
15. Cumings, Abrahamian and Ma'oz, *Inventing the Axis of Evil*, 207.
16. Alfred B. Prados and Jeremy M. Sharp, "Syria: Political Conditions and Relations with the United States After the Iraq War," *Congressional Research Service*, February 28, 2005.
17. Bashar al-Assad Interview: with Clarin newspaper and Telam news agency," May 19, 2013.
18. Alan Taylor, *Colonial America: A Very Short Introduction* (Oxford University Press, 2013) 23.
19. Peter Novick, *The Holocaust in American Life*, (Houghton Mifflin), 1999, 92.
20. Ibid, 93.
21. Nicholas Blanford, "Can the Syrian regime divide and conquer its opposition?" *Time*, April 9, 2011.
22. Anthony Shadid, "Security forces kill dozens in uprisings around Syria," *The New York Times*, April 22, 2011.
23. Jonathan Steele, "Most Syrians back President Assad, but you'd never know from western media," *The Guardian*, January 17, 2012.
24. Nicholas Blanford, "Can the Syrian regime divide and conquer its opposition?" *Time*, April 9, 2011.
25. "Thousands march to protest Syria killings," *The New York Times*, March 24, 2011.
26. Rania Abouzeid, "Assad and reform: Damned if he does, doomed if he doesn't," *Time*, April 22, 2011.
27. Lisa Stampnitzky, *Disciplining terror: How experts invented terrorism.* (Cambridge University Press, 2013).
28. Cumings, Abrahamian and Ma'oz, *Inventing the Axis of Evil*, 207.

Slouching Towards Sirte
NATO's War on Libya and Africa
Maximilian C. Forte

Rwanda and the New Scramble for Africa
From Tragedy to Useful Imperial Fiction
Robin Philpot

The Question of Separatism
Quebec and the Struggle over Sovereignty
Jane Jacobs

The Complete Muhammad Ali
Ishmael Reed

Justice Belied
The Unbalanced Scales of International Criminal Justice
John Philpot & Sébastien Chartrand, Editors

Songs Upon the Rivers
The Buried History of the French-speaking Canadiens and Métis
From the Great Lakes and the Mississippi across to the Pacific
Robert Foxcurran, Michel Bouchard, and Sébastien Malette

The Prophetic Anti-Gallic Letters
Adam Thom and the Hidden Roots of the Dominion of Canada
François Deschamps

Rebel Priest in the Time of Tyrants
Mission to Haiti, Ecuador and Chile
Claude Lacaille

Scandinavian Common Sense
Policies to Tackle Social Inequalities in Health
Marie-France Raynault & Dominique Côté

Printed in September 2017
by Gauvin Press,
Gatineau Québec